THE PORTABLE
ENGLISH
HANDBOOK

THE PORTABLE ENGLISH HANDBOOK

An Index to Grammar,
Usage, and
the Research Paper

WILLIAM HERMAN

The City College of
The City University of New York

Holt, Rinehart and Winston

New York   Chicago   San Francisco   Atlanta   Dallas
Montreal   Toronto

Library of Congress Cataloging in Publication Data

Herman, William.
 The portable English handbook.

 Includes index.
 1. English language—Grammar—1950– I. Title.
PE1112.H38   808'.042   77–27934

ISBN 0–03–020256–6

8 9 0 1 2   059   9 8 7 6 5 4 3 2 1

For my darling daughter
Lisa Jane Herman:
Some day you too will be
a grammar!

Preface

The overriding purpose guiding the organization of *The Portable English Handbook* has been to make it a book that students themselves will use. To achieve this end, the book has five key features: (1) Its index organization makes it *easy* to use. (2) It is complete. (3) It contains many exercises. (4) Its coverage of the research paper is thorough, including an entire model paper. (5) It opens with a thorough and yet concise review of basic grammar.

1. Students will find this book easy to use. For one thing, there is no complicated letter-and-number coding system. Instead, the principal reference section, Part 2 on usage and effective writing, is arranged alphabetically. The two glossaries are also, of course, alphabetical. In addition, Parts 1 and 3 on grammar and the research paper consist of units that progress in a logical teaching and learning order. Also, there are many cross references throughout the book, and the index and the organizational chart on the inside back cover offer further aids to easy access by students.

2. The book is complete. The alphabetical Part 2, "An Index to Usage and the Principles of Effective Writing," contains entries ranging from Abbreviations to Verbs; it concentrates on errors in usage and such important rhetorical matters as Unity, Diction, Coherence, Paragraph Development, and Thesis Statement.

3. The book offers many exercises—"Test Yourself" sections by means of which students can consolidate the gains they make through understanding the text. Virtually every entry in Part 2 contains exercises, and they also appear at critical points in Parts 1 and 3.

4. The book is comprehensive in its treatment of the research paper in Part 3. This section takes the student

through a step-by-step approach to writing a research paper. Sample note cards and reference materials are reproduced at the appropriate stages, and the section ends with a *complete* sample research paper.

5. Part 1, "A Basic Grammar," gives students a basic grounding in the fundamentals they need to know before they start writing. This opening section is intended to be useful both for teaching in the classroom and for independent student study and review. The section clearly explains words, sentences, clusters, clauses, and phrases, in that order, with many examples and exercises along the way.

The book is, as its title denotes, portable—it is no burden to carry around and have handy; this feature is especially important. Finally, I should add that the basic approach to grammar here lays before students only what is essential for their grasp of the writing problems in their own work; I have avoided a top-heavy burden of fine exegesis which could only confuse students and take their attention away from their own writing. I hope, too, that I have written with plain diction and a lively style, so that students will not be led astray by *my* writing.

An *Instructor's Manual* is available. Primarily an answer key to virtually all the exercises, it also includes a list of possible research paper topics. The *Manual* may be obtained through a local Holt representative or by writing to English Editor, College Department, Holt, Rinehart and Winston, 383 Madison Avenue, New York, N.Y. 10017.

• • •

I wish to thank my colleagues in the Department of English of The City College, CUNY, for their generous responses to my sometimes anxious queries. Special thanks are due Professor Arthur Zeiger for reading the manuscript and saving me from a number of potential errors. I should also thank Professor Edward Quinn for performing the same task and for his fine philological distinctions. In addition, I wish to thank Professor

Richard S. Beal, Boston University, and Professor David Skwire, Cuyahoga Community College, who read the manuscript and made constructive comments. My editor at Holt, Harriett Prentiss, was a model of efficiency and unfailing kindness and encouragement. My wife Joanna knows a great deal about making books—and a lot of other things as well—and she generously shared that knowledge with me in the making of this one.

W.H.

To the Student:
How to Use This Book

This book is designed to assist beginning writers in solving certain problems in usage and help them to make their writing clearer, crisper, and more correct. When you and your instructor have identified the specific problems with which you need help, you may use Part 2 (the "Index to Usage and the Principles of Effective Writing") to locate the entries that deal with your problems. In many cases, it will be necessary to read all of Part 1 and work through all of its exercises in order to undertake the work in the Part 2 entries. Again, your instructor can provide guidance in this matter. Students who need special help with the research paper will find that subject dealt with in Part 3.

In addition to the three parts, the book is equipped with a "Glossary of Grammatical Terms." This is useful when you are working on an entry in Part 2 and momentarily forget the meaning of some grammatical term used in that entry.

A "Glossary of Usage" is also included to help you to go directly to some small problem, a word or a phrase, that you're unsure about.

Another way to locate whatever you need in the book is to turn directly to the Index; there you will find every subject dealt with in the book. If, after looking through the table of contents, you still cannot find what you seek, the Index is an excellent source of information and will, in most cases, lead you exactly where you want to go. The chart on the inside back cover will also help you find specific information quickly.

The book is organized in separate units for your convenience. It aims to provide you with a clear guide to what ails your writing and, in doing so, makes suggestions on proper usage and effective writing. In the final analysis, the best sources for solving difficulties are a good book and a helpful instructor. See your instructor for whatever help you do not find here.

Contents

A Basic Grammar Part 1

WHY STUDY GRAMMAR?

Grammar need not frighten you.

Grammar is simply a set of rules that describes how we all speak and write. The frightening word here is *rules,* because it makes us think of penalties for doing something wrong. But it need not. There are all kinds of rules, some of which we don't know are operating, and most of which we fall easily into obeying. For example, you understand what these words you are now reading are saying. The reason for this is that you are obeying the grammatical rules *you* already know.

For all of us, this understanding of some grammatical rules is unconscious, long ago learned and incorporated into our mental processes. The purpose of studying grammar here is to make more of these rules conscious and to do so for a number of very good reasons.

For one thing, grammar is interesting. Language is fascinating when you come to understand that its grammar is a remarkably coherent piece of human knowledge and that most human activities would be impossible without the subtle riches of linguistic communication. More important, however, the study of basic grammar can help you to improve your writing by reminding you of how it works. For example, if you know that a verb must agree with its subject, you are less likely to write "The humor and personal concern of Mr. Jones, my sociology professor, *is* what I like best about the course." Moreover, knowing grammatical terms can help you discuss your writing with instructors trying to make it more effective. If an instructor suggests that you *use subordinate clauses for subordinate ideas,* the suggestion will not get through to you if you do not know a clause from a hammock.

In Part 2 of this book, "An Index to Usage and the Principles of Effective Writing," you will find many suggestions for improving your writing. In order to use that Index intelligently, you will need to understand the basic grammar we are about to discuss. We begin here with Words and Sentences, then Clusters, Clauses, and Phrases.

WORDS

Words traditionally have been placed into classes called *parts of speech* according to their forms and the ways in which they communicate meaning in sentences.

Before we begin to study the characteristic features of these classes, it is important to point out that some words can fall into more than one class, depending on how they are used in the sentence. For example, consider this group of sentences:

The *light* is hurting my eyes.
Let's *light* the Christmas tree.
Kathy has a *light* complexion.
She wore a *light* brown dress.

If your native language is English, you can make out the different meanings of these sentences quite easily. The fact that you *can* make out the different meanings is partly due to your ability to understand the word *light* in a different way in each sentence. In other words, in each sentence you are identifying *light* as a member of a different class, because in each sentence *light* has a different function.

You should be aware that hundreds of words can behave the way *light* does in those four sentences. Good dictionaries always define such words according to each of the various ways in which they can be used, and as we go along you will be able to see the logical processes governing the classification of these words. But you need to know the characteristic features of the various classes.

Nouns

A noun is a word used to name something: a person, a place, an object, an idea. Examples of nouns are such words as *apple, table,* and *car.* The important features of nouns that will help you identify them are the following:

1. Nouns can usually be made into plurals by adding *-s* or *-es:*

apple—apples	peach—peaches	hope—hopes
table—tables	pass—passes	tragedy—tragedies
car—cars	tax—taxes	democracy—democracies
boy—boys	dash—dashes	

2. Nouns can usually be made into possessives to indicate that something belongs to them. This is done by adding *-'s.*

Danny's shoes
democracy's advantages
car's engine

3. Nouns can be preceded by words like *a, an, the, my, each, this, that,* or even another possessive noun (*Judy's,* for example). A whole list of such words will be found below under determiners. These words *signal* that a noun is coming.

a *horse*	that *stadium*
Linda's *boyfriend*	this *chicken*
his *shirt*	an *egg*
my *heart*	Aunt Vicky's *cake*

In a phrase such as "an intelligent young man," the word *an* does its signalling several words away from the noun *man. An* is not signalling that *intelligent* or *young* is a noun.

4. Nouns are in the noun position in the sentence. Notice the position of the italicized nouns in the following sentences, and write in appropriate nouns in the blank spaces.

I bought the *apple.*	This *apple* is beautiful.
I bought the *table.*	This *table* is beautiful.
I bought the *car.*	This *car* is beautiful.
I bought the _____ .	This _____ is beautiful.

I was unhappy with the *apple*.	*Apples* are available in Peoria.
I was unhappy with the *table*.	*Tables* are available in Peoria.
I was unhappy with the *car*.	*Cars* are available in Peoria.
I was unhappy with the _____ .	_____ are available in Peoria.

Some words will fit into the blanks, and some will not. Those that will—words like *axe, closet,* and *house*—are called *common nouns*. Words like *go, do, usually,* or *from* will not fit, and therefore they are not nouns. We do not say, for example, "I bought the *usually*" or "*Froms* are available in Peoria."

However, there are also some nouns that will not fit the blanks: words such as *Italy, Professor Jones,* and *Tom*. These are called *proper nouns,* and they are the names of particular persons, places, and things. What makes them different from common nouns is that they do not ordinarily work with determiners like *the, this,* or *my*.

However, there is a small set of proper nouns, containing such members as *the Netherlands, the United States, the Gobi Desert,* and so forth, that *always* follow a determiner, and it is always the determiner *the*. These will fit some of the blank spaces above. Notice the difference between proper nouns and common nouns in the following pairs of sentences:

Proper   *Freddie* is a very bright student. (no determiner with *Freddie*)

Common   That *boy* is a very bright student. (*that* used with *boy*)

Proper   We all respected *Harriet*.

Common   We all respected the young *woman*.

5. Some nouns are formed by adding certain characteristic word endings (or *suffixes*) either to nouns or to other parts of speech such as adjectives or verbs.

mile + **age** = mileage
deny + **al** = denial
consider + **ation** = consideration
deliver + **ance** = deliverance
provide + **ence** = providence

tenant + **ancy** = tenancy
urge + **ency** = urgency
farm + **er** = farmer
govern + **or** = governor
social + **ism** = socialism
active + **ity** = activity
happy + **ness** = happiness
achieve + **ment** = achievement
hard + **ship** = hardship
dissent + **sion** = dissension
young + **ster** = youngster
introduce + **tion** = introduction

TEST YOURSELF ON
Identifying Nouns

Circle the nouns in each of the following word groups.

1. An American elephant.
2. Judy's notebook.
3. I saw the light.
4. Cheese is available in Wisconsin.
5. The Trail Blazers are a championship team.
6. Alligators are fond of dating crocodiles.
7. I have a boat on the lake.
8. A message from my nose to my brain tells me it's spring.
9. I am going to invite Republicans to my party.
10. The fire is blazing in the fireplace.

Verbs

A verb is used to describe an action or a state of being. A verb says something about what a noun *does* (action) or what it *is* (being).

Karl *plays* basketball. (describes the action of the proper noun *Karl*)
Karl *is* tall. (describes the state of being of the proper noun *Karl*)

The important features of verbs that will help you to identify them are the following:

1. Verbs can change form to indicate a change of time. Not only do verbs describe an action or a state of being, but they also tell us *when* the action is taking place or *when* the state of being was in force. When a verb changes form in this manner, we say that it has changed its *tense*.

Fred *walked* to the movies. (action in the past; *walked* is the past tense—the past time form—of the verb *walk*)
He *is* happy. (state of being now; *is* is the *present tense*—the present time form—of the verb *be*)

One of the surest ways to identify a verb is to look for that word in the sentence which can be changed to a different tense to indicate a change of time. In each of the two sentences that follow, change the time of the action to the future, and you will have identified the verbs—the words that must be changed. For the future tense, you will have to add a word.

By the end of the term, Harry hated school.
Eddie loves orange juice in the morning.

If the words you picked to change were *hated* and *loves*, you have correctly identified the verbs in the two sentences.

2. Nearly all verbs have an *-ing* form. All verbs in the third person singular of the present tense, indicative mood, end in the letter *-s*. In addition, many verbs change to their past forms by adding *-d* or *-ed*. (See below, p. 11, for what is meant by indicative mood.)

-ing Forms   jump*ing*, smok*ing*, act*ing*, play*ing*, try*ing*, do*ing*

Third Person Singular Forms   i*s*, ha*s*, goe*s*, doe*s*, help*s*, play*s*, move*s*

Past Forms   wait*ed*, need*ed*, want*ed*, leap*ed*, pray*ed*, wish*ed*, mov*ed*, lov*ed*

3. Verbs can be single words (*sings*, *worked*, *touched*) or they can consist of several words (*has* *gone, can play, was changing, will have studied*). *Has, can, was, will,* and *have* are called *auxiliary* or *helping* verbs. (For more detailed information about them, see below, pp. 13–16.)

TEST YOURSELF ON
Identifying Verbs

Circle the verbs in the following sentences. Keep in mind the features of verbs you have just read about.

1. Betsy plays the piano.
2. A civil engineer earns a good salary.
3. My sister is jumping rope.
4. Sally waited in the rain for an hour.
5. She trusted Jean to show up.
6. I tried calling her apartment, but she had left.
7. The mail will be late today.
8. I have given you perfect instructions for getting to the lake.
9. The Dean told her that she would graduate with the rest of her class.
10. I am curious about the history of slavery in this country.

TEST YOURSELF ON
Identifying Verbs by Changing Tenses

Identify the verbs in the following sentences by changing their tenses.

Example: Tom *played* basketball for his college team.
Tom *plays* basketball for his college team.
Verb: *played*.

1. Tom played basketball for his college team.
2. George passes his examination easily.
3. The apples were delicious.

4. Your help makes a lot of difference to me.

5. He seemed unhappy.

6. In fact, Arthur works for his father.

7. He will be happy with his birthday present.

8. Frank understood the lesson.

9. The piano piece will end the program.

10. He has taken his father's car to school.

11. We will sit at different tables.

12. He has taken a vacation.

4. Verbs occupy certain typical positions in sentences. In ordinary use, the verb follows the subject (the noun). Notice the positions of the italicized verbs in the sentences below:

People *listen.*
People *play.*
People *come.*
People _____ .

They will *listen* soon.
They will *play* soon.
They will *come* soon.
They will _____ soon.

He *listens* from time to time.
He *plays* from time to time.
He *comes* from time to time.
He _____ from time to time.

These are just three of the positions verbs can occupy in different kinds of sentences. You can see that many other verbs can fit into the blank spaces, for example, *work, drive, approve, study, write,* and so forth. But words like *apple, table, car, ordinary,* or *without* will not fit. We do not say "Please *ordinary*" or "He will *without* soon." Thus an understanding of the position of the verb in the sentence is useful in helping you to identify verbs.

5. Verbs have a property called *voice,* which indicates whether the subject of the verb performs the action or undergoes it. Where the verb is in the *active voice*, the subject does the performing.

John *ate* a rabbit. (*John,* the subject, did the eating)
José *saw* the President. (*José,* the subject, did the seeing)

Where the verb is in the *passive voice*, the subject is being acted on: the subject is *receiving* the action.

John *was eaten* by a rabbit. (*John,* the subject, is acted on)
José *was seen* by the President. (*José,* the subject, is acted on)

Note: Only an *action verb* can have a passive voice. See 7 below for the definition of an action verb. (For more detailed information on voice, see **Voice** in Part 2.)

6. Verbs also have a feature called *mood,* to indicate the manner (or mode) in which they are used: the *indicative mood* is used for statements of fact or other kinds of assertions or questions; the *imperative mood* is used for issuing commands or giving directions; the *subjunctive mood* is used for statements contrary to fact or those that are in the area of possibility or potential.

I *gave* him five dollars. (*indicative:* a statement of fact)
Can you *give* me a lift? (*indicative;* an ordinary question)
Give me five dollars. (*imperative:* a command)
Turn left at the hardware store. (*imperative:* a direction)
If I *were* President, I would declare a holiday. (*subjunctive:* the speaker, "I," is *not* President)

7. Verbs fall into two classes: *linking verbs* and *action verbs.* Linking verbs consist of all forms of the verb *be: is, am, was, were,* and so forth, as well as such other verbs as *seem, become, appear, feel.* They are called *linking verbs* because they link the subject of a sentence (a noun) with either another noun, a pronoun, or an adjective—describing the state of being of the subject.

Frank *felt* anxious.
You *are* gorgeous.
Uncle Al *seemed* quiet.
Fred *is* a dancer.

Action verbs, on the other hand, describe action rather than a state of being. They are divided into *transitive* verbs and *intransitive* verbs.

A transitive verb describes action that is received by something. This something is called the *direct object* of the verb.

Joe Namath *throws* the long **ball.** (*ball* receives the action)
Gravity *moves* the **planets.** (*planets* receive the action)
Women *date* **men.** (*men* receive the action)

Intransitive verbs describe action, too, but they do not act *upon* an object; they have no direct object but simply describe an action performed *by* the subject that also applies *to* the subject.

Christmas trees *burn* easily.
This typewriter really *works*.

Some verbs can be used transitively or intransitively, in different sentences. Notice how the verbs used in the preceding examples can function as transitive verbs:

My stove *burns* coal. (*coal receives the action*)
Charley *works* the tractor. (*tractor receives the action*)

TEST YOURSELF ON
Identifying Types of Verbs

Circle all the verbs you can find in the following sentences. Above each circle, write T if the verb is transitive, I if the verb is intransitive, and L if the verb is a linking verb.

1. I feel wealthy.

2. Charley smokes too much.

3. He is riding his motorcycle.

4. My father plays golf every Sunday.

5. The bomb exploded.

6. Willie loves hats.

7. My brother needs a job.

8. Lawyers are officers of the court.

9. Judges make rulings.

10. My wife is very slender.

11. Jane played the piano.

12. Students read all day long.

Auxiliaries

An auxiliary is often called an *auxiliary verb* or *helping verb*. Very frequently, auxiliaries signal a reader that a verb is coming. Words like those italicized in the following examples are all auxiliaries:

is looking	*did* go	*have* played	*was* laughing
can offer	*may* believe	*would* find	*had* known

The following aspects of auxiliaries will help you to understand their forms and functions:

1. Auxiliaries have different meanings and change the meanings of the verbs they couple with in different ways. For example, they indicate time and therefore change tense.

He *is* playing. He *was* playing.

A subgroup of auxiliaries called *modals* (*should, would, could, can, may, might, must, ought to, have to, shall, will*) add meanings that suggest possibility, ability, obligation, and so forth.

He *can* play.   He *should* play.   He *must* play.

Notice that these modals are always used with the present tense stem of the verb.

2. Auxiliaries are widely used in asking questions.

Did you go?	How *did* you go?
Can you go?	When *can* you go?
Must you go?	Why *must* you go?

3. One auxiliary appears with verbs ending in *-ing:* the forms of the verb *be*.

I *am* playing.
You *are* playing.
He *is* playing.

I *was* playing.
They *were* playing.

He *has been* playing.
They *have been* playing.
They *had been* playing.
They *will be* playing.
They *will have been* playing.

4. Only two auxiliaries are used with past verb forms like *known, played, gone, remembered*; they are the auxiliaries *be* and *have*.

I *am* known.   She *was* known.   He *has* played.
They *are* known.   You *were* known.   He *had* played.
She *is* known.   They *have* played.

5. Auxiliaries act to mark verbs in sentences. Consider this ambiguous sentence:

Senate pledges increase.

This could be a statement about the pledges of the Senate, saying that those pledges have increased in number. Or it could be saying that the Senate is pledging an increase (of something or other, say funds for flood control). The ambiguity in the sentence results from the absence of an auxiliary. We do not know if *pledges* is a verb or a noun; we do not know if *increase* is a verb or a noun. So we can only understand the sentence in both ways. With an auxiliary, the verb is clearly marked and the ambiguity disappears:

Senate pledges *can* increase.
Senate pledges *will* increase.
Senate pledges *may* increase.
Senate *may* pledge increase.

6. The auxiliaries *be (am, is, are, was, were), have (has, had), do (did, does),* and *can* may also occur as verbs; this happens when they appear before a member of some other class of words.

Do *as Auxiliary*   He *does* believe. (*believe* is a verb)

Do *as Verb*   He *does* laundry. (*laundry* is a noun)

TEST YOURSELF ON
Identifying Auxiliaries

Place the proper auxiliary into each of the blank spaces in the following sentences.

1. You _____ visit your sick friend.

2. We _____ need some milk for our coffee.

3. He _____ planning to take a course in physics.

4. He says they _____ trying to climb the rocks.

5. When _____ you take the exam?

6. She _____ gone to the hairdresser's.

7. _____ you continue playing the piano?

8. _____ he see what we _____ doing with the fish?

9. He _____ decided to find out if they _____ taken.

10. He _____ laughing and we _____ crying but nobody _____ paying attention.

For the following group of sentences, supply verbs in each of the blank spaces. Be sure to use the correct verb form.

11. We could _____ the entrance on Grove Street.

12. Can you _____ with us this afternoon?

13. We are _____ to arrive by three o'clock.

14. Did you _____ the dinner was cooked?

15. We should _____ all the windows.

16. We will _____ your apartment on Saturday.

17. I am _____ you to school today.

18. They were _____ him about his mother.

19. May I _____ your word on that?

20. Has he ever _____ you play the guitar?

Adjectives

Let us begin our discussion of adjectives by trying to identify a few nouns. One of the words in each of the following pairs is a noun; underline each.

tasty hamburger	good answer	new moon
beautiful lake	honest man	young turkey
happy parent	hopeless case	typical day

What about the other word in each pair?

What does each *do* to the noun it is paired with?

Each of these words describes further the noun it is paired with; not just *a hamburger* but a *tasty* one; not just *an answer* but a *good* one. Each of these words, a part of speech we call an *adjective*, modifies the noun it is paired with by describing it more specifically. The important features of adjectives that will help you identify them are the following:

1. Adjectives can be changed in form to compare two or more objects. This can be done by adding the ending -*er* to the basic adjective (called the *positive* form) to make the *comparative* form, and the ending -*est* to the positive form to make the *superlative* form.

Positive	Comparative	Superlative
happy	happier	happiest
young	younger	youngest

However, some adjectives form the comparative and superlative by adding the words *more* and *most*.

Positive	Comparative	Superlative
beautiful	more beautiful	most beautiful
honest	more honest	most honest
recent	more recent	most recent

Also, some adjectives form the comparative and superlative irregularly.

Positive	Comparative	Superlative
good	better	best
bad	worse	worst
many	more	most

The comparative form is used to compare two objects.

He is *happier* than I am.
Her cat is *more beautiful* than mine.
My cold is *worse* today. (i.e., "than it was yesterday")

The superlative form is used to compare more than two objects.

I am the *happiest* man in the whole world.
Hers is the *most beautiful* hat I've seen.
He is the *best* player on the team.

2. Adjectives occupy certain typical positions in sentences. Notice the position of the italicized adjectives in the following sentences:

He was *happy.*
He was *lively.*
He was *young.*
He was _____ .

A very *happy* girl arrived.
A very *lively* girl arrived.
A very *young* girl arrived.
A very _____ girl arrived.

The girl looked *happy.*
The girl looked *lively.*
The girl looked *young.*
The girl looked _____ .

Other words that could fit into the blank spaces include such adjectives as *new, old, friendly,* or *sincere.* But words like *apple, play, quickly,* or *from* would not fit in. We do not say "A very *quickly* girl arrived" or "He was *apple*" or "The girl looked *play.*" Therefore, these words are not adjectives. Knowing the position occupied by the adjective in sentences can help you to identify adjectives.

3. Many adjectives have characteristic endings (suffixes) that can help you identify them. Here are just a few:

-al (international)
-ant, -ent (resistant, excellent)
-able, -ible (irresistible, affable)
-ar, -ary (solar, ordinary)
-ful (wonderful, soulful)
-ish (sluggish)
-ive (attentive)
-ous (generous)
-y (funny, sloppy)

Recognition of these suffixes can help you to identify adjectives.

For more information on adjectives, see **Modifiers** and **Dangling Modifiers** in Part 2.

TEST YOURSELF ON
    Identifying Adjectives

The following sentences all contain adjectives; some contain more than one. Identify them by analyzing their positions in the sentence, whether they are in the comparative or superlative degree, the way they end (their suffixes), or some combination of these.

1. She seems courageous.
2. He looked funny in that costume.
3. My father was very kind to my mother.
4. He made her happier than she had ever been.
5. It is childish to be greedy.
6. He was riding a lively horse but his saddle was very old.
7. The greatest batter I ever saw was Ted Williams.
8. He is more confident now that he is in a good school.
9. She was athletic, girlish, and sensitive.
10. Of all the lovely cities of Europe, the one having the largest treasure trove of art is beautiful Florence.

Adverbs

So far we have studied three of the parts of speech: nouns, verbs, and adjectives. Write N above the nouns in the following sentences, V above the verbs, and ADJ above the adjectives.

1. Young dogs eat noisily.

2. Old people often sit.

3. Happy farmers live there.

The words you have *not* marked are all adverbs. Each answers a question about the verb in the sentence.

1. Young dogs eat *noisily*. (*How* do they *eat*? *Noisily*, a way or manner of eating or doing other things.)
2. Old people *often* sit. (*When* do they *sit*? *Often*, which signifies the frequency with which they sit.)
3. Happy farmers live *there*. (*Where* do they *live*? *There*, which signifies a place.)

The adverbs that can replace *noisily* in sentence 1 are called *adverbs of manner*; those that can replace *often* in sentence 2 are called *adverbs of time* or *frequency*; those that can replace *there* in sentence 3 are called *adverbs of place* or *position*. Here is a list of some of them:

Manner	Time	Place
thus	then	there
badly	seldom	here
carefully	never	upstairs
rapidly	again	away
surely	soon	downstairs
sweetly	always	up
even	still	down
just	already	
only		

Adverbs can modify not only verbs but also adjectives, other adverbs, and even whole sentences.

Modifying a Verb   Old people *often* sit. (modifies *sit*)

Modifying an Adjective   She was *rarely* unhappy. (modifies *unhappy*)

Modifying Another Adverb   I spoke *too* harshly to my uncle.

Modifying a Whole Sentence   *Unfortunately,* we cannot have a vacation this year. (modifies the whole sentence beginning with *we*)

The important features of adverbs that will help you identify them are the following:

1. A few adverbs, like adjectives, can change form to compare degrees or qualities by adding the endings *-er* and *-est*.

Positive	Comparative	Superlative
soon	sooner	soonest
quick	quicker	quickest

However, most adverbs form the comparative and superlative by adding the words *more* and *most*.

Positive	Comparative	Superlative
often	more often	most often
rapidly	more rapidly	most rapidly

A few adverbs form the comparative and superlative irregularly.

Positive	Comparative	Superlative
badly	worse	worst
well	better	best

2. Adverbs occupy certain typical positions in sentences. Notice the position of the italicized adverbs in the following sentences:

He drove *in*.	She was lucky *rarely*.
He drove *seldom*.	She was lucky *often*.
He drove *perfectly*.	She was lucky *there*.
He drove _____ .	She was lucky _____ .

You can see that many other adverbs will fit into the blank spaces. For example, in the blank space in column one we could fit words like *up, over, by,* and *away*. These represent a group that generally follows verbs, as in the sentences "He *went away*" and "She *came over*." In the blank space in column two we could fit words like *always* or *again* or *consistently*. All these words are therefore adverbs. However, we could not fit into either of the blank spaces such words as *apple, friend, believe,* or *happy*. We do not say "She is lucky *happy*" or "He drove *believe*." Therefore, these words are not adverbs.

3. Adverbs can often be moved from one position in the sentence to another without changing the meaning of the sentence. This is in contrast to adjectives, which must remain relatively fixed if the sentence is to make sense,

Often she was lucky.
She *often* was lucky.
She was *often* lucky.
She was lucky *often*.

In this group of sentences, *often* is the adverb and *lucky* the adjective. You can see that, whether *often* is made the first, second, third, or fourth word of the sentence, the meaning of the sentence remains essentially the same. By contrast, notice what happens when we try the same movement pattern for the adjective.

Lucky she was often.
She *lucky* was often.
She was *lucky* often.
She was often *lucky*.

Only the last two of these examples make sense. The first two are, of course, nonsense. Sometimes, however, adverbs are not as movable as *often* is in the above examples. (For more details on how to control the placement of adverbs, see **Misplaced Modifiers** and **Dangling Modifiers** in Part 2.)

4. Adverbs frequently end in the suffix *-ly,* and many adverbs can be formed by adding this suffix to an adjective.

Adjectives	*Adverbs*
rapid	rapidly
sweet	sweetly
tense	tensely
brave	bravely
beautiful	beautifully
happy	happily

The difficulty is that not all words ending in *-ly* are adverbs. Some nouns add *-ly* to form *adjectives.** There are not many of these; here are a few:

Noun	*Adjective*
beast	beastly
brother	brotherly
earth	earthly
father	fatherly
friend	friendly
heaven	heavenly
love	lovely
man	manly
neighbor	neighborly
saint	saintly

Recognizing the noun base in these adjectives can help you avoid the mistake of thinking they are adverbs.

---

*Some adjectives ending in *-ly* are *not* formed from nouns, e.g., *unsightly* and *unlikely*.

TEST YOURSELF ON
Identifying Adverbs

Take this test by changing the conditions indicated in each of the sentences below. That is, change the manner (*rapidly* to *slowly*), the time (*now* to *then*), or the place or direction (*here* to *there*, *up* to *down*). The word you change is the adverb.

Example: Gilda walked *slowly* into the lion's cage.
Gilda walked *quickly* into the lion's cage.

1. Gilda walked slowly into the lion's cage.

2. She drove in.

3. He went up.

4. He put the apple here.

5. He answered the question sweetly.

6. She is often absent.

7. He did his homework sloppily.

8. She lived upstairs.

9. He is never happy.

10. She walked over.

Prepositions and *conjunctions*, the next two groups we will study, both act to tie together or connect nouns, verbs, adjectives, and adverbs.

Prepositions

A preposition connects a noun or a pronoun with other parts of the sentence.

The man *in* the truck drove away. (connects *man* to *truck*)
Give me that book *on* the table. (connects *book* to *table*)
He went *to* the movies. (connects *went* to *movies*)

Each of the italicized words in the examples above is a *preposition*. Each preposition, together with the two words that follow it (a determiner, *the,* and a noun), forms what is called a *prepositional phrase:*

in the truck
on the table
to the movies

In these phrases, we would call the word *truck* or *table* or *movies* the *object of the preposition,* the word that the preposition connects to the rest of the sentence. (More on the prepositional phrase will be found below under Phrases.)

Prepositions usually denote direction or position, as you can see from this list:

aboard	around	by	like	till
about	at	concerning	near	to
above	before	despite	of	toward
across	behind	down	off	under
after	below	during	on	until
against	beneath	for	onto	up
along	beside	from	over	upon
alongside	besides	in	since	with
amid	between	inside	through	within
among	beyond	into	throughout	without

In addition to these, there are a number of prepositions in English that consist of more than one word. Here are some:

according to	by way of	in spite of
ahead of	contrary to	in view of
apart from	due to	instead of
as for	in addition to	on account of
as well as	in back of	out of
away from	in case of	up to
because of	in front of	
by means of	in place of	

All the words in the first list above *may* be used as prepositions. Some words on the list—*during, among, with,* and others—are regularly prepositions, but most of the words are also used as other parts of speech. For example, you may recall that the words *in, over,* and *by* were adverbs when used in the following ways:

He drove *in*. He drove *over*. He drove *by*.

But these three are prepositions when used in these ways:

He drove *in* the truck. He drove *over* the bridge. He drove *by* the house.

Prepositions occupy certain typical positions in sentences. Notice the positions occupied by those italicized in the following sentences:

The house *across* the road is mine.
The name *on* the door is my father's.
He wrote an essay *on* Shakespeare.
He was carrying a bag *of* potatoes.
He went *to* the store.
He lived *in* my building.

Words that fit these positions are prepositions. For example, we could say "The house *down* the road is mine" or "The name *over* the door is my father's." But we could not say "He went *apple* the store" or "He lived *believe* my building."

Notice again that the preposition nearly always occurs with a determiner and a noun to form what is called a prepositional phrase.

TEST YOURSELF ON
Using Prepositions

Using the following list of nouns, select twenty of the prepositions listed above and make prepositional phrases by including a determiner where appropriate.

Example: beyond our lake

Nouns: farm, apple, newspaper, automobile, ferry, chair, horse, tomato, pizza, chopsticks, burglary, television set, stadium, football field, day, camp, lake, room, cage, planet

Conjunctions

The word *conjunction* means "the state of being joined." In grammar, conjunctions act to join together words, groups of words, or even whole sentences. Different kinds of conjunctions perform different jobs, and there are three different groups to consider.

1. Coordinating conjunctions

This group consists of the seven words *and, or, but, yet, for, nor,* and *so.* Consider the way *and* does its work:

Apples *and* peaches are delicious.
I bought a red Ford *and* a green Mustang.
My aunt gave my sister *and* my brother some money.
Melons smell *and* taste sweet.
She was young *and* pretty.
I plan to spend the summer working on my uncle's farm *and* studying for my exams.
He will play with us if he has the time *and* if he is not tired.
He is a student, *and* he is my friend.

In nearly all these sentences we can substitute the word *or* for *and. But* can replace *and* only in the last sentence. *But* is commonly used to join pairs of adjectives or adverbs that are somewhat opposed to each other in meaning:

He was poor *but* happy.
He looked quickly *but* carefully.

All seven of the coordinating conjunctions are commonly used to join together two sentences (independent clauses), as in the last sentence above, depending on the relationship between the two sentences.

He was poor, *but* he was happy.
He was dressed, *so* he went out.
He was angry, *yet* he was calm.
He was happy, *for* he had passed his exams.

Note: The punctuation of such sentences is important, and you will find more about the subject in Part 2, under **Comma Rules.**

In addition to these coordinating conjunctions, there are four pairs of what are sometimes called *correlatives:*

both . . . and
not only . . . but also
either . . . or
neither . . . nor

These pairs are used very much as *and* and *or* are used.

Both apples *and* peaches are delicious.
Not only apples *but also* peaches are delicious.
He was *either* young *or* inexperienced.
He was *neither* young *nor* inexperienced.

2. Conjunctive adverbs

This is a group of words used to connect sentences; they act in a sentence like the word *therefore*.

The school year was over; *therefore,* he decided to take a long vacation.
The children were playing in the yard; *therefore,* he took a nap.

The following words are commonly used as conjunctive adverbs:

besides	hence	indeed	subsequently
consequently	however	moreover	therefore
furthermore	in fact	nevertheless	thus

He ate the whole pie himself; *furthermore,* he was not sorry.
He ate the whole pie himself; *moreover,* he was not sorry.
He ate the whole pie himself; *nevertheless,* he was not sorry.

This group resembles the coordinating conjunctions in that both can join two sentences and both can stand directly between the two sentences. But words like *therefore* cannot be used to work in place of *and* in a sentence like "Cows *and* goats eat grass *and* give milk." Another difference between words like *and* and the words in this group is that words like *therefore* can change their position in the sentence and still act as connectors.

The clock struck twelve; *therefore,* Eddie got ready to leave.
The clock struck twelve; Eddie, *therefore,* got ready to leave.
The clock struck twelve; Eddie got ready to leave, *therefore.*

Taking into consideration the fact that words like *therefore* can change position and noticing that they modify the whole sentence to which they are attached you can see why they are called conjunctive *adverbs*; that is, in some ways they act like adverbs.

You should notice one final and important difference between coordinating conjunctions and conjunctive adverbs: when words like *and* join two sentences together, they are preceded by a comma; when words like *therefore* join two sentences together, they are preceded by a semicolon or a period. For more detailed information on punctuating with conjunctive adverbs, see **Comma Rules** and **Fragments** in Part 2.

3. Subordinating conjunctions

Subordinating conjunctions are words used to join a word or a word group to a sentence by subordinating, or making less important, that word or word group. Consider these sentences:

1. John sings well.
2. John is a member of the church choir.

Of the two sentences, which is more important? Obviously, either *could* be more important than the other. But suppose, for example, that we thought sentence 2 were more important. We could then join the sentences together this way:

Because John sings well, he is a member of the church choir.

The italicized portion of the new sentence now corresponds to our old sentence 1. The only difference is that we have added the word *because,* a subordinating conjunction. Of course, we could join our two original sentences together in another way:

Because he is a member of the church choir, John sings well.

Now the italicized portion corresponds to sentence 2 and the new sentence makes old sentence 1 the more important one. Of course, each version of the joined sentences has a different meaning.

Subordinating conjunctions generally act like the word *because*. Depending on the kinds of word groups you want to subordinate, you can use any of the following words as subordinating conjunctions.

after	provided	whatever
although	since	when
as	that	whenever
because	though	where
before	unless	wherever
if	until	whether
lest	what	while

Here are some further examples of how these subordinating conjunctions work:

After we had dinner, we went to the movies.
We went to the movies *after* we had dinner.

Although I am only a student, I have a good knowledge of chemistry.
I have a good knowledge of chemistry, *although* I am only a student.

Whenever I work hard, I get good grades.
I get good grades *whenever* I work hard.

Notice that the subordinated part can occur either at the beginning of the sentence or at the end.

TEST YOURSELF ON
Using Conjunctions

1. Write ten sentences in which a coordinating conjunction joins two sentences. Try to use each of the seven coordinating conjunctions at least once. See p. 26 for examples to use as models.
2. Write eight sentences in which you use each pair of correlatives at least once.
3. Write a dozen sentences using each of the conjunctive adverbs at least once.
4. Take those sentences and change the position of the conjunctive adverb.
5. In how many of the sentences you have written can you substitute a coordinating conjunction for a conjunctive adverb? Try the substitution and find out.

Pronouns

Pronouns are words that can replace nouns. Such words as *he, she, him, them, somebody, mine,* and *this* are all pronouns. An important word associated with pronouns is the word *antecedent*. Consider these examples:

I just saw *Alice. She* seems fine.
Richard put *his* money into real estate.

In the first example we say that the word *Alice* is the antecedent of the pronoun *she*. In the second example we say that the word *Richard* is the antecedent of the pronoun *his*.

Not all pronouns have antecedents in all cases, but you will want to keep the term in mind and be sure that pronouns agree with their antecedents in your writing. For more details on this, see **Pronoun References** in Part 2.

Here are the chief kinds of pronouns and the names they are known by:

Personal

I	me	my, mine
you	you	your, yours
he	him	his
she	her	her, hers
it	it	its
we	us	our, ours
they	them	their, theirs

Reflexive

myself, himself, herself, yourself, ourselves, themselves, yourselves, itself

Relative

who, whose, whom, which, that

Relative pronouns are used to connect a subordinate word group to another part of the sentence.

John, *who* sings well, is a member of the church choir.
The foreign country *that* I like best is Italy.

The antecedent of *who* in the first example is *John*, and the antecedent of *that* in the second example is *country*.

Sometimes a relative pronoun is omitted but understood in a sentence.

The car [that] I liked was a Toyota.

Interrogative

who, whom, which, what

These are used to ask questions.

Who is your friend? Which would you like? What did you say?

Demonstrative

this, that, these, those

These act to *point* to a noun, but they may also be used by themselves.

This hat is mine. (pointing to a noun)
This is mine. (as a pronoun)

Indefinite

Common indefinite pronouns are the following:

one, no one, anyone, everyone, someone
anybody, everybody, nobody, somebody, other
another, anything, everything, something, nothing
all, few, either, neither, none, most, more

Reciprocal

each other
one another

All of the pronouns listed can occupy some of the typical noun positions in sentences, although not all can occupy every noun position.

Sentence with a Noun
The man is over there.

Pronouns Substituted for the Noun
He is over there.
Mine is over there.

Somebody is over there.
Neither is over there.

Sentence with a Noun
I know the *man*.

Pronouns Substituted for the Noun
I know *him*.
I know *hers*.
I know *somebody*.
I know *neither*.

TEST YOURSELF ON
Using Pronouns

A. Use each of the following words in two sentences.

1. many	3. that	5. either	7. all
2. his	4. few	6. several	8. three

B. Replace each of the italicized words in the sentences below with a pronoun. In order to do this, you will—in some cases—have to drop a few words from the sentence.

Example: My old *grandmother* needs false teeth.
            She needs false teeth.

1. My old *grandmother* needs false teeth.

2. My old grandmother needs false *teeth*.

3. My *boss* complained to me.

4. *People* are funny.

5. *Congressmen* are politicians.

6. No *lakes* can ever be emptied.

C. Underline all the pronouns you can find in the following sentences. Some sentences have more than one.

1. His shoes are brown.

2. Mine are black.

3. Everybody knows something.

4. You should be honest with yourself.

5. My brother wanted him to be nice to everyone.

6. Anyone can tell that you have a sunburn.

7. Students are friendly to one another.

8. Nothing bothers me when I myself am driving.

9. She put herself in his position.

10. Much will be gained and nothing lost if you go swimming with us this afternoon.

11. Neither will be enough.

12. Several will be fine.

Determiners

A *determiner* is a word that signals that a noun is coming. Words that act like the definite article *the* are determiners.

the reason   *the* house   *the* man   *the* heart
_____ movie

Words that will fit into the blank space are such words as *every, your, this,* and so forth. Therefore, these are determiners.

Here is a list of frequently used determiners. It is important to note that not all determiners can be used in place of *the* with all nouns. But all determiners can be used with *some* nouns.

the	these	her	few	neither
a	those	its	several	one
an	my	no	any	two
every	our	both	all	three
each	your	some	most	four
this	their	many	more	
that	his	much	either	

Sometimes other words intervene between a determiner and the noun that it is signalling.

The house looked lived in.
The great big, ugly old *house* looked lived in.

It does not matter that in the second of these sentences many words intervene between *the* and *house,* because even though the words are far apart, *the* is a signal to the eye (or ear) that a word like *house* (a noun) is going to appear sooner or later.

Determiners, you will have noticed, are adjectives because they make more specific the noun they are announcing; not just *cats,* but *the cats, my cats, those cats.*

It is worthwhile repeating here what we said at the beginning of our study of words: some words fall into more than one class—as you have probably noticed.

TEST YOURSELF ON
Using Determiners

Fill in the blank spaces in the sentences below with a determiner. Try to use as many of those listed on p. 33 as you can.

1. _____ champion knows

   _____ opponents.

2. _____ subway rider loves riding on

   _____ trains.

3. _____ man said he needed

   _____ time.

4. _____ repairman said he had forgotten

   _____ tools.

5. _____ counterman can serve

   _____ coffee.

6. _____ year we make

   _____ trip to _____

   beach.

7. _____ cars were left in

_____ parking lot

_____ afternoon.

8. _____ professors teach

_____ courses in

_____ spring.

9. _____ birds landed on

_____ window sill

_____ morning.

10. _____ purpose is to make

_____ vacation

_____ pleasant one.

11. _____ people called on

_____ minister after

_____ service.

12. _____ years go into

_____ training of

_____ engineer.

Intensifiers

An *intensifier* is a word that occurs in sentences in the positions in which the word *very* occurs. Notice the positions occupied by *very* in the following sentences.

adj.
He had a *very* good time at the party.

adj.
These *very* beautiful paintings are mine.

adj.
The dog was *very* healthy.
adv.
He wrote *very* often.

adv.
She searched the room *very* carefully.

You can see from the first three sentences that *very* works with adjectives and from the last two that it works with adverbs. But *very* does not work with nouns; we do not say "He had a very *apple* time at the party" or the dog was very *table*."

Neither does *very* work with verbs; we do not say "He wrote very *think*" or "She searched the room very *believe*." If intensifiers *did* work with verbs, then they would modify adjectives, adverbs, and verbs and we would call them adverbs.

The following words act like *very:*

more	quite
most	rather
pretty	really
somewhat	too

He had *quite* a good time at the party.
These *rather* beautiful paintings are mine.
The dog was *really* healthy.
He wrote *pretty* often.
She searched the room *somewhat* carefully.

Intensifiers are adverbs in that they modify adjectives, but they are different from adverbs because they do not modify verbs. (We would not say "He believes *very*" or "He thinks *quite*.")

SENTENCES

Now that we have discussed words, we must begin to speak of sentences. Almost everything we say or write is made up of certain arrangements of words that we call *sentences*. When we speak a sentence, we signal its beginning and end by controlling the sounds of what we say; that is, our voices tell the listener when we have begun and when we have finished. When we write a sentence, we signal these things by beginning with a capital letter and ending with a period, question mark, or exclamation point.

There are three types of sentences, classified according to what effect they are generally intended to have on a listener:

Sentences can be commands or directions on how to do something or go somewhere (imperative sentences):

Turn on the lights.
Make a left turn.

or they can be questions (interrogative sentences):

Are you coming?

or they can be statements (declarative sentences):

I saw Uncle Fred this morning.

In this section, we will be concerned mainly with sentences that are statements. We will begin by studying certain basic facts about all sentences.

1. Every English sentence can be divided into two parts, because every sentence accomplishes two things: (1) it names something (an object, an idea, a person, a place), and (2) it says something about what it has just named.

Part 1 (what is named)	Part 2 (what is said about it)
1. Dogs	*bark.*
2. Birds	*are* beautiful.
3. Cats	*are* animals.
4. Babies	*drink* milk.
(Subject)	(Predicate)

What is named in each of the sentences we call the *subject* of the sentence; the subject is the doer or performer of the action, as in 1 and 4, or it is the thing whose state of being is described by the rest of the sentence, as in

2 and 3. What is said about the subject we call the *predicate* of the sentence.

Even when we make the sentence a bit more complicated, we can still show the basic two-part division.

Subject	Predicate
Babies	*can drink* milk very often.

What is said about babies in the predicate is now a bit more complicated, but the predicate still contains the words that do the saying about *babies*—still the subject, still the doers (the drinkers of the milk).

2. Every predicate contains at least one verb, though it may have an auxiliary and a verb. It can never have *only* an *-ing* verb and still be a sentence. Look at the italicized words in the examples above.

3. To find the subject of a sentence, first find the verb. You do this by understanding that the verb in the sentence is the word that denotes action or a state of being; you may also recall from studying verbs that verbs are words that can change tense.

Joanna *is* beautiful. (the verb: *is;* it denotes a state of being; it can be changed to *was,* the past tense)

Now if you ask the question *who* (or in some sentences *what*) *is,* you get the answer *Joanna.* And *Joanna* is the simple subject of the sentence.

Many sentences have more than one subject; these subjects are called *compound* rather than *simple.*

1. *Dogs* and *seals* bark.
2. *Birds* and *tigers* are beautiful.
3. *Cats* and *squirrels* are animals.
4. *Babies* and *kittens* drink milk.

If you wanted to know the subjects of these four sentences and asked the questions *who* bark (in 1), *what* are (in 2 and 3), and *who* drink (in 4), the answers would be the pairs of words italicized in each sentence; each would then be said to have a *compound subject.*

TEST YOURSELF ON
Locating Subjects

In each sentence below, underline the subject. To find the subject, first locate the verb—the word that indicates action or a state of being and that can change tense; then ask the question *who* or *what* (of the verb); the answer will be the subject.

1. Whiskey burns my tongue.
2. She is beautiful.
3. My father is a policeman.
4. The meat tastes good sometimes.
5. Parents scold their children sometimes.
6. The truckdriver and his helper quit early.
7. Misery loves company.
8. You and he look happy.
9. The pipe blows bubbles.
10. Everybody seemed sad.
11. His pants are bluejeans.
12. My uncle pitches horseshoes.

It may strike you that these basic facts fit well the simple sentences we have used as examples but may not be so useful in analyzing more complicated sentences. The point is a good one, and we should begin to address ourselves to it by learning something about basic sentence patterns.

If you read a page or two of a good piece of writing in English, you will probably notice that there is a good deal of variety in the sentences. Maybe no two of them will look alike to you. But the fact is that these various sentences are built on just a few basic patterns.* These patterns can be modified or combined in a variety of

---

*Just how many of these basic patterns there are is a matter of some argument, but it won't affect what we shall have to say about the main point: that just a few basic patterns underlie all sentences.

ways to produce quite complicated statements, and it is this fact that accounts for the variety you generally find in English sentences. Let us therefore begin to examine these sentence patterns to see how the basic facts—and certain others—apply to them as well as how they can be expanded to make more complicated sentences.

Pattern 1

This pattern consists of a subject (noun or pronoun) and a predicate that is or includes an intransitive verb (one that does not have to act *on* something):

Dogs bark. (*who* bark? *Dogs,* the subject)
Birds sing. (*who* sing? *Birds,* the subject)
He arrived. (*who* arrived? *He,* the subject)

There are a few simple ways in which this pattern can be modified and expanded. For example, we could place determiners in front of the nouns:

My dogs bark.
All birds sing.

Or the verb could have an auxiliary:

My dogs *are* barking.
All birds *can* sing.
He *has* arrived.

We could also add an adverb:

My dogs bark *loudly.*
All birds sing *sweetly.*
He arrived *suddenly.*

Of course, we could add all these things at once:

My dogs *can* bark *loudly.*
All birds *are* singing *sweetly.*
He *has* arrived *suddenly.*

In all these variations, the subject of each sentence remains the same. When the predicate expands, it expands to include the auxiliary and the adverb.

So we can say that this pattern consists of a *subject + predicate.*

Pattern 2

This pattern consists of a noun or a pronoun (*subject*) with a linking verb followed by an adjective (*predicate*). The most common linking verb is *be* (*am, is, are, was, were*), but others like *seem, become, feel, appear, taste,* and *grow* also are used.

Birds are beautiful. (*who* are? *Birds,* the subject; predicate is *are beautiful*)

She feels happy. (*who* feels? *She,* the subject; predicate is *feels happy*)

John looks young. (*who* looks? *John,* the subject; predicate is *looks young*)

As in Pattern 1, we can add a determiner, place an auxiliary before the verb, add an adverb, or do all three at once.

Some birds are beautiful.
She *is* feeling happy.
John looks young *occasionally*.

In these examples, the predicates expand, adding the auxiliary and an adverb to the adjective and the verb.

My dog *had* seemed unhappy *then*. (*who* had seemed? My *dog,* the subject; the predicate is *had seemed unhappy then*)

We call the adjective in each of the predicates the *predicate adjective*. It completes the description of the state of being of the subject. We can say things like "She feels [or *is*] *sad*" or "She feels *young*" or "She feels *old*" or "She feels *pretty*" and always have as the word following the linking verb the predicate adjective. In each case, the predicate adjective completes the statement.

Pattern 3

This pattern consists of a subject (noun or pronoun) with a linking verb followed by a noun (or pronoun). The verbs *be* (*am, is, are, was, were*) and *become* usually occur in this pattern. These verbs tell the reader that the nouns are closely related, if not identical.

Cats are animals.
He is Harry.
She became my wife.

One or both nouns can be preceded by determiners:

These cats are *my* animals.
The bean is *a* vegetable.

In this pattern, we can also add an auxiliary or an adverb or both at once:

These cats *may* be my animals *soon*.

We call the noun *animals* in the first example or the noun *vegetable* in the second example the *predicate noun*. It completes the description of the state of being of the subject. We can say things like "John became a policeman" or "Flounders are fish" or "The cowboy is the hero" and always have as the word following the linking verb a predicate noun. In each case, the predicate noun completes the statement.

Pattern 4

This pattern consists of a subject (noun or pronoun) with a transitive verb (one that acts *on* something) followed by another noun or pronoun. Many verbs can appear in this pattern; a few are verbs like *see, throw, create, deliver*.

Babies drink milk.
He flies airplanes.
Everybody needs a job.

As in the other patterns, we can add determiners, auxiliaries, and adverbs:

Those babies drink *their* milk.
These cats *can* drink *my* milk *often*.

We call the noun *milk* in the first example or the noun *airplanes* in the second or the noun *job* in the third the *direct object*. We say that the subject *does* the action; the direct object *undergoes* or *receives* the action of the verb.

You locate the direct object by asking still another question. Let us go through all the questions needed to identify all the parts of this basic pattern.

Cows chew grass.

Which word can change its tense? (*Chew*, which can be changed to *chewed*. *Chew* is therefore the verb.)
Who chew? (*Cows*, the subject.)
Cows chew *what*? (*Grass*, the direct object.)

Review of Sentence Patterns 1–4

Below are examples of Patterns 1–4. Each part is identified for you. (d stands for determiner.)

predicate

subj.   verb   (intransitive)
Pattern 1: Fish swim.

predicate

subj.   verb (linking)   pred. adjective
Pattern 2: Clowns are   funny.

predicate

d   subj.   verb (linking)   d pred. noun
Pattern 3: A cowboy is   a hero.

predicate

subject   verb (transitive)   direct object
Pattern 4: Mechanics repair   automobiles.

All the patterns we have described can be modified and expanded in a number of ways that we have not discussed. Later on (under Clusters), some of these ways will be discussed; perhaps you have already noticed one or two ways when you read the sections on prepositions and subordinating conjunctions. In any case, let us try one such complicated expansion in case you are still not convinced that underneath these expansions lie basic patterns.

Some big, beautiful *babies* who live in my neighborhood and cry a lot at night should *drink* their *milk* without any help from their mothers, fathers, or baby-sitters.

By looking at the italicized words, you can see that the basic sentence pattern here is *babies drink milk*—Pattern 4.

TEST YOURSELF ON
Identifying Parts of Patterns 1, 2, 3, 4: Subjects, Predicates, Verbs, Direct Objects

A. To each of the sentences listed under "Review of Sentence Patterns 1–4" above add a determiner or adjective or both to the subject and an auxiliary and an adverb to the predicate. In addition, you might add an adjective to the nouns in the predicates of Patterns 3 and 4 (e.g., *happy hero; old automobiles*).

B. Underline the subjects of the following sentences:

1. My mother is a good cook.

2. Summers are too long.

3. He had an idea.

4. Everybody likes ice cream.

5. Some do not.

6. Musicians need formal training.

7. All politicians are the same.

8. She hated her dress.

9. They ordered steak infrequently.

10. A prince is a ruler.

C. Underline all the words that belong to the predicates of the following sentences:

1. My father seldom ate bananas.

2. His friend can play golf now.

3. Al was really a terrible villain.

4. A shopkeeper is really a small businessman.

5. Sharks are always dangerous.

6. Clouds are drifting slowly.

7. His clothes would often be messy.

8. They can travel soon.

D. Describe each word of the predicates you underlined in C by writing above each D (for determiner), VL (for linking verb), VI (for intransitive verb), VT (for transitive verb), ADJ (for adjective), ADV (for adverb), AUX (for auxiliary), PRED ADJ (for predicate adjective), PRED NOUN (for predicate noun), and DIR OBJ (for direct object).

We are now ready to look at three new basic sentence patterns:

Pattern 5

This pattern consists of a noun (or pronoun) followed by a verb, another noun (or pronoun) and then a third noun (or pronoun). The verb in this pattern is a transitive verb, one of a small group that indicate giving or sending or teaching. Some of the verbs are words like *give*, *send*, *mail*, *teach*, *lend*, and *offer*. Here are some examples of Pattern 5:

My brother *gave* his friend a camera. (who *gave*? my *brother*, the subject; my brother gave what? a *camera*, the direct object)

The professor *taught* his students biology. (who *taught*? the *professor*, the subject; the professor taught what? *biology*, the direct object)

Your father *lent* you his car. (who *lent*? your *father*, the subject; your father lent what? his *car*, the direct object.

In these examples, you can see that we have identified all the parts except the noun following the verb in each. In each example, the second noun is called the *indirect object*. The indirect object is the person or thing *to* or *for whom* the direct object is given, taught, lent.

My brother gave a camera—to whom? to his *friend*. (indirect object)

The professor taught biology—to whom? to his *students*. (indirect object)

Your father lent his car—to whom? to *you*. (indirect object)

This pattern, then, consists of *subject + verb + indirect object + direct object*. You can see that the second noun (the subject is the first noun) is the indirect object and the third noun the direct object; you can also see that the second and third nouns refer to different things. When they refer to the *same* things, we have a slightly different pattern: Pattern 6.

Pattern 6

This pattern consists of *subject + verb + direct object + noun* (or pronoun). The verbs in this pattern are transitive verbs like those in Pattern 4.

d	subject	verb	d	direct object	d	noun
	We	considered	the	cowboy	a	hero.
	They	called	the	policeman	an	officer.
My	committee	elected		Jim		chairman.

Notice that in this pattern the second noun is the direct object and the third noun, which really refers to the same thing as the direct object, is called the *object complement*. A complement is something that *completes* something else. Thus the object complement completes the meaning of the direct object by identifying it further: *cowboy:hero; policeman:officer; Jim:chairman*.

Pattern 7

This is only slightly different from Pattern 6. It is the same except that the object complement is an adjective instead of a noun.

d	subject	verb	d	direct object	adjective
	We	considered	the	cowboy	foolish.
	That movie	made		my friends	angry.

Like the first four patterns studied, these can also be expanded.

My very generous and loyal *brother gave his friend* Charlie who lives in California *a camera* as a birthday present.

You can see by reading the italicized words one after the other that this sentence is a complicated expansion of a basic sentence pattern: Pattern 5.

TEST YOURSELF ON
Identifying Parts of Patterns 5, 6, 7: Indirect Objects, Object Complements (Nouns and Adjectives)

Circle the words in the following sentences that are either indirect objects or object complements. Mark the circles IO (for indirect objects), OCN (for *o*bject *c*omplements that are *n*ouns), or OCA (for *o*bject *c*omplements that are *a*djectives). Probably you will need to find the direct object before you can locate the other parts.

1. My wife bought me a wedding present.

2. Frank thought the cop a hero.

3. During the meeting, we elected Jim our spokesman.

4. The boys considered the girls beautiful.

5. Sally taught her sons arithmetic.

6. Afterwards, Uncle Joe sent Aunt Mina a letter.

7. His tailor made my friend a suit.

8. The people thought the mayor foolish.

9. I found the teacher interesting.

10. We made the beach a paradise.

11. After the party, we found the host happy.

12. He lent his brother the bike.

CLUSTERS, CLAUSES, PHRASES

Now that we have studied basic sentence patterns and learned how their parts are related, we are ready to tackle sentences with parts more complicated than single words. These complicated parts are strings of words called *phrases* and *clauses*, and they appear in still larger strings called *clusters*.

Clusters

When studying sentences, we noted an important fact about all sentences: they can be divided into two parts called the subject and the predicate. We can also divide a sentence into two parts in another way, very similar to but not identical with subject and predicate; that is, we can say that a sentence consists of a *noun cluster:* the string of words surrounding and including the subject; and a *verb cluster:* the string of words surrounding and including the verb. Consider this sentence:

The strong, young *men* in the truck, who are laborers, often *go* into that diner when they want lunch.

As you can see from the italicized words, this is nothing but an expansion of Sentence Pattern 1 (*subject + intransitive verb*) by means of strings of words surrounding and including both the subject and the verb. Thus the noun cluster is

The strong, young men in the truck, who are laborers,

and the verb cluster is

often go into that diner when they want lunch

Let us begin by examining the noun cluster:

The strong, young men in the truck, who are laborers,

The first noun in the cluster is *men*; we will call this the *headword* of the cluster. Notice that it is preceded by a determiner and two adjectives. Although we have not seen one noun modified by two adjectives before, it should not be difficult to understand that the procedure is a sound one; we have all spoken and written sentences referring to things like "the pretty little girl" and "the happy old man." Here the two adjectives are *strong* and *young*.

The next part of the cluster following the headword includes the words *in the truck*. This group consists of a preposition followed by a determiner and a noun. In the section on prepositions, we said that such a group of words is called a *prepositional phrase*. In this cluster, the prepositional phrase *in the truck* acts to make more specific the word *men*; not just *men*, but *men in the truck*. Since the phrase acts to modify the word *men* (a noun), we call it an *adjective phrase*. The *kind* of word the phrase begins with—a preposition, its headword—leads us to call it a prepositional phrase, but in *function* it acts as an adjective, even though it comes *after* and not *before* the noun. It's easier to recognize it by watching for the preposition, but it's more important to know how it acts.

We shall say more below about phrases and identify other types, but for now let's continue to look at the other part of the noun cluster:

who are laborers

We touched briefly on structures like this when we spoke of relative pronouns. You will remember that *who* as a relative pronoun subordinates or makes less important the group of words to which it is attached. Therefore we call such structures subordinate *clauses*.

This clause consists of a relative pronoun (*who*) and a predicate (*are laborers*). *Who* acts like a noun (subject) here. See what happens when we substitute *men* for *who:*

The men are laborers.

Now men is the subject of a sentence: Pattern 3 (*subject + linking verb + predicate noun*). A clause, therefore, has a predicate and a subject, but unlike a sentence a subordinate clause cannot stand alone:

subj.   predicate

Subordinate Clause   who are laborers (has subject and predicate but cannot stand alone; it is *dependent*)

subj.   predicate

Sentence   The men are laborers. (has subject and predicate and
can stand alone; it is *independent*)

Now look at the original noun cluster again:

The men in the truck who are laborers

Although the clause (*who are laborers*) is different in
form from the phrase (*in the truck*), it too makes more
specific the headword of the cluster, *men;* not just *men,*
but *men who are laborers.* Since the whole clause acts
to modify the word *men* (a noun), we call it an *adjective
clause.* This type of subordinate clause generally begins
with the words *who, whom, whose, which* or *that.*

You may already have noticed the major difference
between a clause and a phrase.

Phrase   in the truck (*has no* subject and *no* predicate)

Clause   who are laborers (*has* subject and predicate)

Keep this mind as we proceed to look at the verb cluster; we will mention this fact again.

Structures similar to the ones we have just described
occur in the verb cluster.

often go into the diner when they want lunch.

The first verb in the cluster is *go*; we will call this the
headword of the verb cluster. But before we come to
go, we find the word *often*; however, you have seen the
word *often* used before, and you know it is an adverb
modifying the headword *go.*

The next part of the cluster consists of the words *into
the diner.* By now you may be able to recognize it as
a prepositional phrase—it begins with the preposition
into and has also a determiner and a noun. But unlike
the phrase in the noun cluster, *into the diner* acts to
make clear *where* the men *go*; since it makes the *going*
more specific, it modifies *go,* and we call the phrase an
adverb phrase.

The last part of the cluster consists of the words *when they want lunch*.

We also touched briefly on this type of structure when we studied subordinating conjunctions. Recall that the word *when* is a subordinating conjunction and makes less important or subordinates the group of words to which it is attached. As you can see, the words that follow *when* (*they want lunch*) make a whole sentence (Pattern 4) by themselves, with subject (*they*) and predicate (*want lunch*); therefore, we can call *when they want lunch* a subordinate clause.

Although it is different in form from *into the diner*, it too acts to make more specific the word *go*: it makes clear *when* the men *go*. Thus the clause modifies *go* (a verb), and we call it an *adverb clause*.

Notice that it differs from the adjective clause *who are laborers* in two respects:

1. In the adjective clause, *who* is both the relative pronoun and the *subject* of the clause; in other words, *who* is part of the clause. But in the adverb clause *when they want lunch*, *when* is *not* part of the clause (*they* is its subject), but only introduces and connects it to the sentence.

2. An adverb clause can be moved around in the sentence without changing the meaning of the sentence.

The strong, young men in the truck, who are laborers, often go into the diner *when they want lunch*.

When they want lunch, the strong, young men in the truck, who are laborers, often go into the diner. (in this form, we would still say that *when they want lunch* is part of the verb cluster, because it still modifies the verb)

An adjective clause cannot be moved in this way without changing the meaning.

One last note about noun clusters: they can appear anywhere a noun can appear.

Pattern 1   *The strong, young men in the truck, who were laborers*, smiled. (*subject*)

Pattern 2   *The strong, young men in the truck, who were laborers*, felt hungry. (*subject*)

Pattern 3   The heroes were *the strong, young men in the truck, who were laborers.* (*predicate noun*)

Pattern 4   He noticed *the strong, young men in the truck, who were laborers.* (*direct object*)

Pattern 5   The carhop served *the strong, young men in the truck, who were laborers,* their morning coffee. (*indirect object*)

Pattern 6   We considered hard workers *the strong, young men in the truck, who were laborers.* (*object complement*)

Perhaps you can now see more clearly how complicated statements can be made by expanding the basic patterns.

Clauses

In the preceding section, we learned a little about an adjective clause and an adverb clause. In this section, we will review adjective and adverb clauses and learn about a third type: noun clauses.

1. Adjective clauses

Cats are animals *that can scratch.*

The italicized group of words is an adjective clause. It modifies the noun *animals* by making it more specific; not just *animals,* but *animals that can scratch.* The word *that* is part of the clause. You can substitute *animals* for it and get a sentence:

Animals can scratch.

An adjective clause can modify a noun regardless of where the noun is positioned in the sentence.

Chairs *that are covered in velvet* look elegant. (modifies *chairs*)
I don't like professors *who lecture all the time.* (modifies *professors*)
Bob was the attorney *whom the court had appointed.* (modifies *attorney*)

Three points about adjective clauses are worth noting here:

1. We usually make this distinction in using *who* and *which*: when the noun being modified refers to a person, we use *who*; when it does not refer to a person, we use *which*. But we often use *that* in place of either:

The *doctor who* treats me is a graduate of Mount Sinai.
The *law which* was passed in 1964 prohibits discrimination in housing.

or

The *doctor that* treats me is a graduate of Mount Sinai.
The *law that* was passed in 1964 prohibits discrimination in housing.

2. Frequently, in both speech and writing, we use adjective clauses and omit the subordinating conjunction.

The girl *I met* lives in Mill Valley. (*whom* or *that* is omitted between *girl* and *I*)

This happens only when we can turn the noun modified into a direct object if we make a sentence out of it and the clause words.

The *girl I met* lives in Mill Valley.
I met the girl.
The *party he gave* was a lot of fun. (*that* or *which* is omitted between *party* and *he*)
He gave the party.

3. Sometimes a *which* clause can modify a whole sentence—not just one noun in it.

He scored 87 points in one game, *which is a record for our team*.

2. Adverb clauses

Babies drink milk *when they are hungry*.

The italicized group of words is an adverb clause. It modifies the word *drink* by answering the question: *when* do babies drink milk. They don't drink it all the

time, only *when they are hungry*. The adverb clause differs from the adjective clause in two ways: 1. its con-
necting word (*when*, in this case) is not part of the
clause but stands at the beginning of it; 2. it can be
moved around in the sentence and still do its job.

Babies drink milk *when they are hungry*.
When they are hungry, babies drink milk.

Adverb clauses begin with one of the subordinating
conjunctions listed on p. 29 (words like *whenever, although, if, until, unless,* and so forth).

3. Noun clauses

What I am eating tastes good.

The italicized group of words is a noun clause. Occupy-
ing the place of a noun, it is the subject of the sentence.
You can test to see if this is true by asking the question:
what tastes good. The only satisfactory answer is *what
I am eating*. Therefore, the clause is the subject. But
the noun clause can also occur in most of the other positions typically occupied by nouns (that is, as predicate
noun, direct object, or in the position of a noun in a
prepositional phrase).

That is *what I am eating*. (predicate noun)
I love *what I am eating*. (direct object)
I am satisfied *with what I am eating*. (object of a preposition)

Noun clauses are very commonly signalled by words
like *whoever, whatever,* and *what*.

I can supply *whatever you need*.
Whoever runs will be short of breath.
What needs fixing can go to the repair shop.

TEST YOURSELF ON
Clauses

A. Using the words *who, whom, which,* and *that*, construct
clauses that modify the following words:

Example: 1. money: clauses constructed using *that* and *which:* money *that I spent yesterday,* money *which was given to me*

1. money

2. people

3. little boys

4. apples

5. laws

6. women

B. Using words such as *although, unless, because* (or any of those listed on p. 29), construct clauses to go with the following simple sentences:

Example: 1. The Scholarship Fund gave me what I asked for.
clause constructed to go with this sentence: *Although my grades weren't as good this year as they were in 1977,* the Scholarship Fund gave me what I asked for.

1. The Scholarship Fund gave me what I asked for.

2. It has hair on it.

3. Onions give me indigestion.

4. I can see my brother.

5. Parades make me nervous.

6. The office was empty.

C. Underline the clause in each of the following sentences and above each write ADV if the clause is acting as an adverb, N if it is acting as a noun, or ADJ if it is acting as an adjective.

1. What I want for supper is fish.

2. Until you come home, I have to babysit for our little brother.

3. The car that pleases me most gives good gas mileage.

4. Whatever you do is all right.

5. The man whom I pointed out is my uncle.

6. I don't know what will happen next.

7. Although I came early, the show was sold out.

8. I am disappointed because my grades were not higher this term.

9. The basketball court that is in the gym is occupied day and night.

10. The thing that hurts most is indifference.

Phrases

When we studied clusters we identified a particular kind of phrase as a prepositional phrase (*preposition + determiner + noun*). You saw that this type of phrase could be used as an adjective or an adverb, and that all phrases differed from clauses in that phrases had no subject and predicate. There are other types of phrases that can be used as adjectives and adverbs, and some of these can be used as nouns, too.

1. Phrases used as adjectives

1. The man *in the blue suit* spoke quietly. *Pattern 1*
2. The birds *flying toward the barn* are beautiful. *Pattern 2*
3. My father is a man *known for his kindness. Pattern 3*
4. I need shoes *to wear to the wedding. Pattern 4*

The italicized part of each sentence is a phrase used as an adjective. The phrase in Example 1 should be familiar: it's a prepositional phrase used as an adjective. The phrases in Examples 2 and 3 are somewhat different. Each begins with a verb. *Flying,* an *-ing* word, we call a *present participle; known* in Example 3 we call a *past participle*—it is normally used with an auxiliary, as in

He had known. Since both phrases begin with a participle, we call them *participial phrases*—but both are here *acting* as adjective phrases.

Notice that these two phrases, *flying toward the barn* and *known for his kindness,* consist of their headwords (*flying* and *known*) plus a prepositional phrase. But this type of phrase need not be structured this way. For example, we could say "The birds *flying there* are beautiful" and "My father is a man *known to be kind.*" However, they would still both be participial phrases acting as adjectives.

In Example 4 above, the italicized phrase modifies the word *shoes* by making it more specific; not just *shoes,* but *shoes to wear to the wedding.* This type of phrase has two headwords: *to* and *wear. To wear* is the infinitive form of the verb *wear.* So we call this type an *infinitive phrase* according to its form, but it is functioning as an adjective and is an adjective phrase.

2. Phrases used as adverbs

He spoke *in the afternoon. Pattern 1.*

The italicized group of words is a phrase used as an adverb. You may recognize it by its construction, *preposition + determiner + noun,* as a prepositional phrase. This phrase tells *when* he spoke, modifying the verb *spoke.*

There is one other kind of phrase that can be used as an adverb:

To avoid fatigue, he rested.

The italicized group of words is an infinitive phrase used as an adverb; it modifies the verb *rested.*

3. Phrases used as nouns

Riding a motorcycle can be dangerous. *Pattern 2*

The italicized group of words is a phrase used as a noun. It occurs in the noun position and acts as the subject of the sentence. You can test to see if this is true by asking *what* can be dangerous. The only satisfactory answer is *riding a motorcycle,* because the sentence does not say that *riding* can be dangerous or that a *motorcycle* can be dangerous.

You will notice in this phrase that the word *riding* resembles a verb in having the *-ing* ending. Here this word is not used as a verb. Instead we call it a *gerund,* that is, a verb form that acts as a noun—as in the sentence "*swimming* is fun." Therefore, for purposes of recognizing the form of the phrase, we would call *riding a motorcycle* a *gerund phrase* because it begins with a gerund; but it acts like a noun and is called a *noun phrase* by function.

This type of phrase can occupy other noun positions:

I like *riding a motorcycle.* (*direct object*)

An infinitive phrase can also be used as a noun and occupy some typical noun positions:

To ride a motorcycle can be dangerous. (*Pattern 2. subject*)
I like *to ride a motorcycle.* (*Pattern 4. direct object*)
He asked me *to ride a motorcycle.* (*Pattern 6. object complement*)

Occasionally, a prepositional phrase is used as a noun in the subject position:

Over the fence is out.
After supper is all right.

But these uses are not common.

TEST YOURSELF ON
Phrases

Underline each phrase you find in the sentences below and above each write ADJ if the phrase is being used as an adjective, ADV if it is being used as an adverb, or N if it is being used as a noun. Some sentences have more than one phrase.

1. He traveled in the afternoons.

2. The cameras carried in stock were all cheap.

3. After a few minutes, he saw the sun set over the trees.

4. Known for his pure tenor voice, he often gave concerts in the park.

5. To love deeply is my goal in life.

6. I saw him riding a bicycle.

7. Come up to my house for an hour.

8. He wants to study chemistry.

9. I saw the shoplifter running down the street.

10. She stood next to my brother.

If you have worked your way carefully through this part of the book, you should now be ready to tackle any of the entries in Part 2. These entries all focus on specific writing problems or principles of effective writing. Most of them cannot be understood without reference to some of the ideas discussed in Part 1. Thus you should continue to use this part as a reference, or, if you prefer, to use the *Glossary of Grammatical Terms*—or both. The improvement it can make in your writing is worth the effort.

An Index to Usage and the Principles of Effective Writing

Part 2

Note: Cross-references in **boldface** type are to other entries in Part 2. Cross-references in regular type are to sections in Part 1.

ABBREVIATIONS

Abbreviations can be useful in saving the writer time and space, but not all abbreviations are acceptable in essay writing. Over the years there has developed a set of conventions (agreements) that tell us when we may and when we may not use abbreviations. Here they are divided into two classes, the appropriate and the inappropriate.

Appropriate

Forms of address and titles

It is permissible to use such abbreviations as *Mr.*, *Mrs.*, *Ms.*, *Messrs.* (plural of *Mr.*), *Mmes.* (plural of *Mrs.*), *St.*, *Jr.*, *Sr.*, *M.D.* (Doctor of Medicine), *D.D.S.* (Doctor of Dental Surgery), *A.B.* (or *B.A.*, Bachelor of Arts), *M.A.* (Master of Arts), *Ph.D.* (Doctor of Philosophy), and *Esq.* (Esquire; a title appropriately used only by attorneys).

Conventional foreign words and phrases

The following abbreviations of certain useful foreign words and phrases may be used:

c *or* ca. (about)	i.e. (that is)
cf. (compare)	v. (see)
e.g. (for example)	viz. (namely)

Technical terms

The following technical terms may be abbreviated:

BTU (British Thermal Unit)	kmh (kilometers per hour)
cc (cubic centimeter)*	mpg (miles per gallon)
cm (centimeter)	mph (miles per hour)
gm (gram)	rpm (revolutions per minute)
km (kilometer)	

*cm^3 is preferable in technical writing

Organizations, institutions, government agencies, trade unions

You are probably familiar with the abbreviations for some institutions, organizations, government agencies, and trade unions—as well as other groups—because it is now common practice to use the abbreviations of their names, either as individual letters or as *acronyms*. An acronym is a pronounceable word formed from the first letters or the first few letters of several words. The point to remember when using an acronym or another kind of abbreviation for a group or organization is to write out the full name at least once, giving the abbreviation in parentheses. After the first spelling out, you may use the abbreviation alone.

The Committee on Dental Education (CODE) issued a stern warning about the use of kangaroo flakes in toothpaste. CODE officials noted that very few kangaroos have had good check-ups this year. CODE stated that fluorides are the most effective additives for toothpaste.

Here is a brief list of some common abbreviations for well-known groups; some of them are acronyms, as you can see:

ACTION (American Committee to Improve our Neighborhoods)
AFL/CIO (American Federation of Labor/Congress of Industrial Organizations)
AGO (Adjutant General's Office, U.S. Army)
CARE (Cooperative for American Relief to Everywhere)
CBS (Columbia Broadcasting System)
FBI (Federal Bureau of Investigation)
GSA (General Services Administration)
HEW (Department of Health, Education and Welfare)
UN (United Nations)
UNESCO (United Nations Educational, Scientific, and Cultural Organization)
VISTA (Volunteers in Service to America)
WHO (World Health Organization)

Expressions of time

These may be abbreviated:

1434 B.C. (before Christ)
A.D. 953 (anno domini; in the year of Our Lord)
8 A.M. *or* 8 a.m.
7:29 P.M. *or* 7:29 p.m.
EST (Eastern Standard Time)
DST (Daylight Saving Time)
MST (Mountain Standard Time)
CST (Central Standard Time)
PST (Pacific Standard Time)

Inappropriate

It is inappropriate to abbreviate in the following ways in written text. (Many of these abbreviations are acceptable in addresses and certain short references.)

Titles

Wrong   *Prof.* Smith and *Sen.* Smith are brothers.
Right   *Professor* Smith and *Senator* Smith are brothers.

Given names

Wrong   Geo., Wm., Thos., Ed., Jas., Theo.
Right   George, William, Thomas, Edward, James, Theodore

Places

Wrong   I plan to spend my vacation in *N.M.*
Right   I plan to spend my vacation in *New Mexico.*

Wrong   Of all the underdeveloped areas, *S.A.* has the highest economic growth rate.
Right   Of all the underdeveloped areas, *South America* has the highest economic growth rate.

Wrong   To get to Sarah's, take County *Rd.* to Closter.
Right   To get to Sarah's, take County *Road* to Closter.

Wrong   Jerry lives at Elm *St.* and Carson *Ave.*
Right   Jerry lives at Elm *Street* and Carson *Avenue.*

Days of the week, names of the months, and holidays

Wrong   The King died on *Tues.*
Right   The King died on *Tuesday.*

Wrong   The academic calendar runs from *Oct.* to May.
Right   The academic calendar runs from *October* to May.

Wrong   For *Xmas,* I'd like a new bathrobe.
Right   For *Christmas,* I'd like a new bathrobe.

Units of measurement

Wrong   ins., ft., yds., mi., lbs., oz.
Right   inches, feet, yards, mile, pounds, ounces

Academic courses

Wrong   Richard is failing *eco.* and *psych.* this term.
Right   Richard is failing *economics* and *psychology* this term.

Miscellaneous items

Do not use the ampersand (&) unless it is part of an official company name, for example, *Earl H. Rovit & Son, Inc.* In ordinary circumstances, use *and* in place of &.

Do not abbreviate ordinary words through laziness or because you are uncertain about their spellings. Do not, for example, substitute *thru* for *through,* *tho* for *though,* *yrs* for *yours* or *mtns* for *mountains.*

TEST YOURSELF ON
Abbreviations

By using abbreviations where appropriate, correct the errors in the following sentences. Place the letter C next to sentences that you think are correct.

1. _____ Mister Tuten took the stand and stated that at 8

ay em, when the accident took place, he was traveling at 55 miles per hour.

2. _____ The physician on duty administered 100 cubic centimeters of insulin.

3. _____ He said he was able to get through the winter by taking a short vacation in Florida at Christmas time.

4. _____ By using the Panama Canal, ships can avoid going around the tip of S.A.

5. _____ The Council to Rehabilitate Urban Military Back Yards announced a fund-raising drive today. Officials of the Council to Rehabilitate Urban Military Back Yards set their goal at $3,000,000 and said they hoped to reach it by St. Pat's day.

6. _____ Many species of fish inhabit this lake, e.g., pike, perch, and catfish; some specimens have measured as much as twenty inches and weighed as much as fourteen pounds.

7. _____ On Mon., Wed., and Fri. I go from eco to philo and then on to gym.

8. _____ Driving west toward California, you can pass through Ill. and Kan.

9. _____ Before I started my diet on Thurs., I weighed 242 lbs.

10. _____ The mtns look toward Penn on one side and W.Va. on the other.

11. _____ Gail & Grace have both broken up with their boyfriends.

12. _____ His parents hope that Joseph Young, Junior will grow up to be like Joseph Young, Senior.

ACTIVE VOICE
See **Voice.**

ADJECTIVALS
An adjectival is any word, phrase, or clause that can act as an adjective in a sentence. See **Modifiers.**

ADVERBIALS
An adverbial is any word, phrase, or clause that can act as an adverb. See **Modifiers.**

AMBIGUITY
When something can be read in two or more ways then we say it is ambiguous, that is, it has ambiguity. *Mail leaves tomorrow* could mean that *the mail will leave tomorrow* or that the writer of the message wants *his leaves* mailed tomorrow. See Determiners, Auxiliaries; **Modifiers, Pronoun References, Shifts.**

ANTECEDENTS
An antecedent is what a pronoun may sometimes refer to and must always agree with. See **Pronoun References, Shifts;** Pronouns.

APOSTROPHE

The apostrophe is a mark used by convention (agreement) to signal contractions, possessives, and certain special plurals.

Contractions

The rule for contracting two words into one is to use the apostrophe in place of the missing letter or letters.

```
are not = aren't
Bud is = Bud's (see also Possessives, below)
cannot = can't
it is = it's (but its, possessive)
let us = let's
we have = we've
would not = wouldn't
you will = you'll
```

Possessives

In English, there are two ways to express possession, ownership, and similar relationships when using nouns.

The *office of the manager* is located at the top of the stairs.
The *manager's office* is located at the top of the stairs.

Both ways are correct. In general, we would use the first method (using the word *of*) for nouns that stand for something inanimate and the second (using an apostrophe and -s) for nouns representing something animate.

Animate Judy's room; Mark's office; Franny's eyes; Colin's book

Inanimate the light of the moon; the color of the paint; the score of the game

Nevertheless, it is valuable to know that both forms mean the same thing: possession. For if you are having trouble with the apostrophe -s (*'s*) form, you can determine whether or not the *'s* is needed by using the fact we've just noted. For example, suppose that one of your essays contained the following phrases, and that you were unsure whether an apostrophe were needed in any of them.

1. Charlies horse
2. Clarences cross
3. Janeys boss
4. Marks loss
5. the Smiths went

Using the fact noted above—that the *of* form and the *'s* form both mean the same thing—we can try to see whether any of the five phrases can be turned into the alternative *of* form.

1. Charlies horse = the horse of Charlie
2. Clarences cross = the cross of Clarence
3. Janeys boss = the boss of Janey
4. Marks loss = the loss of Mark
5. the Smiths went ≠ the went of Smith

We can see clearly that the first four examples can be changed into the alternative form and therefore need an apostrophe in the original form—as follows:

1. Charlie's horse
2. Clarence's cross
3. Janey's boss
4. Mark's loss

Example 5 needs no apostrophe because it contains no possessive.

TEST YOURSELF ON
   Changing from One Form of Possession
   to the Other

Using the rule you learned, change the following into the alternative possessive form:

1. the outcome of the game

2. the tirade of Lenny

3. the argument of the Mayor

4. the future of the boy

5. the impatience of my father

6. the wit of Eddie

7. the engine of Phil

8. the winged chariot of time

9. the ale of Gail

10. the acting of Colin

Forming the possessive of singular nouns and indefinite pronouns

In order to form the possessive of singular nouns and indefinite pronouns* that do not end in -s simply add *'s*.

my father's cigarette
my mother's comb
TV Guide's features
everybody's future

a doctor's appointment
anybody's game
teacher's pet
nobody's fault

Forming the possessive of plural nouns

To form the possessive of plural nouns, add *'s* to nouns with an irregular plural (e.g., *children, men, women*); but add *only* an apostrophe to plurals ending in -s.

Irregular Plurals
men's clothing
women's liberation
children's growth

Regular Plurals
the boys' hats (the hats belong to more than one boy)
his parents' devotion (the devotion of two people: mother and father)
students' grades

Note: Never use an apostrophe for any of the possessive personal pronouns. That is, *his, hers, its, yours, ours, theirs, mine* already indicate possession and need no additional marks to indicate that fact.

Forming the possessive of nouns ending in -s, -x, and -z

The rule here is the same as the previous one for plurals ending in -s.

Marx' philosophy	the Joneses' garage
Lefty Gomez' career	Ulysses' voyage
the boss' daughter	Venus' orbit

However . . .

In the case of plural nouns ending in any of these letters (-s, -x, -z), you have a spelling option based on how you pronounce these possessives. For example, if you actually *say boss-es* in pronouncing *boss'* then you may spell it to conform with the pronounciation. Thus the following alternative spellings would also be correct:

Marx's philosophy
Lefty Gomez's pitching
the boss's daughter

Forming the possessive of two or more nouns

Place the *'s* after the last item in the series of nouns if you want to indicate joint ownership; place the *'s* after each item if you want to show individual possession but talk about both items in the same sentence.

I stayed at *Fred and Ed's* house. (they own the house together)
I have sympathy for *Fred's and Ed's* troubles. (each man's troubles are his own; the speaker declares sympathy for that which belongs to each man—and does so in the same sentence)

Forming the possessive of compound nouns

In a compound noun, the last word takes *'s*:

my mother-in-law's generosity
the Attorney General's order
my brother-in-law's book

Special Plurals

The apostrophe is used to form the plurals of certain signs, numbers, letters, and words.*

Count up all the +'s and −'s.
On her quizzes, she had all *8*'s and *9*'s.
He had trouble pronouncing his *s*'s and his *th*'s.
Don't use too many *which*'s in your writing.

TEST YOURSELF ON
The Correct Use of the Apostrophe

Each of the sentences below has either a misplaced or an omitted apostrophe. Supply the apostrophes where needed and strike out those that are superfluous.

1. The womens' liberation movement grows stronger every day because of it's militant posture.

2. During the 50s, the outspoken would'nt speak; their's was the silent age.

3. Charleys horse had a Charley horse before Tuesday's race's.

4. The Attorney Generals office is flooded with work; Federal crime's seem to be happening at a record rate.

5. If you get 90s and 100s on your exams, your grade index this term will be higher than Max'.

6. If she wont give you her book's, thats all right; Grandmas grammars are hers to give.

7. Its in your pant's pocket.

8. My mother-in-laws kindness to others has made her famous in Waterbury.

---

*The apostrophe is sometimes also used for plural dates: "The 1800's were a time of change." However, it is preferable to write *1800s* for this kind of date.

9. Harry's and Frank's book is likely to be published this year.

10. Mrs. Gonzalez's fathers sister was the first member of his family to arrive in the United States.

11. My father-in-laws' story-telling is always fascinating.

12. I'm tired of Linda Ronstadts; play someone elses records.

13. Anybody's troubles are my trouble's.

14. Ham and egg's is my favorite dish.

15. Peoples interests are determined by the complicated fact's of their lives.

APPOSITIVES

An appositive is a noun, or some structure that can take the place of a noun, that is set right next to a noun to further explain or define it. It is set in *apposition*—in the next position in the sentence—to the noun which it will expand on. An appositive can be a single word or a group of words. In the following examples, the first noun is in italics and the appositive is in boldface.

The *teacher*, **Davis,** spoke slowly. (word)
McGinnis' *skill,* **stuffing a basketball through a hoop,** earns him a large salary. (phrase)
The *teacher*, **a physics professor,** spoke slowly. (clause)

An appositive can occur in a sentence in various positions where nouns occur.

That was *Eddie,* **my friend.**
He liked my *car,* **a '57 Chevvy.**

A useful fact to understand about appositives is that this structure is really an abbreviated clause.

The *teacher*, **Davis,** spoke slowly. (the appositive *Davis* is really a *part* of the clause *whose name is Davis*)
McGinnis' *skill,* **stuffing a basketball through a hoop,** earns him a large salary. (the appositive, *stuffing a basketball through a*

hoop, is really a *part* of the clause *which is stuffing a basket-ball through a hoop*)

There is another important fact about appositives that you should understand. Some are not essential to complete the meaning of the sentence; these are therefore called *nonrestrictive*. They are set off by commas. The appositives are italicized in the examples:

The doctor, *Allan Peters,* treated me for the flu. (the essential meaning is "The doctor treated me for the flu.")
For Christmas, I got a camera, *a Kodak Instamatic.* (the essential meaning is "For Christmas, I got a camera.")

However, some appositives *are* essential to the meaning of the sentence; these are called *restrictive*. They are *not* set off by commas because they *belong* to the noun they are set beside.

The gas station attendant *John* gave my car a lube job. (the essential meaning here is not that *the* gas station attendant gave my car a lube job, but that the gas station attendant named John did the job—there was more than one attendant and *John* identifies the correct one)
I was helped through college by my Aunt *Martha.* (if the speaker had had only one aunt, then the word *Martha* would have been nonessential; as it is, *Martha* identifies one of the aunts and is an essential word)

(See also **Comma Rules,** 5, for more on restrictives and nonrestrictives.)

TEST YOURSELF ON
Appositives

A. Underline the appositives in the following sentences.

1. My instructor, John Davis, liked to give difficult assignments.

2. We went to the garage, an old building on North Main Street.

3. My sister Jean Diamant works for the State of New Jersey.

4. We all liked Murray, our class president.

5. The old man, white-haired and frail, spoke too softly.

6. We thought of him as a character, someone different from the rest of us.

B. The following sentences all contain appositives, but they are all improperly punctuated. First, underline the appositive; then decide whether or not to set it off by a comma or commas. *Remember:* If the appositive is essential to the sentence (restrictive), do not use the comma or commas; if the appositive is nonessential (nonrestrictive), do use the comma or commas.

1. We slept that night in the tent an old piece of canvas with a dozen holes in it.

2. The Colonel Thomas Jones commanded the regiment as if he were a drill sergeant.

3. The police arrested two people a pickpocket and a burglar.

4. My aunt who lives in California Rebecca Rose is a movie producer.

5. We had to read *War and Peace* a book by someone named Tolstoy.

6. The cop we liked best O'Reilly treated us like human beings.

7. We were in the hands of the mediator the one who would decide.

8. Arthur Hopkins was a law professor a status he had achieved at a very young age.

9. The fighter we were eager to see Jackson was up against a tough opponent.

10. The author of the book Grace Paley will be autographing copies at Macy's today.

AUXILIARIES

Auxiliarics or helping verbs are the following: forms of the verb *be* (*am, is, are, was, were*); *has, have, had; do, did; can, could; be able to; may, might; would; should; must; ought to; shall* and *will*. For detailed information on how auxiliaries are used, see Auxiliaries.

BUSINESS LETTERS

In a world as complex as this one, nearly everyone has to write a business letter at some time or other. But what is a business letter as opposed to, say, a letter to a friend?

It is, first and foremost, a formal piece of communication that says you mean business. The formality, expressed in both the writing style and the conventions of typography and layout we shall discuss, declares the writer a serious and reliable individual with serious business to transact. This impression is distinctly different from that conveyed by an ordinary informal letter to friends or relatives, where the primary purpose is to convey personal and intimate information.

You may have to write a business letter in applying for a job or a place in a professional school; you may have to write one making an inquiry or a complaint. Whatever the purpose of your business letter, it should follow these conventions:

1. Type business letters on plain white bond paper, 8½×11 inches in size.

2. Use standard business envelopes, 3⅝×6½ inches or 4⅛×9½ inches.

3. Be sure to pay careful attention to all six parts of the business letter: the heading, the inside address, the salutation, the body of the letter, the complimentary close, and the signature (handwritten and then typed).

Sample Letter: Modified Block Style

1. Heading { 105 Wedgwood Drive
Waterbury, Conn. 06705
April 11, 1977

Mr. Richard Appleman
Manager, Architect's Service Corporation } 2. Inside address
54 East 8th Street
New York, N.Y. 10003

Dear Mr. Appleman: 3. Salutation   4. Body

This letter is in answer to your advertisement
for a summer architectural apprentice published in
the March issue of <u>Architectural Digest</u>. I wish
to apply for this position and believe I am
well-qualified.

As an architecture student at the University of
Connecticut, Storrs, I have completed thirty
credits of courses in mechanical drafting, design,
and stress and materials. My sophomore project, a
design for a domed stadium, won second prize in
the Architecture Department's competition. Last
fall, I was employed part-time in the Department
of Buildings here in Waterbury. The job required
me to read blueprints and I am thus familiar with
building specifications and details.

Should you wish to see my employment folder, you
may contact Ms. Katherine Roe. She is empowered
to send you my resume and letters of recommendation.

        Ms. Katherine Roe, Director
        Office of Student Employment
        University of Connecticut
        Storrs, Connecticut 06268

I am available for an interview at your
convenience any time after 12 noon on Fridays, or
during the entire week of April 18. Should you
wish to telephone, I can be reached at (203)
755-5900.

5. Complimentary close   Yours sincerely,
6. Handwritten signature   *Peter S. Mudd*
6. Typed signature   Peter S. Mudd

The sample letter is typed in modified block style. If it were done in full block style, the heading and the closing would, like the rest of the letter, be flush with the left-hand margin. (The main styles are listed at the back of *Webster's New Collegiate Dictionary*.)

1. The heading

Notice that no part of this three-line heading is indented and that there is no end punctuation. The lines are single spaced. When letterhead stationery is used, the date is sometimes centered two or three spaces below the printed material.

2. The inside address

Four to six spaces separate the heading from the inside address. Like the heading, the address is in block form. Notice that the address is spelled out without abbreviation, except the state; if an address is judged to be too long, certain abbreviations can be used—for example, *3512 Runnymede Pl., N.W.*

3. The salutation

The salutation (or greeting) is flush against the left-hand margin and placed two spaces below the last line of the inside address. Notice the colon following the name of the addressee.

Where it is known, always use the surname of the addressee. Where it is not known, you have a choice of the following:

```
Dear Sir or Madam:
Dear Sir:
Dear Madam:
Gentlemen:
```

The salutation "To Whom It May Concern" is generally used when a letter is not addressed to a particular company or organization.

4. The body of the letter

This is normally single-spaced, with double-spacing used to separate paragraphs. Paragraphs should be flush with the left-hand margin if you are using the full block or modified block style (or they should begin with equal indentations, depending on your use of other styles).

The subject matter should be appropriately organized into paragraphs—that is, each paragraph should be devoted to one general idea. Use the plainest and most direct writing style, and avoid informal phrasing.

5. The complimentary close

Business letters have a variety of closes: *Yours truly, Very truly yours, Yours sincerely, Sincerely yours*. Occasionally, it is appropriate in a business letter to use *Cordially yours,* or *Cordially*—when you are on very friendly terms with the recipient. *Note:* The second word of the complimentary close begins with a small letter.

6. The signature

The handwritten signature.

The handwritten signature goes between the close and the typed signature. Do not in handwriting indicate your official capacity or title.

The typed signature.

The typed signature may be followed by your official title or capacity.

Yours sincerely,

William J. Mudd, M.D.

Sincerely yours,

Douglas Hurban
Professor of Physiology

Women have generally been accorded the option of enclosing in parentheses either Ms., Miss, or Mrs. beside their typed names. A married woman may choose to add Mrs. together with her husband's name in parentheses.

Yours sincerely,

Janet Miller

(Ms.) Janet Miller

Yours sincerely,

Louise Johnson

Louise Johnson
(Mrs. John Johnson)

Envelopes

The envelope should be addressed as follows:

```
Peter S. Mudd
105 Wedgwood Drive
Waterbury, Conn. 06705



          Mr. Richard Appleman
          Manager, Architect's Service Corp.
          54 East 8th St.
          New York, N.Y. 10003
```

TEST YOURSELF ON
Writing Business Letters

Write the following business letters:

1. to your local light and power company requesting a clarification of their new rate schedules for both electricity and natural gas fuel;

2. to the manager of a seashore hotel in Florida requesting a room reservation with a terrace facing the ocean;
3. to your Congressman, urging him or her to vote for a bill that you are interested in seeing passed;
4. to a former employer, requesting that a letter of recommendation be sent to the placement office of your college, where your folder is on file.
5. to a former professor, requesting a letter recommending your admission to medical school; remind the professor of the course you took and the progress you have made since that time.

CAPITALIZATION

The use of capital and lower case (small) letters follows a number of clear rules. We can number these for convenience as follows:

1. Beginning a sentence

Capitalize the first words of sentences.

Lasagna and pizza are Italian delicacies.
Travel agents are now offering charter flights to Mars.

2. The pronoun *I* and the interjection *O* (or *Oh*)

Capitalize these no matter where they occur in the sentence.

Doug says *I* am an astronaut.
He had O such an elegant jacket!

3. Days of the week, months, holidays

Capitalize all of these no matter where they occur in the sentence.

Tuesday	April	Memorial Day
Friday	August	Easter
Sunday	January	Christmas

4. Titles of books, plays, movies, TV shows, short stories, poems

Capitalize all of these no matter where they occur in the sentence. Articles and pronouns are not capitalized unless they begin the title.

The Sun Also Rises (book)
Caesar and Cleopatra (play)
Star Wars (movie)
The Fitzpatricks (TV show)
"Asparagus Soup" (short story)
"Lycidas" (poem)

Important note: These titles should also be either italicized or enclosed in quotation marks, as they are above. See **Italics** and **Quotation Marks** for further information.

5. Proper names, proper adjectives, and titles

Capitalize the proper names of persons or geographical locations. Capitalize official titles but only when the title accompanies the name of the person holding the title.

Capitalize an official title when (a) it is used in place of a name to refer to the titleholder or (b) when it is used with the titleholder's name. Do not capitalize when the title refers to the office but not the person.

James Greene   Oneonta, New York
Kathy Roe   Niagara Falls
Olive Piper   Mount McKinley
Bronxite   New Englander
Middle East   Ninth Street
Lake Erie   Mars
Italian   Venus
Israeli   Sirius II
Westerly, R.I.

Judge Constance Baker Motley is presiding. The Judge is late today. [Used in place of name of Mrs. Motley.]
Senator Moynihan
We are electing a senator today. (refers to office but not to specific senator)

Vice-President Mondale
Corporal Zeiger
General Custer
The General lost his head today. (refers to General Custer)
Reverend Justice

6. Historical events, historical terms, historical artifacts

Use a capital letter for items such as the following:

the Civil War	the Enlightenment
the Declaration of Independence	the Augustan Age
the Magna Carta	the Battle of the Marne

7. Terms associated with colleges and universities

Use a capital letter for courses that are specifically designated by number. Use a lower case letter for those that are not so designated (except languages, which are always capitalized). Use a capital letter for academic titles or where the title alone is used to refer to the person holding it.

Biology 137
Math 11
French
anthropology (as in "I am taking anthropology this term.")

Dean Theodore L. Gross

The Dean (referring to Dean Gross)
Professor Blanche Skurnick
Dr. Gerald Gould

8. Miscellaneous items

Use a capital letter for the names of public or private buildings

the White House	the Gardner Mansion
the Flatiron Building	the Kennedy Center
the World Trade Center	the Renaissance Center

Use a capital letter for the names of both private and public organizations

the Agriculture Department
the United Nations
the New York Yankees
Hadassah
the Modern Language Association
the Missouri Historical Society

Use a capital letter for virtually all references to things religious: deities, churches, adjectives based on these.

Hindu
God
the Lord
Anglican
Christ
Moses
the United Methodist Church
Catholicism
Christian
the Bible
Genesis
the Bhagavad Gita
Mosaic

Use a capital letter for products referred to by brand name:

| Xerox | Rice Krispies | Chevrolet |
| Scotch tape | Kleenex | Sony |

TEST YOURSELF ON
Capitalization

Read carefully each of the following sentences. Where there is an error in capitalization, indicate the error by writing CAP in the space provided. Then correct the error. If the sentence is correct, write C in the space.

1. _____ On friday we are taking the venus Special to Mars.

2. _____ Senator Moynihan made his maiden speech in

congress today; the senator spoke on rock 'n roll.

3. _____ To be mayor of New York is a little crazy.

4. _____ He didn't say i was a graduate of City college—he said I was a prisoner.

5. _____ An arabian knight is oil right.

6. _____ President Carter favors a policy of lasting peace in the Middle East.

7. _____ The level of pollution in lake Erie is superseded only by the level of pollution in the Passaic river, according to measurements conducted by the Environmental protection administration, made last january.

8. _____ The work of a college president would be no challenge to the Dean.

9. _____ Next semester, I plan to take chemistry, Biology 101, mathematics, History 98, and Physics.

10. _____ The junior colleges in this state are suffering great great decreases in student enrollment.

11. _____ This year we plan a big Memorial day parade followed by a dinner dance in the evening.

12. _____ At the University of Michigan, we are required to take classes in english.

13. _____ During World War II, spam was invented.

14. _____ Amy Carter is one of the youngest residents of the white house.

15. _____ The judge will now charge the jury.

16. _____ He was a christian gentleman.

CASE

In grammar, the word *case* refers to the capacity of a noun or pronoun to show its function in a sentence by means of its form. For example, you might write four sentences like the following:

1. *I* was happy.
2. *Mine* are blue.
3. He gave *me* an orange.
4. *We* invited *them*.

Example 1 uses *I* as the subject. Example 2 uses *mine* as the subject, but *mine* clearly suggests possession, something that belongs to the writer of the sentence. Example 3 uses *me* as the indirect object. Example 4 uses *we* as the subject and *them* as the direct object.

Now you would *not* write, in place of these sentences, "*Me* was happy" or "*I* are blue" or "He gave *we* an orange" or "*Us* invited *they*."

In writing the sentences correctly (Examples 1–4 above), we have used the proper *case* for the pronouns. *Them* and *me* are always used as objects; *mine* or *my* are always used to mean possession. As you will see below, *I* and *we* are used not only as subjects but in other positions in the sentence too.

This system of cases is an essential feature of some languages other than English; in those languages, adjectives and nouns and pronouns may have as many as five different sets of endings (or cases) to show the function of the words in sentences. But in English there are only three cases: *nominative, possessive,* and *objective.*

You need not worry about nouns; they have just two case forms: (1) the common form, for example, *doctor,* which is used to indicate all of that word's functions in a sentence (subject, object, and so forth) except possession; and (2) the possessive form, for example, *doctor's,* which of course indicates possession.

It is the case of pronouns that requires the writer's attention. The three cases—nominative, possessive, and objective—can be summarized as shown in the following table.

Nom.:	I	we	you*	he	she	it*	they	who
Poss.:	my, mine	our, ours	your, yours	his	her, hers	its	their, theirs	whose
Obj.:	me	us	you	him	her	it	them	whom

Following are the rules for the proper use of each case.

Nominative

A. Use the nominative case for the word in the subject position in the sentence. We need hardly say more about this rule, since few of us are likely to write sentences like "*Us* have a date tomorrow," or "*Me* want an apple."

B. Use the nominative case *who* in a clause where it is clearly the subject of the verb; do not be tempted into using *whom* by the words that intervene between *who* and its verb.

clause
There is a professor *who I know works hard to make contact with students.* (*who* is here the subject of *works;* you should not make the error of thinking that *whom* should replace it because of the words *I know*)

clause
He saw some men in uniform *who he thought were Marines.* (*who* is the subject of *were;* do not think that *whom* should replace *who* because of the words *he thought*)

*As you can see, *it* and *you* do not change in the objective case, only in the possessive.

C. In formal writing, use the nominative case after forms of the verb *be* (*is*, *are*, *was*, *were*, and so forth). Many good writers and speakers use the objective case, but formal writing requires the nominative.

Formal It is *I*. It might be *they*.

Informal It's *me*. It might be *them*.

D. Use the nominative case, in formal writing, after the conjunctions *as* and *than*. In these constructions, the pronoun is the subject of an omitted verb. In informal writing and in speech the objective case is frequently used.

Formal He is hungrier *than I* [am]. (*am* in this sentence is omitted but understood by the reader, and *I* is the subject of *am*; therefore, *I* must be in the nominative case)

Informal He is hungrier *than me*. (here the conjunction *than* is made into a preposition, with *me* as its object)

Formal We are as intelligent *as they* [are]. (*are* is omitted but understood by the reader; they is the subject of *are* and is therefore in the nominative case)

Informal We are as intelligent *as them*. (*as* is made into a preposition, with *them* as its object)

E. Use the nominative case when the pronoun appears as part of a compound subject.

Jack and *he* played cards last night. (the compound subject of this sentence is the words *Jack* and *he;* the whole sentence really combines two sentences: "*Jack* played cards last night" and "*He* played cards last night")

F. Use the nominative case of a pronoun in an appositive where that pronoun explains or further identifies a noun that is either the subject or the predicate noun.

appositive

It was the *coach, he* alone, who held the team together. (*coach* is the predicate noun; therefore, *he,* the appositive pronoun, is in the nominative case)

appositive

Those *two*—the policeman and *he*—prevented a robbery. (*two* is the subject; therefore, *he,* the pronoun in the appositive, is in the nominative case)

Note: Not all pronouns in appositives are in the nominative case. See Objective, below, for examples of appositive pronouns in the objective case.

Possessive

A. Use pronouns in the possessive case to indicate possession, source, authorship, and similar relationships.

I liked *his* speech very much.
I know *whose* house that is.
The legislature has *its* power limited by the judiciary.

B. In formal writing, use the possessive case of a noun or a pronoun before a *gerund*. A gerund is the *-ing* form of a verb that is used as a noun; for example, *swimming* is a gerund when used in the sentence, "Swimming is fun." In informal writing, you will sometimes see the objective case used instead of the possessive.

Formal   There was a good reason for *his* working hard.
Informal   There was a good reason for *him* working hard.

Formal   She was glad about *Charley's* organizing the concert.
Informal   She was glad about *Charley* organizing the concert.

Notice the subtle difference in meaning in the last pair of examples. In the first, the emphasis is on the organizing of the concert. In the second, the emphasis is on Charley.

Objective

A. Use the objective case where the pronoun is the object of a verb.

The weird noise troubled him. (*him* is the object of *troubled*)
Whom did you invite? (*whom* is the object of the verb)

It is important to understand that where the object is a compound construction containing, say, a proper name and a pronoun, the pronoun must be in the objective case.

The club elected Paul and *me* co-chairmen. (*Paul* and *me* are the objects of the verb *elected;* therefore *me* is in the objective case; do not say "Paul and *I*" in a construction like this. You would not say "The club elected *I* chairman.")

B. Use the objective case when the pronoun is the object of a verbal. A verbal is either a verb ending in *-ing* or an infinitive, that is, a verb with the word *to* preceding it (*to work, to play,* and so forth).

Knowing *him* was a pleasure. (*him* is the object of *knowing*)
Whenever I see babies, I want to kiss *them.* (*them* is the object of *to kiss*)

Note: An exception to this rule occurs when the infinitive is the verb *to be* and the subject of the infinitive is unexpressed; then formal usage requires that the nominative case be used after the infinitive.

Formal I wouldn't want *to be he.*
Informal I wouldn't want *to be him.*

C. Use the objective case for a pronoun that is the object of a preposition.

Three of *us* went to the movies last night. (*us* is the object of the preposition *of*)
He is the professor for *whom* I worked hardest. (*whom* is the object of the preposition *for*)

It is important to note that on occasion two pronouns will be objects of the same preposition. Both must then be in the objective case.

Bob and I both wanted the job; the boss would have to choose between *him* and *me.* (both *him* and *me* are objects of the preposition *between*)

D. In formal writing, use the objective case *whom* in a clause where it is clearly the object of the verb. In informal writing, *who* is widely used instead of *whom*.

Formal She is the visitor *whom* we expected. (*whom* is the object of *expected*)
Informal She is the visitor *who* we expected.

Formal   *Whom* are you criticizing? (*whom* is the object of *are criticizing*)
Informal   *Who* are you criticizing?

The word *whom* is now used less and less, even among well-educated writers and speakers. Still, in certain cases, *whom* is the much-to-be-preferred formal choice.

Whom do you want to see?
Whom are you waiting for?

Note: Whom is *always* used when the pronoun directly follows a preposition.

For *whom* are you waiting?
I don't know to *whom* he spoke.

E. Use the objective case of a pronoun following the conjunctions *as* and *than* if that pronoun is the object of a verb that has been omitted from the sentence.

He likes her more *than* [he likes] *me.* (*me* is the object of *likes*)
I treated her as fairly *as* [I treated] *him.* (*him* is the object of *treated*)

F. Use the objective case of a pronoun that appears in an appositive when that pronoun explains or further identifies a noun that is an object.

appositive
The coach fired two *players,* Colin and *me* (*me* is in the objective case because it further identifies the noun *players,* the object of *fired*)

Note: Do not use the reflexive pronoun *myself* in place of the objective pronoun *me.*

Wrong   My aunt willed her estate to my brother and *myself.*
Right   My aunt willed her estate to my brother and *me.*

TEST YOURSELF ON
Using the Correct Case of Pronouns

Select the proper case of the pronoun from the choices in parentheses in each of the following sentences. Make your choices in accordance with correct formal usage.

1. She talked to Ed and (I, me) for a long time.
2. I can't imagine (his, him) accepting the job.
3. He didn't look it, but Paul was as tired as (I, me).
4. The Mayor, (he, him) alone, was responsible for slum conditions in our city.
5. The blue jeans fitted Bob as well as (I, me).
6. Somehow, Richard thought he was better than (I, me).
7. When Betty ran to answer the phone, she knew it was (he, him).
8. They never found out the names of the vandals (who, whom) they believed were destroying the highway signs.
9. Chris and (he, him) got drunk together last night.
10. The two of them—Irv and (he, him)—drove to California in three days.
11. I can do the job without (his, him) instructing me every minute.
12. The girls considered Jim and (I, me) the most attractive bachelors they knew.
13. (Who, Whom) are you waiting for?
14. They gave medals to two swimmers, David and (me, I).
15. After the party, the host was as tired as (I, me).

COHERENCE

The word *coherence* means "a sticking together." When we use it to refer to writing, we mean (1) that the parts of a sentence stick together to form a correct and logical utterance; (2) that the sentences in a paragraph are in logical and smoothly connected order; and (3) that each paragraph in a piece of writing is logically and smoothly connected to the ones that precede and follow it.

Achieving Coherence in Sentences

Many different kinds of errors contribute to the lack of coherence in sentences. Some of these are discussed in separate entries (**Dangling Modifiers, Diction** (especially Idioms), **Misplaced Modifiers, Parallel Construction, Pronoun References, Shifts**). In order to achieve coherence in the sentence, it is necessary to avoid the following kinds of errors as well.

1. Avoid split constructions

A. Do not needlessly separate the subject of the sentence and the verb.

Poor   *Lisa,* after gathering together her clothes, books, and papers, *packed.*
Better   After gathering together her clothes, books, and papers, Lisa packed.

B. Do not needlessly separate the verb and its complement.

Poor   The truck driver delivered, after driving all night in a terrible rainstorm, the new boiler we had ordered.
Better   After driving all night in a terrible rainstorm, the truck driver delivered the new boiler we had ordered.

C. Do not needlessly split an infinitive. To do so may destroy the coherence of the sentence. A split infinitive, however, does not always lead to incoherence; sometimes it cannot be avoided and produces perfect clarity.

Awkward   He asked me *to as quickly as possible drop over* to his house. (notice how this very nearly produces a "squinting modifier": was he asked quickly or was he supposed to drop over quickly?)
Correct   He asked me *to drop over* to his house as quickly as possible.

Awkward   I promised *to immediately try out* for the football team.
Correct   I promised *to try out* for the football team immediately.

Appropriate IBM expects *to more than double* its business this year.

Appropriate *To just miss* the train is a bad start for anybody's day.

2. Avoid illogical subjects and complements

A. Do not carelessly use a modifying phrase or clause as the subject of a sentence.

Wrong *Because he drove too slowly* made him miss the first inning of the game. (the adverb clause cannot be the subject of *made*)

Right Because he drove too slowly, he missed the first inning of the game.

Right Driving too slowly made him miss the first inning of the game.

Wrong *By using power tools* will save a lot of hard work. (the italicized phrase cannot be used as the subject of *will save*)

Right Using power tools will save a lot of hard work.

Right The use of power tools will save a lot of hard work.

B. Do not use *when* or *where* as part of the complement of the verb *is*.

Wrong The thing I like to do most at parties *is when* I'm dancing.

Right The thing I like to do most at parties *is dance*.

Wrong A vacation *is where* you relax.

Right A vacation is *a period of relaxation*.

3. Avoid using mixed or incomplete comparisons

A. Do not use comparisons that mix two comparative constructions.

Mixed My biology course is as interesting, *if not more interesting* than, my chemistry course. (the modifying, italicized, phrase is misplaced, making the main clause read: "My biology course is as interesting than my chemistry course")

Unmixed My biology course is as interesting as my chemistry course, if not more interesting.

Correct (but stilted) My biology course is as interesting as, if not more interesting than, my chemistry course.

Mixed   Willie Mays was one of the greatest, if not the greatest, players in all of baseball history.
Correct   Willie Mays was one of the greatest players in all of baseball history. He may even have been *the* greatest.

B. Do not use inexact or incomplete comparisons.

Inexact   New York City is farther from Albany than Newark. (confusion: which place is farther from which?)
Exact   New York City is farther from Albany than Newark *is.* (both terms of the comparison are filled in here)
Exact   New York City is farther from Albany than *it is from* Newark. (again, the comparison is now exact)

Inexact   I like to watch television because it has more varied entertainment. (more varied than what?)
Exact   I like to watch television because it has more varied entertainment *than other* media.

Incomplete   Her prospects for a job after graduation looked lower than a laborer. (is a laborer *low?*)
Complete   Her prospects for a job after graduation looked lower than a *laborer's.*
Complete   Her prospects for a job after graduation looked lower than *those of* a laborer.

4. Avoid omitting necessary words

A. Do not omit words that are necessary to maintain parallel structure in the sentence. (See Parallel Construction for a complete explanation of the term.)

Wrong   He told her that she was intelligent but she lacked confidence. (the omission of *that* between *but* and *she* makes it uncertain whether she was *told* she lacked confidence or whether she thought so herself)
Right   He told her *that* she was intelligent but *that* she lacked confidence.

B. Do not omit necessary parts of verbs. When the two parts of a compound construction are in different tenses or there is a change of number between them, be sure to include all the parts of *both* verbs.

Wrong   Freedom *has* and always *will be* the most cherished American ideal. (*be* goes properly with *will* to form the future tense; but *has* needs *been* to form the present perfect)

Right Freedom *has been* and always *will be* the most cherished American ideal.

Wrong Jack *was fishing* and the other men *sleeping*. (Jack is singular and properly takes the singular auxiliary *was;* men is plural and needs the plural *were*)

Right Jack *was fishing* and the other men *were sleeping*.

Note: It is permissible to omit parts of compound verbs when both parts of the construction are in the same tense.

She *had read* the assigned books and [had] *done* the required term paper. (the tenses are the same, so the bracketed *had* may be omitted)

C. Do not omit words through sheer carelessness; careful proofreading can usually pick up these errors. But notice how careless omissions give a special incoherence to sentences.

Omission He took a five-mile walk the pool. (a reader might think that the letter *p* in *pool* should be an *f*—what was actually omitted was the word *to*)

Complete He took a five-mile walk *to* the pool.

Omission The moon gave him the *feeling wonder* and *romance*. (did the moon give him three separate things, the italicized words? No. The word *of* has been omitted)

Complete The moon gave him the feeling *of* wonder and romance.

TEST YOURSELF ON
Revising Incoherent Sentences

Each of the following sentences is plagued by one of the problems we have been discussing in this section. Analyze each problem, then write out what you consider to be a good revision of the sentence; be prepared to explain why you think your version is superior.

1. In the basket is where I put the apples.
2. Because cheating the consumer is so widespread that we need a permanent Department of Consumer Affairs.
3. Jack, after the heat, the crowds, and the excitement, fainted.

4. The doctor wanted, because he suspected a kidney problem and needed to be sure, a urine sample.
5. The invitation said that I was to only reply if I couldn't make it.
6. A good disco is where they play music for dancing.
7. Professor Gould is one of the best, if not the best, teachers in the department.
8. A Toyota is built better and gets better gas mileage.
9. The actor's makeup looked like a clown.
10. Northerners are just as friendly as the south or west.
11. Loneliness is when you are starved for intimacy.
12. The bookcase I built myself cost far less than a carpenter.
13. The music instructor told her that she had talent but she needed to improve her technique.
14. In lower Manhattan are a pair of skyscrapers reaching toward the clouds and which provide great sightseeing for millions of visitors.
15. He was working and still does at the packing plant.

Achieving Coherence in Paragraphs

Most kinds of writing require that sentences be written one after another to form coherent paragraphs. A coherent paragraph is one in which (1) there is a logical order to the sentences: some principle governs why each sentence in the paragraph occupies its particular place there; and (2) there are clear connections—smooth bridges—between those sentences.

1. To assure that your paragraphs have coherence, choose the appropriate logical plan with which to govern the order of your sentences. Usually, the subject of your paragraph will suggest the right plan to follow. If you are telling a story, a common plan is the chronological one; you order your sentences according to time. If your paragraph is describing something, say a house, then a common plan of organization would have you describe the house from the inside out or vice-versa: we call this a spatial plan. Here are examples showing the difference a plan can make in the coherence of your paragraphs.

Incoherent (sentences without order)

Last night, my father discovered that our car had been stolen. The detectives didn't hold out much hope for its return, but they said they would be in touch if there were any news. They took down all the information about the car and were very polite. My father asked my mother if she thought I had taken it without permission, but she assured him I hadn't. He just couldn't believe it wasn't parked in the usual place, and ran down the hill to see if maybe the brakes had given out and it had rolled down. When he was finally convinced that the car had been stolen, he phoned the police. After they left, my father was depressed.

Coherent (chronological order imposed)

Last night, my father discovered that our car had been stolen. He asked my mother if she thought I had taken it without permission, but she assured him I hadn't. He just couldn't believe it wasn't parked in the usual place and ran down the hill to see if maybe the brakes had given out and it had rolled down. When he was finally convinced that the car had been stolen, he phoned the police. The detectives took down all the information about the car and were very polite. They didn't hold out much hope for its return, but they said they would be in touch if there were any news. After they left, my father was depressed.

Incoherent (sentences without order)

A spiral ramp hugging the wall goes whirling up as far as the eye can see, leaving a huge cone of space in the center. The entrance hall is also very dramatic. When you first approach the museum, you notice that it's very different from the buildings around it—ordinary high-rise apartment houses. It is low, first of all, almost squat in appearance. The squat impression made by the outside is lost on the inside. The building is made of massive geometric forms: cones, tubes, rectangles, and squares, all solidly connected to form a unitary, dramatic mass of concrete, with here and there a strange vertical slit in the facade. Everything inside is airy and light, turning and curving. From the top of the ramp, what you see is so slender and spacious you can hardly believe it's the same building you saw from the outside.

Coherent (spatial order imposed)

When you first approach the museum, you notice that it's very different from the buildings around it—ordinary high-rise apartment houses. The museum is low, first of all, almost squat in appearance. It is made of massive, geometric forms: cones, tubes, rectangles, and squares, all solidly connected to form a unitary, dramatic mass of concrete, with here and there a strange vertical slit in the facade. The entrance hall is also very dramatic. A spiral ramp hugging the wall goes whirling up as far as the eye can see, leaving a huge cone of space in the center. Everything inside is airy and light, turning and curving. From the top of the ramp, what you see is so slender and spacious, you can hardly believe it's the same building you saw from the outside.

TEST YOURSELF ON
Making Coherent Paragraphs

A. Write a coherent paragraph that incorporates all the following information about Ralph Ellison. Begin your paragraph with sentence 1.

1. Ralph Ellison, the distinguished American novelist, was born in Oklahoma in 1914.
2. Afterwards, he became interested in sculpture, and finally, of course, in writing.
3. While attending school in Oklahoma City, he had a decisive experience when he heard Lester Young play the saxophone.
4. Probably the whole experience helped orient him toward art in general.
5. In 1965, *Invisible Man* was voted the most distinguished novel to have been published in the previous twenty years.
6. Hearing the great jazz player prompted him to go to Tuskegee Institute, in 1933, with the intention of studying music.
7. Since 1952, he has also published a collection of essays, *Shadow and Act;* from 1958 onwards, he has taught literature at various colleges.
8. Ellison started publishing in 1937, but it wasn't until 1945, after service in the Merchant Marine in World War II, that he began his famous *Invisible Man*.

B. Both of the following paragraphs are incoherent because the sentences are poorly arranged. Impose some orderly plan on each and make coherent paragraphs of them.

1. Most Americans have become increasingly interested in leisure activities these days. There is so much intensity invested in these activities that we can fairly say Americans now have two jobs: one is real work, the other real play.

Jobholders work fewer hours and thus have more leisure. Besides, Americans have always been sociable and sociability goes hand in hand with leisure. The reasons have to do with changes that have taken place in American life in the last twenty-five years. Interest in health has grown, and this has led many to take an active role in sports. Moreover, the idea has gained prominence that self-fulfillment means gaining skills in pleasureable leisure activities like photography, sailing, woodwork, painting, and many others.

2. The outside of the building is typical of old farmhouses in this part of the country. So is the blackened tin funnel that was once used to lead cooking fumes to the outside. Inside, the house has been modernized—a new stove, a refrigerator, wall heaters—but the old wood stove is still there. A chimney squirts into the air from the top of each addition. Even a faded print on the living room wall, showing the original house without the additions, testifies that what used to be is not entirely gone. The furniture also reflects the original identity of the house. It is a white frame square, with two little additions—afterthoughts—sloping off either side of the square.

2. To assure that there are clear connections between your sentences, you must keep in mind the following four considerations.

A. Present your ideas from a consistent point of view. This means that you must speak, in each sentence, from the same position or vantage point. You must not needlessly shift tense, number, or person within a paragraph.

Shift in Tense

In the story, Tom *went* to Canada to make a life as a hunter and trapper. Then he *goes* to Alaska to search for gold. His restlessness *was* emphasized repeatedly. Thus by the end of the story, he *is* a sad man.

Shift in Number

Young *people* who look for security in their jobs rather than satisfaction are likely to be disappointed. A young *person* needs to choose a career that will stimulate his imagination while it is young and responsive. *They* can always gain security later on, at the appropriate age. *He* must be wary of experiencing the worst possible regret: looking back on life and knowing *he* hasn't lived.

Shift in Person

Now more than ever, *parents* need to pay close attention to children's gaining basic skills like reading, writing, and mathematics. *You* need to do more than help them with their homework. *You* cannot expect children to honor those skills if *you* don't. Therefore, a *parent* must set an example for *children*.

B. For the purpose of presenting parallel or coordinate ideas, use parallel construction in sentences that follow each other.

My mother has passed along to me certain rules for getting along with others. Don't argue with parents; they'll think you don't love them. Don't argue with children; they'll think themselves victimized. Don't argue with husbands and wives; they'll think you're a tiresome mate. Don't argue with strangers; they'll not want to be friends. My mother's rules can be summed up in two words: don't argue.

Most of us feel that the troubles we encounter are not of our own making. We think that the system has failed us. We think that our loved ones have failed us. We think that circumstances have failed us. It rarely occurs to us that the failure has been our own and that it might be temporary and perhaps even reparable.

(See Parallel Construction for more information.)

C. Repeat key words and phrases to keep before the reader the flow of your thought. If you fail to do this, gaps in your thought are created. Pronouns referring precisely to their antecedents can also serve this bridging function.

A *magic show* works by carefully directing our *attention*. But the *show directs* our *attention* where the *magician wants* it to be. *He wants* us to look away from the *place* where his transformations go on. For that *place* has no *magic*; it's a *work place*. The *magical* quality of the *show* depends on our not seeing the *work*. When we do not look at that *work*, we see the *magic*, and our *attention*—focussed on the right *place*—is well rewarded.

D. Use transitional devices where they are necessary to further this bridging function between sentences. A transitional device is a word or a phrase that can serve as a point of reference (*finally, at last*) or that can actually indicate the relationship between one sentence and the next (*consequently, as a result*).

Soon, he was able to walk. *Afterwards,* he was even able to swim a little and he managed a few minutes in the pool every day. *Consequently,* when spring came, his physical condition had improved considerably. He was stronger, could walk without tiring, and was able to swim as long as he wanted to. *However,* he was still depressed by the ordeal of the accident and the recuperation period during which he was unable to work. *On the whole, though,* he had much to be thankful for.

Here is a list of some of these transitional devices, classified according to meaning:

Time

after a while, afterwards, at last, at the same time, in the meantime, immediately, later, soon

Place

here, there, nearby, close by

Addition

again, also, besides, further, furthermore, in addition, likewise, moreover, next

Result

as a result, accordingly, consequently, hence, therefore, thus

Comparison

likewise, similarly, in such a manner

Contrast

after all, and yet, however, in contrast, in spite of, nevertheless, on the contrary, on the other hand, otherwise

Concession

it may be true, I admit, naturally, of course

Summary

in brief, in short, on the whole, to conclude, to sum up, finally, to summarize

Illustration and Example

for example, for instance, to be specific, in particular, indeed, in fact, that is, to illustrate

See also **Transitions.**

TEST YOURSELF ON
Revising Incoherent Paragraphs

The following paragraphs contain confusing shifts in person, tense, or number, or lack smooth transitions. Eliminate the shifts wherever they appear and add transitions where necessary to make them all coherent.

1. My parents always argue with me about my wanting a moped. They said the machines were dangerous, but I believed they were not. Mopeds go only twenty miles an hour. It ran cheaply and had no license or insurance requirements. They have been sold cheaply too.

2. Cooking is both easy and fun if one observes certain basic rules. First, you should have the right utensils. As the saying goes, "a cook is only as good as his pots." A cook should buy only fresh ingredients. You ought to learn how much heat to apply to particular foods. Save good recipes.

3. A professor I know who is older than I am says that rock and roll is terrible music. I said it's just a form of what he used to think was popular music when he was young. He says rock and roll lyrics can't be heard because the music is too loud. He said the lyrics are foolish. I pointed out that though he may be right about the lyrics, they have not been more foolish than *his* kind of pop music. The degree of loudness is a matter of taste.

Achieving Coherence Between Paragraphs

As you might have expected, the rules for achieving coherence between paragraphs are identical with those that apply to achieving coherence *within* paragraphs. For example:

[1] Strong faith, no matter where it is directed, can also erase anxiety, fear, and doubt from the human soul. These are often direct causes of many modern illnesses both real and imaginary. Faith seems to have a calming and soothing effect on a troubled mind. Thus in a sense the patient often cures himself by his own strong *faith, faith* which is stimulated by the efforts of the *healer* and reinforced by the *group traditions* surrounding the *healing* ceremony.

[2] Nonmedical *healing,* whether it be on the *folk or mass culture* level, contains many more components than power and *faith.* There are always rudimentary elements of auto-suggestion, crowd hysteria, thought transference, and subtle forms of hypnotism lurking in these rituals, but the healing ceremony always centers on these two key ingredients. When the balance between the two is right, when the patient and audience exhibit deep, sometimes emotional, faith, then this strange power called healing begins to flow. What this force really is, modern science, psychology, and technology have not as yet determined. Perhaps it is a creation of man's imagination. Perhaps it is a substantial and measurable force. But whatever it is, it should be considered an intrinsic part of both popular and folk medical belief.

—Greg Johnson, "A Classification of Faith Healing Practices," *New York Folklore Quarterly,* Summer 1975

Notice in the example that the words *faith, healer, healing* constitute a bridge from paragraph 1 to paragraph 2 and that the idea "group traditions" acts as a bridge to the idea "folk or mass culture level."

COLLOQUIAL

See **Diction.**

COLON

The colon is a mark of internal punctuation that can be used according to the following rules:

1. Use the colon to introduce a series of items explained in the main clause of the sentence.

In order to enjoy camping, you need the right supplies: a tent, a sleeping bag, good walking shoes, foul weather gear, waterproof matches, and the right kind of food.
He had a bad group of symptoms: headache, nausea, fever, and an itchy rash.

2. Use the colon to direct the reader's attention to a final fact or explanation.

You lack the one thing that rich people have: money.
One quality is essential for the good teacher: patience.

3. Use the colon to introduce a direct quotation of some length and formality.

The problem was clearly outlined by the Mayor, who put it this way: "The cities are in a state of decay. Our lives, our children's lives, and the future of cities everywhere depend upon how we choose to confront the renewal of the urban environment. Either we undertake rebuilding our cities with enthusiasm or we suffer the consequences with shame."

Longer direct quotations can of course be introduced by a comma, too, but a comma *should* be used when the material is more informal and shorter:

John smiled and answered softly, "You can do as you please."

4. Use a colon for the purposes of mechanical separation.

Matthew 8:10 (separating chapter and verse in Biblical citation)
Dear Mr. Kojak: (after the salutation in a formal letter, to separate it from the main body)
2:32 a.m. (separating numbers in a time designation)

Note: Do not use a colon interchangably with a semicolon.
Do not use a colon after a verb or a preposition in a sentence to introduce a series.

Wrong   My priorities *are:* home, country, and God.
Right   My priorities are as follows: home, country, and God.
Right   My priorities are home, country, and God.

Wrong   This summer I am planning *to:* study French, get a part-time job, and swim a half-mile every day.

Right   This summer I am planning to do the following: study
French, get a part-time job, and swim a half-mile every day.
Right   This summer I am planning to study French, get a part-
time job, and swim a half-mile every day.

TEST YOURSELF ON
the Use of the Colon

In each of the sentences below, insert colons where they are
needed or change their position after inserting another word.

1. It is now 245 p.m.

2. Whatever he wanted from Sarah, he got love, affection,
   kindness, money, or food.

3. The things that need repairing around the house are: the
   rain gutters, the front steps, the upstairs storm windows,
   and the leaks in the attic.

4. What do I spend my money on? I spend my money on:
   food, clothing, shelter, movies, medicine, skateboards,
   lobsters—a lot of things!

5. You need only one thing for a perfect golf swing, control.

COMMA FAULT

Another term for **Comma Splice.** Both apply to independent clauses joined *only* by a comma.

Wrong   We were very tired, we went to bed early.
Right   We were very tired, *so* we went to bed early.

For more detailed information, see **Run-on Sentences.**

COMMA RULES

The comma is used to separate sentence elements. It
is the most frequently used of all the punctuation marks.
Its appearance signals the reader that something is in-

terrupting the flow of the main statement (main clause), that something is being added or subtracted, usually something that is not so closely related to that main flow of thought. The specific rules given below are aimed at insuring that a writer's flow of thought is presented with clarity; they should be applied with that aim in mind. When there is a conflict between applying these rules and your own sense of the fitness of a comma placement, consult your instructor.

1. Use a comma to separate independent clauses joined by the coordinating conjunctions *and, but, or, nor, for, so, yet.*

Greene has washed and cleaned his old car, *and* he hopes that it will attract a buyer.

The plan was to leave on Sunday morning, *but* we found that we couldn't get ready on time.

We can stay home and have leg of lamb for dinner, *or* we can eat out and have pizza.

Jones could not name any of the original thirteen states, *nor* could he identify any of the original signers of the Declaration of independence.

Note: A comma may be omitted between short independent clauses.

I laughed and he cried.
I asked but he didn't answer.

2. Use a comma to separate items in a series. These items may consist of words, phrases, or clauses.

Series of Words   I'd like a big bowl of fruit with *apples, pears, peaches,* and *plums.*

Series of Phrases   He liked *going to the movies, eating at fancy restaurants,* and *visiting museums.*

Series of Clauses   She liked him *when he was thoughtful, when he was kind,* and *when he was relaxed.*

Note that in each of these examples, there is a comma as well as the word *and* between the last two items in the series. In the case of items in a series, you have the option of following the practice in the above examples or of omitting the comma just before the *and* preceding the final item. Both procedures are correct; probably the retention of the comma is more formal than its omission. But whatever you choose to do, *be consistent*. Do not use one system with one series and another with a second series.

The series of words separated by commas in the first of the above examples are nouns. A series of adjectives can present a slightly different problem in punctuation. For example, consider the following sentences:

They were *energetic, pretty, intelligent,* and *sensitive* girls.
They had an *interesting European summer* vacation.

In the first example, we could substitute the word *and* for each of the commas—energetic *and* pretty *and* intelligent. We could also alter the order of these adjectives; it would make little difference to the sense of the sentence if we wrote "sensitive, pretty, energetic, and intelligent." Therefore the adjectives in this example are *coordinate adjectives* and are properly separated by commas.

By contrast, the adjectives in the second example are not coordinate. We could not logically join them by the word *and* (interesting *and* European *and* summer is illogical). And we could not alter the order of these adjectives: we could not say "summer European interesting vacation." In fact, the word *interesting* really modifies *European summer vacation;* the word *European* then modifies *summer vacation* and the word *summer* modifies *vacation*—there are layers of modification, so to speak. Where we have such a series of adjectives that are not coordinate we do not use commas to separate them.

Coordinate   It was a *happy, productive,* and *prosperous* season in his life.
Not Coordinate   He was wearing a *light green* belt.

Coordinate   His remark was *foolish, rude,* and *embarrassing.*
Not Coordinate   Last night we went to a *lively little* party.

3. Use a comma to separate introductory elements from the rest of the sentence. These elements can be words, phrases, adverb clauses, or transitional expressions.

Introductory Word   Usually, he took a nap after lunch.

Introductory Phrase   Coming through the alley, the car swerved to avoid a garbage can.

Introductory Clause   Although he had already eaten dinner, he sat down to have a sandwich.

Transitional Expressions   In other words, I'm in love.
On the other hand, meat loaf is fattening.

Note: Certain introductory elements do not need to be followed by a comma, if they are short and omitting the comma does not cause a lack of clarity in the sentence.

Probably he won't win.
Naturally he found what he was looking for.

But note too how confusion can enter a sentence when a comma that *should* come after an introductory element is omitted:

After he ate the horse took a romp in the fields.
Because he needed to hit the catcher choked up on the bat handle.

Readers of the first sentence will suffer momentary confusion because they will grasp the meaning unit *he ate the horse,* and readers of the second suffer the same confusion because they will grasp the unit *he needed to hit the catcher.* Of course, neither sentence intends to generate such meanings, so each needs a comma—following *ate* in the first and following *hit* in the second—to make its meaning clear.

As we have shown, introductory adverb clauses should be set off from the rest of the sentence by a comma. The need for a comma when the adverb clause comes at the end of a sentence depends on the relationship of the adverb clause to the main clause of the sentence. When the information contained in the adverb clause is essential to the meaning of the sentence, no comma is needed.

I will keep knocking *until they open the door*.

The speaker here tells us that *until they open the door*, the speaker will keep on knocking; therefore, that information is essential—it gives the motive for the information in the main clause—and no comma is needed.

I came to this school *because the engineering courses are so good*.

This states the essential reason that the speaker came, and so the clauses need not be separated by a comma.

However, when the adverb clause merely gives nonessential explanatory material, a comma should be used between it and the main clause.

Our seats were in the last row of the balcony, *although we had ordered a pair in the orchestra*.

Here the italicized clause has no *essential* relationship to the main clause: it gives no *reason* that the seats were in the balcony (far from it, in fact: it suggests a contrast), nor any motive for the seats being where they were. Therefore, it needs a comma, as if to emphasize the separateness of its information from that in the main clause.

4. Use a comma to set off a parenthetical element at the beginning of a sentence; use one comma before and one after a parenthetical or appositive element that occurs in the middle of a sentence. A parenthetical element is one which is not essential to complete the meaning of the sentence but which supplements a part or parts of the sentence.

Parenthetical Element at Beginning of Sentence
To be frank, I'm completely broke.
Certainly, he has a right to do what he wishes.

Parenthetical Element in Mid-Sentence
The car, *you see,* is in the garage.

Appositive Mr. Morris, *the patient in room 950,* has been wheeled down to occupational therapy.

Appositive   My uncle, *Harry Jackson,* was a stingy millionaire.

It should be clear from the above examples that appositives and parenthetical elements do not affect the meaning being delivered by the sentence; they can be omitted without loss of meaning.

Notice that if only one comma is used in each of the last two examples, some confusion in meaning results.

Mr. Morris, the patient in room 950 has been wheeled down to occupational therapy. (meaning, possibly, that the speaker is addressing a Mr. Morris and advising him that the patient in room 950 has been wheeled down)

My uncle, Harry Jackson was a stingy millionaire. (again, it is not clear that *my uncle* and *Harry Jackson* are the same person)

5. Use commas to set off nonrestrictive elements in a sentence. Another way of talking about a parenthetical or appositive element is to say that it is *nonrestrictive:* it does not *restrict* or essentially modify what it refers to; therefore, it *must* be set off by commas. On the other hand, if the element in question is *restrictive* or is essential to what it modifies, it must *not* be set off by commas.

Restrictive Element   The audience *that gave him the most applause* pleased him the most. (no commas necessary)

Nonrestrictive Element   The audience, *which paid a fortune for its seats,* applauded for five minutes.

Sentence 1 is not about the *audience*—it is about *the audience that gave him the most applause*. Therefore, the clause must not be separated by commas from the subject word *audience;* the clause is part of the complete subject (italicized in this paragraph), and if it were separated the sentence would lose its essential meaning. On the other hand, the second sentence *is* about the *audience;* it is only incidental, not essential, information that this audience paid a fortune for its seats. Therefore, the clause in that sentence must be separated from *audience* by commas.

Try to figure out which of the following sentences contain restrictive elements and which nonrestrictive elements. Answers follow immediately below.

1. People who live in glass houses shouldn't throw stones.
2. Students who take this film course are guaranteed an exciting experience.
3. My doctor who is on vacation this month leads a busy professional life.
4. The foreman at the factory who was a conscientious worker was taking evening courses in business administration.
5. The man leaning over the edge of the balcony is being reckless.

Answers: 1, 2, and 5 all contain *restrictives*. In these, no commas should be used. But commas *are* needed in 3 and 4 because they contain *nonrestrictive* elements.

3. My doctor, who is on vacation this month, leads a busy professional life.
4. The foreman at the factory, who was a conscientious worker, was taking evening courses in business administration.

The reason that we need commas in these examples is that in each, the material between the commas is not essential to the writer's message. In 3, it is only incidental that the doctor is on vacation, not essential. Similarly, in 4, the material between the commas is also incidental; it has nothing to do with the main message of the sentence—that the foreman is a conscientious worker.

On the other hand, the reason we do not use commas in 1, 2, and 5 is that, in each, the italicized material is essential to what is being said about the subject.

1. People *who live in glass houses* shouldn't throw stones.

This writer doesn't mean that "people shouldn't throw stones" and that incidentally those people live in glass houses—although "People shouldn't throw stones" is a grammatical sentence and may even be a pretty good rule to live by. The writer means that *only people who live in glass houses* shouldn't throw stones; therefore, we must have *people* and all the words that follow it as one single unit, unbroken by commas.

2. Students *who take this film course* are guaranteed an exciting experience.

The writer of this sentence doesn't mean that "students are guaranteed an exciting experience," and, incidentally, that those students are taking this film course. "Students are guaranteed an exciting experience" is a grammatical sentence and may even be true, but the writer of 2 really means that *only students who take this film course* receive the guarantee. Therefore, we must take these words as a single unit, unbroken by commas.

Try analyzing 5 as we have just analyzed 1 and 2.

6. Use a comma to separate a contrasting element from the rest of the sentence; a comma emphasizes the contrast.

He came to the dance with me, *and not with you.*
She says she loves exercise, *but doesn't do it.*

7. Use a comma to achieve clarity, even in places where you ordinarily might omit it.

In brief, dresses will be longer this year.
People who like to see wild bir*ds, w*alk through the woods.
Whatever he *did, did* no good.
The soldier droppe*d, a bullet* in his leg.

8. Use a comma in dates, addresses, and letter forms.

Dates   August 4, 1977 (or 4 August 1977)
           Friday, November 30, 1973

Address   Waterbury, Connecticut

Letter Forms   Dear Mary Lea,
                Yours sincerely,

TEST YOURSELF ON
     the Use of the Comma

A. 1. Construct five compound sentences, each with two independent clauses; use the coordinating conjunctions *and, but, or, nor,* and *so* once each—and place commas in the correct position.

2. Construct five sentences, each beginning with an adverb clause and followed by a simple main clause. Place the comma in the correct position.

B. Some of the following sentences use the comma correctly; next to these, place the letter C. In the others, either there is a comma missing or too many commas are used. Supply those that are needed; cross out those that are superfluous.

1. _____ The boys in the back of the room are noisy.

2. _____ Women, who are very poor drivers should have their licenses revoked.

3. _____ During the summer days are long.

4. _____ Above all the rooftops are filled with TV antennas.

5. _____ I saw you talking to a pretty slim girl.

6. _____ I'd like to be rich married secure and famous.

7. _____ The ship, which docked yesterday is the *Queen Elizabeth II*.

8. _____ People, who live beyond their incomes, shouldn't complain about money.

9. _____ I will keep taking the test, until I pass it.

10. _____ I need to buy a gray, summer suit and a pair of white seersucker pants.

11. _____ Wherever you're going to get there requires planning and purpose.

12. _____ On Friday, November 30, 1973, I met my wife, and my life, has not been the same, since.

13. _____ In fact I stole the books.

14. _____ George, who is very nearly my age, is much further along in his career than I am in mine.

15. _____ The revolution in education which so many educators talk about has yet to take place.

16. _____ A college really consists of a group of students who want to learn, a group of teachers who want to teach, and a good collection of books.

17. _____ I paused but he went on.

18. _____ Either he goes or I go.

19. _____ He eats drinks and talks too much.

20. _____ Usually living alone is a matter of personal choice.

COMMA SPLICE

When two independent clauses are joined only by a comma, and *not* by a comma and a coordinating conjunction, we call the error a comma splice.

Wrong We went to work very early, we came home very late.
Right We went to work very early, but we came home very late.

For a detailed discussion of this problem, see **Run-on Sentences.**

CONTRACTIONS

When two words are joined together with one or more letters omitted and an apostrophe in its place, we have a contraction.

do not = don't   is not = isn't   we will = we'll

See **Apostrophe** for more detailed information.

DANGLING MODIFIERS

A dangling modifier is a phrase or a clause that either modifies no word in the sentence or refers to the wrong word.

Dangling Participial Phrase *Walking home from school,* the fire engine came screeching around the corner.

The thing to notice about this example is that it *says* one thing but *intends* to say another. Because *walking home from school* modifies *fire engine*, it *says* that the fire engine, as it was walking home from school, came screeching around the corner. Clearly this is ridiculous.

It *intends* to say that as *someone* was walking home from school, the fire engine came screeching around the corner, or that, walking home from school, *someone* saw the fire engine come screeching around the corner.

Therefore, to correct the dangling phrase, we must get *someone* into the action, either by giving the phrase something to modify in the main clause (*the fire engine came screeching around the corner*):

Walking home from school, *I saw* the fire engine come screeching around the corner. (now the phrase modifies the word *I* in the main clause)

or by turning the phrase into a dependent clause and getting the *someone* into the action that way:

As I was walking home from school, the fire engine came screeching around the corner. (now someone—*I*—has been gotten into the action by appearing in the italicized clause)

How you decide to correct this dangling modifier depends on where you want to place the emphasis. Since emphasis naturally falls on the subject of the main clause, you would use the first revision if you wanted to emphasize the speaker, *I*, and the second if you wanted to emphasize the *fire engine*.

Writers who produce dangling modifiers do so usually because they write hastily and do not proofread carefully. Learn to recognize and correct the various kinds of dangling modifier likely to appear in your work.

1. Recognize and correct dangling participial phrases

These are similar to the example just discussed.

Dangling   *Smoking a cigar,* the horse stood on its hind legs. (the phrase seems to modify *horse*—the wrong word)
Revised   *As I was smoking a cigar,* the horse stood on its hind

legs. (phrase turned into a clause—a person getting into the action)

Revised   Smoking a cigar, *I* saw the horse stand on its hind legs. (now the phrase clearly modifies the new subject of the main clause: *I*)

Dangling   Our summer passed happily, *swimming and playing baseball.* (note that the dangler can come at the end, not just at the beginning of the sentence; the summer did not swim and play baseball—*we* did; therefore, the phrase modifies the wrong word)

Revised   *We* passed our summer happily, swimming and playing baseball. (note that the addition of the word *we* as the new subject does the correcting job nicely)

Revised   *Because we were swimming and playing tennis,* our summer passed happily. (the phrase has been converted into a clause)

Dangling   *Lying on my back on the raft,* the stars burned brightly in the sky. (it is not the *stars* that are lying on the speaker's back—but the speaker; the phrase is modifying *stars,* the wrong word)

Revised   *As I was lying on my back on the raft,* the stars burned brightly in the sky. (the phrase is turned into a clause)

Revised   Lying on my back on the raft, *I* could see the stars burning brightly in the sky. (adding the word I—a new subject —to the main clause gives the phrase the correct word to modify)

2. Recognize and correct dangling gerund phrases

A gerund is an *-ing* word that functions as a noun. A gerund implies the presence of a *someone*.

Dangling   *After drilling my tooth,* my cavity stopped aching. (the *cavity* did not do the *drilling*)

Revised   *After the dentist drilled my tooth,* my cavity stopped aching. (the phrase is now a clause)

Revised   *After drilling my tooth,* the dentist stopped my cavity from aching. (now the phrase refers clearly to the new subject of the main clause: *dentist*)

Dangling   *In planning a college education,* careful preparations are needed. (*careful preparations* cannot do the *planning;* a *someone* is needed)

Revised In planning a college education, a *student* needs careful preparations. (the someone, in the form of a *student* has been added to the main clause; now the phrase correctly modifies *student*)

3. Recognize and correct dangling infinitive phrases

An infinitive phrase has for its headwords the *to* form of a verb: *to play, to work, to love,* and so forth.

Dangling To become a movie star, talent and luck are needed. (*to become a movie star* does not logically refer to *talent* and *luck,* the subjects of the main clause; people become movie stars)

Revised To become a movie star, one [or a *person*] needs talent and luck. (now the phrase refers logically to *one*—or a *person*)

Revised If you want to become a movie star, you need talent and luck. (the phrase has been converted into a clause)

Dangling To make a delicious stew, fresh ingredients must be used. (the *ingredients* do not cook the stew; people do)

Revised To make a delicious stew, you must use fresh ingredients. (we have supplied the subject in the main clause, *you,* to which the phrase can logically refer)

Revised If you want to make a delicious stew, you must use fresh ingredients. (the phrase has been converted into a clause)

4. Recognize and correct dangling elliptical clauses

An *elliptical* expression has words missing. An *elliptical* clause is missing either a subject or a verb; these are understood instead of being stated. You can correct dangling elliptical clauses either by making the subject of the elliptical clause agree with the subject of the main clause or by supplying the missing subject and verb.

Dangling When driving, my seat belt is always fastened. (the *seat belt* is not *driving;* the italicized clause is missing the words *I am,* so the implied subject, *I,* does not agree with the *seat belt* of the main clause)

Revised When driving, I always fasten my seat belt. (now the implied subject, *I,* is the same as the new subject of the main clause)

Revised   When I am driving, my seat belt is always fastened. (with the missing words supplied, the clause is expanded and refers, properly, to *is fastened*)

Dangling   When at the age of six, my Uncle Fred gave me my first haircut. (*Uncle Fred* was not *at the age of six* when the haircut was given—the speaker was: *I was* are the words missing)

Revised   When at the age of six, I was given my first haircut by my Uncle Fred. (the implied subject of the clause now matches the new subject—*I*—of the main clause)

Revised   When I was at the age of six, my Uncle Fred gave me my first haircut. (the missing words supplied expand clause it and make it modify, properly, the verb *gave*)

Note: Some verbal phrases do not intend to modify any single portion of the main clause. Rather, they make statements about the whole sentence. These are called *absolute constructions;* using them puts the writer in no danger of creating a dangling modifier.

Considering the time, we're not doing badly.

Parking regulations having been suspended, we decided to leave the car on 12th Street.

The air being nippy, we brought along our parkas.

Winning being impossible, we figured we'd just have fun playing.

TEST YOURSELF ON
Recognizing and Correcting Dangling Modifiers

Some of the following sentences are correct; place a C next to them. For those that have dangling modifiers, underline the dangling modifier; then correct it according to the methods just discussed.

1. _____ Before leaving for California, hotel reservations must be made.

2. _____ Being an American, his knowledge of Italy was limited.

3. _____ Arriving in Chicago, his suitcase was in California.

4. _____ To understand one's spouse, good communications should exist.

5. _____ After putting my son to sleep, I settled down with a good book.

6. _____ After changing my shoes, my girlfriend took me for a walk.

7. _____ To understand true happiness, you need to know true love.

8. _____ Although planning to get married, my girl's parents didn't know it.

9 _____ His eyes caught the glint of a strange sea shell walking barefoot on the beach.

10. _____ Listening to the concert, the Rolling Stones seemed like the funkiest group in the world.

11. _____ My examinations were passed, sweating and praying.

12. _____ To travel in grand style, money is essential.

13. _____ Driving through Ohio, I decided to stop in Akron.

14. _____ If sleepy, your car can be very dangerous.

15. _____ Before going up for a parachute jump, the airplane was thoroughly inspected.

16. _____ While visiting in France, the wine was excellent.

17. _____ On opening the garage door, the cat and dog came leaping out.

18. _____ While relaxed, I am able to jog two miles easily.

19. _____ In cooking the roast, the meat was impregnated with vegetable juices.

20. _____ When a baby, my Great Aunt Sarah died.

21. _____ To operate on a patient, a careful diagnosis must first be made.

22. _____ Stephen kept watching the traffic light till green.

23. _____ Knowing what he liked, I was able to buy him a
satisfying birthday present.

24. _____ To sleep comfortably, a good mattress and peace
of mind are required.

25. _____ To understand how automobiles work, the Chevy
was taken apart.

DASH

The dash is a mark of internal punctuation that has
the separating effect of the comma or parentheses but
that confers emphasis on what follows it. (See **Parentheses** for a brief discussion of the differences in the use
of the three marks.)

If you use a typewriter, the dash is made by striking
the hyphen key twice: --. If you write by hand, make
the dash twice as long as the hyphen. In either case, do
not leave a space before or after the dash—run it directly up against the letters of the preceding and following words. The dash may appropriately be used in the
following circumstances.

1. Use the dash to set off a final appositive that is
short and would benefit from emphasis.

What was in the package was what he feared and desired—
poison.
After he read the thesis, one word came to mind—nonsense.

2. Use the dash to set off nonrestrictive appositives
that would benefit from emphasis or that need dashes
for clarity.

My doctor—my friend for thirty years—always told me the truth.
Three girls—Jackie, Leslie, and Margo—came to my birthday
party.

Note that we could replace the dashes in the last example with commas, but see what confusion might result
if we did:

Three girls, Jackie, Leslie, and Margo, came to my birthday
party.

In this sentence, we cannot be sure that the names
given are those of the three girls; it is possible, in this
case, that six people came and that Jackie and Leslie
are men. The dashes, however, clear up any possible
confusion.

3. Use a dash to set off a series of items, occurring
either at the beginning or the end of a sentence, where
the items are separated by commas.

Beginning of Sentence Love, friendship, caring for children,
personal fulfillment, protecting nature's bounties, concern for
others—these are the values that free men strive for.

End of a Sentence We look for the same qualities in an athlete
that we find in a soldier—agility, stamina, strength, courage,
and competetiveness.

4. Use a dash to off parenthetical elements that
abruptly interrupt the sense of the sentence.

In the blackness of the mine shaft, we started climbing slowly—
what else could we do?—until at last we saw a pinpoint of
light.
The character of the voting population—8,500 registered Democrats—makes it impossible to elect a Republican to office.

TEST YOURSELF ON
the Use of the Dash

In some of the following sentences, the dash is used correctly;
place a C next to these sentences. In other sentences, it is possible to use the dash to improve the clarity, emphasis, and
meaning of the sentence; in these, insert a dash where you
think it would be helpful.

1. _____ You owe me one thing, loyalty.

2. _____ There is a possibility that we who have paid our
rent will be evicted from our apartment.

3. _____ The pilgrims went devoutly to Rome—Catholicism's holy city.

4. _____ That's what I would call it—a crying shame!

5. _____ The crises in his life, divorce, separation from his children, the loss of his job, the attack of pneumonia, these were all too much for him.

6. _____ I notified the Dean of my decision, resignation.

7. _____ Job training programs, increased educational opportunities in the professions, Federally sponsored housing, improved day-care facilities, all these are necessary to begin the attack on poverty.

8. _____ The defeat of communicable diseases and the increase in the food supply—those have been partly responsible for the rise in world population.

9. _____ One of the world's great religions Islam was begun by an Arab merchant, Mohammed.

10. _____ He drove in a cold fury not for one minute taking his eye off the prisoner beside him.

DICTION

Diction means "the use of words." The use of words always involves choice, and in this entry we will discuss the considerations that govern a writer's choice of words. Before we do so, however, we must consider two preliminary matters: 1. the sources where writers can find words and 2. the standards commonly applied to the use of language.

Sources

1. Dictionaries

The dictionary is an invaluable source of words. It is not just an alphabetical list of definitions; for each word, a good dictionary will also give such information as the part of speech the entry belongs to (i.e., noun, verb, preposition, etc.), its level of usage (archaic/obsolete, informal/colloquial, nonstandard, dialect, slang, etc.), plural spelling, pronunciation, synonyms and antonyms, and more. You should become familiar with the use of the dictionary and take advantage of what it has to offer. The following are recommended in the event that your instructor does not suggest a particular dictionary:

The American College Dictionary
The Random House Dictionary
Webster's New Collegiate Dictionary
Webster's New World Dictionary
The American Heritage Dictionary

2. Dictionaries of synonyms and antonyms

Dictionaries of synonyms and antonyms are especially valuable in helping you to expand and enliven your vocabulary and to help you with using exact expression—a crucial aspect of good diction. To use one, you need to know (roughly) the word you want to use. If you look up this particular word in a thesaurus (another name for a dictionary of synonyms and antonyms), you will find many more words having various shades of meaning similar to that of the word looked up. The following are recommended:

Roget's International Thesaurus
A Dictionary of Synonyms and Antonyms, by Joseph Devlin

3. Other people's writing

An important source for fresh and lively words is your reading. When you read, do so with a sharp eye for what is well said. It is not only permissible, it is desirable to use—in your own way—words and expressions that other writers have used well. This does not mean that you should, in response to a writing assign-

ment, *lift* (plagiarize) a whole essay or even a couple of
sentences from someone else's writing and try to pass
them off as your own; rather it means that you should
feel free to incorporate into your own work the best
words and expressions that other writers have used and
that seem to you especially eloquent.

Standards

Good English is a relative term. Linguists define it as
the level useful to the particular situation in which it is
spoken and written. Thus good English varies from one
social or regional group to another and from one particular kind of writing and speaking to another. What is
good for speakers and writers in Southern Australia differs from what is good for users of the language in Western Ireland—or Middle America. Many kinds of variations have been described for speakers of our language;
but the most important for our purposes are the distinctions made between *Standard* and *Nonstandard* English, and, within Standard English, the distinction between *formal* and *informal*.

Standard English is the spoken and written language
used by well-educated people when they wish to communicate as effectively as they can. People who use
Standard English enjoy a certain measure of social prestige; their language is used routinely in business, law,
science, the humanities, and whenever an occupation or
a profession requires written communication. Journal-
ism, literature, and the great bulk of printed matter also
use Standard English. On the other hand, *Nonstandard*
English is the term given to the speaking and writing
characteristics of the relatively uneducated. Writers
and speakers of Nonstandard English have usually had
little opportunity to use written communication, and,
more often than not, they have had little formal education.

Standard

Most people today feel politically powerless. A relatively
small group participates in nominating candidates for office, and

not many more go to the polls to elect these candidates. More important, few citizens have access to government at any level. Thus politicians are not in touch with the real needs of their constituencies. The people know it, and this is the source of the feeling of powerlessness. Unfortunately, that feeling leads to apathy.

Nonstandard

We was asking ourselfs the other day what we would be doing if we was rich. Charlie didn have no idea, he say it couldnt never happen anyway, so whats the difference. Herbie said he buy himself a car—a Cadillac—a house, a boat, and so many pair of shoes he couldn't never wear them out, cause he couldn't never wear em at all. Me, I say if I was rich, I just keeps on *buying.* I don't care *what.*

The advice given in this book is directed toward helping you to achieve competence in Standard English. Since most students using this book will be seeking to enter into the world where Standard English is considered the appropriate level of spoken and written communication, we adhere to this standard. What we mean by good diction, then, will refer to Standard English.

Within Standard English, good diction depends on three basic considerations: the use of language that takes into account both your subject matter and your audience; in other words, the levels of usage called *formal* and *informal* and the appropriate uses of the *colloquial* and *slang;* the use of the *exact* word that will convey your *exact* meaning; and the use of words that are fresh, clear, and concrete.

Levels of Usage: Subject Matter and Audience

1. Formal

The formal level is appropriate whenever you want to establish an impersonal relation to your subject and your audience. It is a useful level for conveying serious information to an audience wanting exact information, because formal writing strives for clarity and precision. Serious books and articles in science, social science, technology, law, and the humanities employ the formal level. Characteristically, the formal is found mainly in writing, but it is also used in speeches, lectures, and discussions—such as those commonly held at formal meetings. Formal writing is characterized by seriousness of tone, complexity of sentence structure, and elaborate vocabulary—all in the interest of conveying exact, serious, and clear information.

Ginseng is the perennial herb *Panax* native to North America and Asia. Asiatic ginseng (*Panax schinseng*) has been known in Asia for centuries and particularly prized by the Chinese as an important item in their herbal formulary. They have used ginseng as a virtual panacea, prescribing it for conditions ranging from flatulence to pneumonia. The demand for ginseng in America is a recent development. For the purpose of export, China and Korea have developed the North American *Panax quinquefolius*. Here ginseng root is also virtually a panacea, but most users employ it to enhance natural vitality.

2. Informal

In recent years, it has become increasingly difficult to separate the formal from the informal. Still, there are distinct differences. The informal is the everyday language employed by well-educated people. It is the language used in private letter-writing, ordinary conversation, and even books and articles that aim to catch the attention of an audience at home with a familiar tone.

Policemen make friends with other policemen. It isn't that they're not friendly; they're just busy. In fact, they spend so much time on the job, they don't have much time for socializing. So they just naturally tend to be friendly with the people they see most: other policemen. Most policemen enjoy each other's company, but most wish they had a wider range of acquaintances.

Note that this sample of the informal is conversational in tone; that it has a speaker's vocabulary, uses contractions, and has a less complicated sentence structure than the formal sample. All but the most sternly academic, scientific or legal writing has some informal cadences in it.

An important thing to bear in mind—regardless of whether your writing is formal or informal—is to maintain consistency of tone, except when you are so well in control of your material that you are able to mix tones purposefully.

Unintentionally Mixed Tones

The beauty of the uninhabited desert regions *doesn't do a thing for me.*

Revised to Maintain Formality

The beauty of the uninhabited desert regions *does not impress me.*

Intentionally Mixed Tones

The President's tour of European capitals must be described as a *bust*—considering that he failed to negotiate any of the trade agreements he had hoped for.

Some discussions (and some dictionaries) regard the *colloquial* level as synonymous with informal or Nonstandard or both. But the word *colloquial* really means *spoken* and can be used to describe a wide range of language that appears in Standard, Nonstandard, formal, or informal writing.

Here is a small list of words and expressions that are considered colloquial, along with their more formal counterparts:

Colloquial	*More Formal*
boss	superior, supervisor
bug	germ
brainy	intelligent
flunk	fail
hunch	premonition
job	position
kid	child
snooze	nap
splurge	spend lavishly
stump	puzzle
alibi	excuse
funny	strange
phone	telephone
guy	man
slob	unkempt person

3. Slang

Slang is highly informal language, mostly spoken, rarely used in written Standard English—but not absolutely forbidden there. Slang consists of both newly coined words and expressions and new and extended meanings attached to older words. It develops from attempts to find fresh and colorful language—funny, pungent, surprising. It also develops as a kind of shorthand, and that is frequently at the root of its downfall. As shorthand, slang comes to be so overused that it falls into disuse. For example, *heavy,* a "heavy" expression of the late sixties and early seventies, is no longer in frequent use by those who habitually use slang. *Groovy* has also been banished by many slang users, and *let's tip,* meaning *let's leave* (on the analogy of "let's tiptoe out"), is so short a piece of shorthand that it never really caught on.

Nevertheless, slang has its place in both formal and informal writing and it is unwise to suppose that slang is "bad" English. In fact, many words and expressions that began as slang have passed into general (formal) usage, and our language is richer for having them. The use of slang, like the use of other words, should be determined by audience and subject matter. Some purists would object to a slang expression like the following:

The new Woody Allen movie is *a real kick in the head.*

although, conceivably, it might prove a highly effective concluding sentence for a first paragraph reviewing that movie, especially if the review were addressed to a suitable audience (the subject matter is certainly suitable for slang expression).

Woody Allen is a comic on his way up; Diane Keaton is a lovely, scatter-brained, painfully shy Midwestern singer-model; *Annie Hall* is a hilarious and touching film that depicts the bittersweet progress of an on-again, off-again romance between a New York ethnic and a middle American. Conclusion: *the new Woody Allen movie is a real kick in the head.*

Examine carefully the following three examples. Are these effective uses of slang? Can you think of a way to improve the one or ones you think are ineffective? Can you think of contexts in which one or more of them might be effective?

I didn't want to get hung up on a 9-5 caper but I needed the money that this gig had to offer, so I rapped about it with my old lady and got a good handle on the whole shebang. Then I said okay.

To me his apartment was pure raunch. It looked like he had pigged out there over the weekend.

Man, don't get all bent out of shape!

TEST YOURSELF ON
Identifying Slang and Colloquial Language

Using your own sensitivity to language, put a C next to those words or expressions below that strike you as colloquial and an S next to the ones that seem to be slang. After you have marked all of them, look each of them up in a good dictionary and check the dictionary labels against your answers. How many did you get?

1. bitch (verb)
2. freak (fan, enthusiast)
3. flunky
4. jazz (noun)
5. bust (verb)
6. cool it
7. awful
8. cop (noun)
9. stuff (belongings)
10. mad (angry)
11. sloppy
12. cute

TEST YOURSELF ON
Selecting the Proper Level of Usage for a Specific Piece of Writing

Think about each of the specific pieces of writing listed below and for each one choose the proper level of usage. Prepare to defend your choice with a logical argument.

1. A report to the Board of Directors of IBM Corporation on the sales prospects of a new product: a tiny, portable minicomputer.

2. A review of the movie, *Star Wars*, written for an underground newspaper.
3. An introduction to the form of popular music called "Punk Rock," written for *Time* magazine.
4. The same—written for the Sunday magazine section of your hometown newspaper.
5. An article for the campus newspaper on a recent budget crisis at your college.
6. An account of your football (or basketball or baseball) team's fortieth consecutive loss—written for your school newspaper.
7. An essay written for a course in sociology giving an account of how your family (including aunts, uncles, and cousins) celebrates weddings.
8. A speech at a fraternity or club dance announcing the dissolution of the club or fraternity.
9. A basic explanation of enzymes for a scientific journal.
10. A review of children's literature published in the past year —for a journal of psychology.

Using Exact Words to Convey Exact Meaning

Writers who care about their work—which is another way of saying writers who care about their readers— will expend the time and energy necessary to write with precision, that is, they will go over what they have written to make sure that the words they have used convey their exact meaning.

1. Precise expression

Writers who want to increase the precision of their word choices must be prepared to acquire the habit of rereading and then revising their written work. They must develop the habit of *seeing* and changing constructions like the following:

Inexact   Americans are *totally* interested in sex.

It's hard to say exactly *what* this sentence intends to express; it may mean something like "Americans are *completely* interested in sex" but more likely a word like *exclusively* or *solely* or *only* was intended, instead of either *totally* or *completely*. The writer may have meant to say that "Americans have an *absorbing* interest in sex"—but the failure to be exact asks the reader to consider many possibilities.

Inexact   Lisa was asked to testify as an *uninterested* observer of the burglary.

Here the writer simply confuses two words: *uninterested*, which means "without interest," and *disinterested*, which means "free of bias; impartial." Obviously, then, the exact expression would be "Lisa was asked to testify as a *disinterested* observer of the burglary."

Inexact   We swam until we were tired, played volleyball on the sand, ate too much seafood, and got bad sunburns. We had a *nice* time.

Here the offending word is *nice;* it's simply too vague and doesn't in the least describe what has gone before. Better would be "We had an *exhausting but exhilarating day.*"

TEST YOURSELF ON
Using Exact Expressions

In each of the following examples, the italicized word or phrase is not as exact as it should be. Supply a better expression in each case.

1. Corruption in the District Attorney's office was *first known* in the *Times.*
2. He *fulfilled* the court orders.
3. By the time the summer was over, he *knew* his desires.
4. Summer jobs for students were *not easy.*
5. Unemployment was an important *fact* in our economy.
6. Many of those who were flower children have *lost their appeal* for working on the land.
7. Her *immaturity* may improve as she gets older.
8. The rural atmosphere *subjects* a person to the beauties of nature.
9. He decided to *except* the job.
10. After the meal, he felt *nice.*

2. Idioms

An idiom is an expression whose meaning cannot be determined by the ordinary meanings of the words employed in it. Native speakers of English have no trouble recognizing the idiom in the sentence "A gunman *held up* the supermarket." They would not think that the gunman *lifted high*, but rather that he *robbed*, the supermarket. Thus we could not literally translate *held up* into, say, French, and expect a Frenchman to understand it to mean *robbed*. Logic also offers no help in understanding idioms. Because it is *customary* in English to say "He was acquitted *of* the charges" rather than "He was acquitted *from* the charges," we say that the use of certain prepositions after certain words is idiomatic—that is, not logical but just peculiar to our language.

Although most native speakers of English automatically use idiomatic expressions, some writers have difficulty with verbs or adjectives that must be followed by particular prepositions in order to deliver their intended meaning. Here is a brief list of some troublesome combinations:

absolved by, from   I was *absolved by* the court. I was *absolved from* blame.

accompany by, on   I was *accompanied by* Tom. I was *accompanied on* my trip by Tom.

acquitted of   He was *acquitted of* all charges.

adapted to, from, by   The gasoline engine can be *adapted to* air-conditioners. The movie script was *adapted from* a novel; it was *adapted by* William Goldman.

agree to, on, with   We *agree to* the terms. We *agree on* a course of action. He *agreed with* me.

angry with, at, about   Terry was *angry with* me, *angry at* her mother, and *angry about* her situation.

argue with, for, against, about   I *argued with* Harry *about* air pollution; he *argued for* and I *argued against* government controls.

capable of   He was *capable of* being deceitful.

compare to, with   *Compared to* me, he's a saint. He *compared* a Volkswagen *with* a Toyota.

communicate with, about   I asked him to *communicate with* me soon. The two countries *communicated about* agriculture.

confide in, to   Can I *confide in* you? Then I want to *confide to* you that I broke the law once.

conform to, with   You must *conform to* (or *with*) this standard.

conformity with   You must act in *conformity with* prevailing customs.

connect by, with   The hose is *connected by* a coupling. I am *connected with* the English Department.

correspond to, with   I *correspond with* my colleagues regularly. A French province *corresponds* roughly *to* an American state.

describe as, to   It was *described as* a blessing. I *described to* him my latest project.

despair of   He *despaired of* ever understanding algebra.

differ about, from, with   We *differ about* the best wine to drink with fish. My ideas *differ from* his. I beg to *differ with* you.

*different from**   My plans are very *different from* yours.

enter into, on, upon   We *entered into* an agreement. The United States entered *on* (or *upon*) a new era in foreign relations.

free from, of   We were *free of* him at last. I need to be *freed from* my obligations.

identical with   Your hat is *identical with* mine.

independent of   He is *independent of* his family.

interest in   He *interested* himself *in* politics.

live at, in, on   He *lives at* 525 East 89th Street. He *lives in* an elegant mansion. He *lives on* his independent income.

---

*Different than is the colloquial usage when a clause is the object of the prepositional phrase. *Formal:* The farm looks different *from what* I had expected. *Colloquial:* The farm looks *different than* I had expected.

listen to, at   He *listened to* nobody. She *listened at* the door.

necessity for, of   The *necessity for* vitamins has been proven. There is no *necessity of* your catching cold.

object to   I don't *object to* your statement.

overcome by, with   Sarah was *overcome by* sadness. Arthur was *overcome with* admiration.

parallel between, with   There is a *parallel between* his attitudes and his behavior. The course of his career ran *parallel with* mine.

persuade of, to   I was *persuaded of* the rightness of his argument. I was *persuaded to* accompany him on the trip.

preferable to   Hawaii is *preferable to* Alaska for a vacation.

superior to   His stereo set is *superior to* mine.

vary from, in, with   Ideas *vary from* one another just as shoe sizes *vary in* width. My mood *varies with* changes of weather.

worthy of   He is *worthy of* my sympathy.

   Idiomatic expression also requires that some verbs be followed by a gerund and some by an infinitive.

Infinitive	*Gerund*
able to go	capable of going
like to go	enjoy going
eager to go	cannot help going
hesitate to go	privilege of going
need to go	purpose of going
ask to go	consider going
consent to go	deny going
want to go	put off going

TEST YOURSELF ON
Using Correct Idiomatic Expressions

In each of the blank spaces, write the correct idiomatic expression needed for the sentence. The expression required may be a preposition, an infinitive, or a gerund.

1. With   fish   dinners,   white   wine   is   preferable

_____ red.

2. I hesitate _____ him what I think of him. (use a form of *tell*)

3. He lives comfortably _____ his pension.

4. They argued _____ who would do a better job as mayor.

5. He was described _____ me as a liberal, which was quite different _____ what I had been led to believe.

6. She was capable _____ making her feelings known.

7. Because she was angry _____ me, I was overcome _____ guilt.

8. I was not eager _____ (use a form of *leave*) school, but there was a necessity _____ doing so.

9. We entered _____ a contract; therefore, we were legally connected _____ each other.

10. George confided _____ his friends that he was breaking up with Kathy.

Fresh, Specific and Concrete Language

A writer's language should be fresh, specific, and concrete; it should avoid cliches and try to make a vivid impression on the reader. Plain language can do this if it strives for a proper balance between the abstract and the concrete, the general and the specific.

1. Clichés

The word cliché (pronounced *clee-shay*) comes from the French word for stereotype plate or printing block. Hence any word or expression whose freshness or clarity has been lost through constant usage is called a cliché, a stereotype. Such words or phrases are also called tired, stale, trite, or worn out. Writers who habitually use clichés not only use tired words but also present the reader with tired ideas.

Nevertheless, we all use clichés in ordinary conversation. In those circumstances, they are frequently forgiven—perhaps because we make up for the tired expression with a lively presence. In any case, whether your writing is formal or informal, you should develop an ear for clichés and avoid using such expressions as the following:

the beginning of the end	the last straw
better late than never	mother nature
bigger and better	neat as a pin
cool as a cucumber	on balance
a crying shame	pretty as a picture
deep, dark secret	right on
do justice to	rotten to the core
free as a bird	sadder but wiser
hard as nails	tell it like it is
hot under the collar	variety is the spice of life
last but not least	viable options

Writers who persistently use clichés are not in control of their material. Writers who are in control of their material can *use* clichés to make fresh points.

The fact that Harry was so often late for appointments made it obvious that he would never be known as *a regular guy.*

My response to what you've just proposed is *wrong on.*

The bigger the better simply does not apply to things like budget deficits and the headaches they invariably bring on.

TEST YOURSELF ON
Identifying Clichés

Circle any words or expressions you find in the following passages that you think are clichés; then supply better—fresher—words or expressions to replace them.

A. Although I was financially embarrassed, I decided to eat out anyway. I didn't care that I was getting to be fatter than a pig, I wanted to do justice to a great meal—and the bigger the better. I settled on McDonald's and started eating like there was no tomorrow. I had six Big Macs, four large orders of fries, and three large shakes. Last but not least, I topped the whole thing off with four apple turnovers. That, however, was the last straw. My stomach really started to growl, and later on that evening I realized that I had eaten myself sick. The next morning I was, believe it or not, sadder but wiser.

B. In this day and age, the American way of life demands that college students get on the ball and learn more than just the stuff taught in classes. Students should get out and mingle. This is the only way to develop a well-rounded personality and the ability to get along with others. There are all kinds of things students can do to become more interesting personalities. They can join a club, attend dances, or just start being friendly—straight from the shoulder—with their fellow students in class. Hitting the books isn't the only way to go in college. If you want to get what you pay for, you have to pass the acid test. Beyond a shadow of a doubt, if you want to get more out of life, you have to put more into it.

2. Concrete and abstract language

Writers should use the concrete wherever possible. A concrete word is one that appeals directly to the senses —it points to something that exists. Thus *engine* is a concrete word: we can see, hear, and feel one when we lift the hood of a car. But what the engine supplies, *power* (or *energy*), is an abstract word: *power* cannot be directly perceived; but many concrete things deliver power: *an engine, a turbine, a locomotive, a football fullback,* and so forth. We would not say, giving the reason that we would not buy a specific car, ''The Ford had no power'' if we meant that it ''had no engine,'' but

we might say "The Ford had no power" if we meant
that its engine wasn't efficient. So both abstract and
concrete language have their uses. But the advice still
holds: writers should use the concrete word whenever
they can, because the mind's ability to perceive a concrete word makes the writing more vivid. This policy
also applies to sentences. Sentences with abstract ideas
can be made clearer by supporting them with concrete
illustrations.

Sentence Containing Needlessly Abstract Words

The *grounds* were *sloppy* and the *planks* on the porch were
    bad.

Revised to Supply Concrete Words

The *front yard* was *littered with broken furniture and rusted
    tools* and the *steps* of the porch were *rotted and splintered.*

Abstract First Sentence of a Paragraph

When dealing with institutions, people are made to feel small.

Concrete Follow-up Sentence

They are made to fill out needlessly complicated forms, to spend
    long hours waiting on line, and frequently to visit an office
    several times in order to get what they came for.

3. Specific and general language

The terms *specific* and *general,* applied to words or
expressions, mean much the same as is meant by the labels *concrete* and *abstract*—with this difference: *specific* and *general* attest to the relative degrees of con-
creteness of a particular set of words.

meat—poultry—chicken
animals—primates—gorillas
military—soldier—Pvt. Mudd
foliage—trees—oak
clothing—trousers—blue jeans

Note that as you read from left to right, the words become more specific—the reader is better able to *picture*
the concrete object; though we would not say that the
words in the left-hand column are abstract, they are
more general terms than those in the other two col-

umns. Good writing requires that the writer use the more specific term whenever possible. Although it is true that good writers use general terms as well as specific ones, more often than not there is a loss of freshness and clarity in writing when writers abandon control of their work and use constructions like the following:

General Shade was provided by a big *tree* on the *grass.*
Specific Shade was provided by a *spreading maple* on the *lawn.*

General College students are forced to waste a lot of time.
Specific A college student's time is often wasted by waiting on registration lines, filling out forms, and making more than one trip to a professor's office to obtain a grade. (notice how this idea gets expanded by having to be made more specific)

TEST YOURSELF ON
Using Specific, Concrete Language

A. For each of the italicized words in the sentences below, find at least two other words that convey a more specific meaning.

1. He *slept* for half an hour.
2. He *ate* his food as if it were his last meal.
3. He decided not to *tell* that he'd had an accident.
4. She *called* for help.
5. Al didn't want to *show* his feelings.
6. He *ran* all the way home.
7. He *worked on* his essay for an hour; then he gave up.
8. Out of the corner of his eye, he *noticed* someone approaching.
9. He *walked* lazily down to the corner market.
10. They *wrote* their compositions in class.

B. Follow each of the general statements in the sentences below with two more sentences, giving concrete details to illustrate them.

Example: When I woke up this morning, I felt as if I'd been drugged.
Follow-up with concrete details: My head ached dully, and my vision was blurred. When I tried to move, it felt as if I were walking through water.

1. When I woke up this morning, I felt as if I'd been drugged.
2. My garden is growing beautifully.
3. I don't think my parents understand that I'm an adult.
4. Most college freshmen have special problems.
5. Registering for classes at this college takes its toll on a student.

DOUBLE NEGATIVE

The use of an additional negative to reinforce an already negative statement is called a double negative and is not acceptable in Standard English.

Double Negative   *Nobody* loves me *no* more.
Revised   *Nobody* loves me *anymore.*

Triple Negative   He *never* had *no* faith in *nobody.*
Revised   He *never* had faith in *anyone.*

ELLIPSIS

The omission of a portion of quoted text is called ellipsis. Spaced dots (ellipsis points) are used to indicate where text has been omitted.

The Full Text Being Quoted

Mr. Ross Alexander's play moves across the stage like a dream of yesterday, stinging us with its wit and wisdom, arguing our case before an ethical court, lifting our spirits as we contemplate our battered selves.

—Edward Quinn

A Portion Quoted from This Text with Some Words Omitted

Quinn says "Alexander's play moves . . . like a dream . . . arguing our case . . . lifting our spirits. . . ."

The spaced dots in this quoted portion are ellipsis points. When the ellipsis comes at the end of a sentence, use a period followed by three spaced dots to indicate omitted material.

Ellipsis points are also used to indicate a pause or an unfinished statement, especially in dialogue.

"Be careful, John. If you're not . . ."
"I don't know . . . I just don't know."

END PUNCTUATION

The punctuation marks that end sentences—periods, exclamation points, and question marks—suggest how a reader is to understand the whole sentence. Internal punctuation (colons, commas, dashes, parentheses, and semicolons) indicate relations of the parts of the sentence. See **Colon, Comma, Dash, Exclamation Point, Parentheses, Period, Question Mark, Semicolon.**

EXCLAMATION POINT

The exclamation point (!), which always signifies strong emphasis, should be used as follows.

1. Use the exclamation point to mark the end of an exclamatory sentence, phrase, or clause. An exclamatory expression is an abrupt, forceful outcry—very emphatic.

How he must be suffering! (sentence)
What a tragedy! (elliptical clause, i.e., one with words missing: full clause is "What a tragedy this is!"
No kidding! (phrase)

A single exclamation point does the job. Don't use more than one for extra emphasis.

2. Use the exclamation point to emphasize a form of direct address or an interjection when there is strong feeling being conveyed.

George! I need help!
Hurray! We won!

3. Use an exclamation point to add emphasis to an imperative sentence (a command) where strong feeling is being conveyed.

Shut your mouth!
Stay away from me!
Give me an answer now!

4. Do not use an exclamation point for (a) statements that are not exclamatory; (b) ordinary forms of address; (c) unemphatic interjections; or (d) mild commands.

Wrong   That's too bad!
Wrong   George! I'd like to speak to you.
Wrong   Well! we've arrived.
Wrong   Turn left at the corner!

Note: When the exclamation point is overused, it gives your writing an air of phony excitement—almost hysteria—and robs you of the opportunity to provide real emphasis where it is needed. So use the exclamation point sparingly.

TEST YOURSELF ON
Using the Exclamation Point Appropriately

Some of the sentences below use the exclamation point appropriately; next to these, place the letter C. In the rest, strike out the exclamation points that are unnecessary.

1. _____ War is hell!

2. _____ How the mighty have fallen!

3. _____ College courses ask too much of a student!

4. _____ Get your hands off me!

5. _____ How he must have suffered!

6. _____ This coffee is terrible!

7. _____ I need aspirin!

8. _____ What a crazy man!

9. _____ Turn the car around!

10. _____ What big teeth you have, Grandma!

FRAGMENTS

The word *fragment* means a piece or a part; therefore, a sentence fragment is a piece of a sentence. Beginning writers frequently write pieces of sentences because they distrust the *length* of what they are writing, and they think that if they insert a period after they have written a certain number of words their writing will "look" better. This is an error. Length is not the main factor in determining when to end one sentence and begin another.

[A.] Whenever I try to hold a long and serious conversation with my parents about my career. [B.] They get me angry by raising irrelevant issues and arguments.

The writer of this material decided to put a period after the word *career* because the string of words looked long. In fact, however, the portion that is marked A is an incorrect *sentence fragment*. The reason it's a fragment is that it is a dependent clause; that is, it has a subject (*I*) and a finite verb (*try*)—which all sentences need —but it also has a subordinating conjunction, *whenever*. The whole structure hangs from this conjunction —which signals us that the structure must be connected to an independent clause—and therefore it cannot stand alone.

We can make A independent and therefore able to stand alone by eliminating *whenever;* this detaches the clause from what it depends on and makes it a whole sentence—an independent clause.

The second method of correcting the fragment error is to take the fragment, A, and hook it on to an independent clause. This we can do by substituting a comma for the period after *career* and making the capital letter in *they* into a lower-case letter, for the B portion of the example *is* an independent clause.

Original Example

Whenever I try to hold a long and serious conversation with my parents about my career. They get me angry by raising irrelevant issues and arguments.

Example Corrected by the First Method

I try to hold a long and serious conversation with my parents about my career. They get me angry by raising irrelevant issues and arguments.

Example Corrected by the Second Method

Whenever I try to hold a long and serious conversation with my parents about my career, they get me angry by raising irrelevant issues and arguments.

Which of the corrections do you think is better?

In this case, the second method is better because retaining the word *whenever* establishes a clear relation between the two parts.

Fragment

While I was listening to some punk rock on the stereo the other night. Someone came along and stole my car.

Corrected by First Method

I was listening to some punk rock on the stereo the other night. Someone came along and stole my car. (grammatically correct, but gives no sense of how the two parts are related)

Corrected by Second Method

While I was listening to some punk rock on the stereo the other night, someone came along and stole my car. (also grammatically correct, but a better correction because the two parts are better related)

TEST YOURSELF ON
Correcting Sentence Fragments

The following are all incorrect. Rewrite each as a complete sentence.

1. They wouldn't let Agnes on the basketball court. Because she wasn't wearing sneakers.
2. I'm worried about my final exams. Which come in about three weeks.
3. Professor Urban took me out for an expensive dinner. Although he had mentioned to me that he was short of money.
4. Unless I'm given the salary I want. I won't take the job.
5. Whenever he hears the Beatles sing ''Yesterday.'' He's reminded of the sixties.

Another kind of sentence fragment is made when beginning writers mistake verbals for verbs and think that the structure containing a verbal can stand alone. (See Phrases.)

verbal
Incorrect   Joey has an overwhelming desire. *To leave town.*

verbal
Incorrect   Arthur believes he has one purpose in life. *To teach.*

verbal
Incorrect   Uncle Bud is happy doing only one thing. *Running.*

Even if you haven't written much, you would not be likely to make the errors in these examples, because in each case the verbal is limited to just a few words. The problem remains the same, however, when these verbals are extended into long verbal phrases.

Incorrect   Joey has an overwhelming desire. *To leave town in order to start a new career.*

Incorrect   Arthur believes he has one purpose in life. *To teach youngsters the fundamentals of mathematics.*

Incorrect   Uncle Bud is happy doing only one thing. *Running ten miles a day to prepare himself to run in marathon races.*

The italicized phrase in each of these examples is dependent and cannot stand alone. Each must be connected, with or without a comma, to the sentence that precedes it. Besides having no subjects, these phrases have no finite verbs—only verbals—and a sentence must have a subject and a finite verb.

A third type of fragment appears when you punctuate prepositional phrases as if they were complete sentences (see Phrases). But only complete sentences should be punctuated as such.

prepositional phrase
Financial aid at this college is given. *To students.*

prepositional phrase
Financial aid at this college is given. *To students who show need.*

prepositional phrase
Financial aid at this college is given. *To students who show need and whose records are outstanding.*

Once again, it is unlikely that beginning writers will make the error shown in the first example, because the prepositional phrase there consists of only two words. But in the other two examples, the possibility is greater because the number of words is greater. In all three examples, of course, the period after the word *given* is incorrect and creates the fragment that follows it.

A fourth type of fragment is created when you fail to recognize that a portion of what you are writing is really a final appositive and not a sentence.

appositive
This summer, I'm spending my vacation with George. *A friend.*

appositive
This summer, I'm spending my vacation with George. *A friend, a sportsman, a very funny guy.*

The first example contains an error that a beginning writer probably won't make, because the appositive consists of only two words. But the error in the second example is more likely to be made because the appositive has more words. In fact, appositives can be quite long and complicated, but no matter how long they are, they cannot stand as sentences. To correct the fragments above, change the period to either a comma or a colon.

TEST YOURSELF ON
Recognizing and Correcting Sentence Fragments

A. Turn the following sentence fragments into sentences by crossing out a word in the fragment.

1. Until I reached home.
2. Although he seemed like a nice enough man.
3. Whenever I have gone to the movies.
4. Unless the college gives me some financial support.
5. Because you have dry skin.
6. If I saw her at a party.
7. After the doctor changed my bandage.
8. Since he wasn't a practicing Christian.

9. While the cows were being milked.
10. As my uncle walked through the door.

B. Correct the following fragments by adding an independent clause to the beginning or the end of each.

Example

Fragment: Which cost me twelve dollars.
Fragment connected: His birthday present was a shirt, which cost me twelve dollars.

1. Which cost me twelve dollars.
2. Although I rarely eat at a restaurant.
3. If I never buy another automobile again.
4. Running along the side of the road.
5. To understand auto mechanics.
6. In the woods behind my house.
7. A friend, a teacher, an adviser.
8. To students who are able to undertake advanced studies.
9. Unless I hear from you tonight.
10. To people who are interested in art.
11. Traveling all over the world.
12. Enough time, enough equipment, enough spirit.

C. Read carefully each of the following examples. Underline a sentence fragment wherever you see one, and correct it. Some of the examples are complete sentences, containing no fragments; next to these, write C.

1. _____ Horses racing together through the surf.

2. _____ When Americans celebrate a holiday, they usually have a picnic and a parade.

3. _____ The Founding Fathers had a wish. To leave to us a good model for democratic living.

4. _____ She cooked a large and elaborate dinner. To impress her husband's parents.

5. _____ Last summer we visited Niagara Falls and then crossed over into Canada. Which is what I had always wanted to do.

6. _____ Although I am not at all sure what I will do after graduation. I am very sure that I want to spend four years studying ecology.

7. _____ They drove 3,000 miles across the country to see their son's graduation. An event that they had yearned to see for four long years.

8. _____ The black experience in America has been a frightful one. Which accounts for the revolutionary tone of recent black writing.

9. _____ Although television programming seems innocuous, its effects are not.

HYPHEN

The hyphen is used between words or between prefixes and words to indicate that the hyphenated structure should be taken as a unit (*anti-war, twenty-two, low-level*); to separate prefixes from words when the combination is spelled like a word with another meaning (e.g., *re-creation,* "a creation again," and *recreation,* "leisure"); and to divide a word at the end of a line of text to show that it continues on to the next line. This last use is a matter of convention; we will begin with it.

1. Use a hyphen when you must divide a word at the end of a line of text and continue it onto the next line. When you must do this, place the hyphen between syllables. A syllable is a unit of spoken language consisting usually of a vowel alone or a vowel with one or more consonants. Good dictionaries give the proper syllables of a word in each entry. Here is the proper syllabication of a few multisyllable words. Notice that each syllable is pronounceable.

a-bove	con-ver-sa-tion	pa-tience
ac-tor	dis-trib-ute	pic-ture
bap-tism	hy-dro-gen	rev-er-end
bi-cy-cle	op-po-nent	sep-a-ra-tion
bur-y		

It turned out on Friday that our *conversa-
tion* had been unnecessary. We were really agreed on everything.

After graduating from college, Henry became an *actor,* something I had not thought possible when I knew him.

If you are unsure of the proper syllabication of a word, consult a good dictionary. But never leave a single letter on one line even if it *is* the proper syllabication. And never divide a word of one syllable, such as *France* or *trout.*

Wrong   There was a line of low, threatening clouds a-
bove the mountains.
Right   There was a line of low, threatening clouds above
the mountains.

Wrong   We decided it would be in our best interest to *bur-
y* the hatchet and be friends again.
Right   We decided it would be in our best interest to *bury*
the hatchet and be friends again.

Wrong   In the fall, when we finally left for *France,* we were very excited.
Right   In the fall, when we finally left for *France,*
we were very excited.

2. Use a hyphen to join words or words and prefixes together. The hyphen used in this way is, in most cases, a transitional mark. For example, usually (but not always), when words are first linked to each other, they are written separately—as in *basket ball.* Later, this word became *basket-ball,* and it is now, of course, always written *basketball.* Thus just how to use the hyphen for any compound word at any particular moment is difficult to determine, because usage is continually changing and even good, recently published dictionaries are likely to be behind the times. Still, the dictionary is the soundest authority and should be consulted when the writer is doubtful about some case of hyphenation.

The following rules were accurate when this book was written.

A. Words beginning with *all, self* and *ex* (meaning *former*) are always hyphenated.

He is a *self-made* man.
In Washington, the President's staff is *all-powerful*.
The *ex-President* has hardly any influence on national policy.

B. When the root word is a proper noun or proper adjective, use a hyphen to separate prefixes.

anti-Nixon   un-American   pro-Carter

C. Prefixes ending in a vowel are frequently hyphenated, especially if the root word begins with the same vowel.

anti-intellectual	semi-invalid	pre-election
re-educate	de-escalate	re-evaluate
co-ordinate		

Note: Some constructions with a double vowel are acceptable without hyphenation.

cooperate, preeminent, preexisting.

D. Certain prefixes are hyphenated to avoid confusing a word with another whose spelling is identical.

A work of art is a *re-creation* of experience. (to avoid confusion with *recreation*, "leisure")
Since the math teacher couldn't follow his logic, he had to *re-prove* the theorem. (to avoid confusion with *reprove*, "rebuke")
Now that my wife has emptied our closets, we have to *re-store* all our things. (to avoid confusion with *restore*, "return to a former condition")

3. A good many compound nouns are hyphenated; a good many others are not; and some are written as single words. (A compound noun is one that consists of more than a single word.)

Hyphenated	*Un-hyphenated*	*Single Words*
air-brake	bus boy	blackbird
bull's-eye	diving board	headache
cave-in	first cousin	highway
free-for-all	high school	landslide
bee-sting	ice cream	madman
merry-go-round	oil spill	newsstand

Remember: If you are unsure about a particular case, consult a good dictionary.

4. Compound adjectives—groups of words that when taken together act like a single-word adjective—are usually joined together by hyphens.

able-bodied seaman	*low-level* official
devil-may-care attitude	*middle-of-the-road* politician
double-parked car	*out-of-work* actor
fence-busting outfielder	*two-tired* stadium

Note: When these adjectives are in the predicate adjective position, following a linking verb, the hyphen is omitted.

The actor is *out of work.*
His car was *double parked.*

5. Hyphens are used between parts of compound numbers—twenty-one to ninety-nine—and in specifying fractions. Hyphens are also frequently used to connect numbers in specifying dates.

This is my *twenty-second* birthday.
My professor is only *thirty-one* years old.
He is taxed *two-fifths* of his income.
The meetings will take place September *4-11.*
My vacation runs *July 31-August 14.*

Note: Do not use a hyphen in noncompound numbers.

one hundred twelve

TEST YOURSELF ON
the Appropriate Use of the Hyphen

Some of the sentences below contain uses of the hyphen that are correct; next to these, write C. Some sentences, however, contain word groups that need a hyphen. Insert a hyphen wherever you think one is missing.

1. _____ Sarah is a well trained teacher, but she would
rather be a well paid researcher.

2. _____ Resort the laundry so that we can get all the white things together.

3. _____ Everything Jeffrey does is self-serving.

4. _____ Call in a carpenter; those book shelves are not a doityourself job.

5. _____ Ed's colorblindness is due to a genetic defect.

6. _____ If you don't like spaghetti and meat balls, you're unItalian.

7. _____ Coal mine caveins are preventable.

8. _____ That actor used to be an able bodied seaman.

9. _____ Ex naval officers frequently become business executives.

10. _____ The all-powerful Internal Revenue Service takes two-fifths of my income in taxes.

11. _____ He was a semiinvalid and a proCarter pseudoliberal.

12. _____ He scored a bullseye in target shooting, but she was uninterested.

IDIOM

See **Diction.**

INTERNAL PUNCTUATION

See **End Punctuation.**

ITALICS

Italics is the name given to the typeface in which these words are printed. On the other hand, the typeface in which these words are printed is called roman.

In hand-written manuscripts or typescripts, underlining is the equivalent of italics. Italics are conventionally used in the following special cases.

1. Use italics for the names of books, plays, movies, TV shows, newspapers, magazines, ships, aircraft, musical compositions.

Shakespeare's *Hamlet*
Melville's *Moby Dick*
The New Yorker (magazine)
The Los Angeles *Times* (note that the name of the city is not in italics here)
S.S. Rotterdam, Queen Elizabeth II
The City of Birmingham (name of aircraft)
Beethoven's *Ninth Symphony*
Star Wars (movie)
All in the Family (TV show)

2. Use italics for foreign words and phrases that have not become part of the English language.

He lived in Peekskill but kept a small *pied-à-terre* in New York. (*pied-à-terre* = temporary or secondary lodging place)
Writing poems was his whole *raison d'être*. (*raison d'être* = reason for being)
Dave is known as a *bon vivant*. (a person who enjoys good food and other pleasant things)

Note: Some foreign words and phrases *have* become part of the English language and should not be italicized. Here is a small list of them:

| cliché | gamin | guru | genre | lacuna |
| café | bona fide | ensemble | elite | Gesundheit |

3. Use italics for words and phrases considered for themselves.

The word *elegant* is derived from Old French.
The term *end of the line* is a cliché.

4. Use italics for scientific terms in Latin.

The constellation Great Bear (*Ursa major*) is in the northern hemisphere.
For genetic research, the species of mosquito known as *anopheles* is most useful.

5. Use italics for giving special emphasis to ordinary words. You should achieve emphasis by placing the important word or words in an emphatic position in the sentence—not by carelessly using italics. Italics should be reserved for words that cannot be emphasized enough by ordinary work on structure.

Weak I'm talking about *love,* as an emotion.
Revised Love is what I'm talking about. (here the position of *love* as the subject gives it enough emphasis without italics)

Weak He said he would *never* marry.
Revised To the question of when he would marry, he replied with one word: never. (the final position of the word in the rewritten sentence is very emphatic; note, too, that the sentence has been designed to emphasize *never*)

Proper Use of Italics

What's important is not what she *was,* but what she has *become.* (italics point up the contrast between *was* and *become*)

Charley is henpecked not because he has a wife but because *his wife has him.* (italics call attention to the reversal)

TEST YOURSELF ON
the Use of Italics

Some of the following sentences show the correct use of italics. Next to each of these, write C. Some sentences, however, need to have italics added or removed; in these, make the appropriate corrections.

1. _____ The current craze for *nostalgia* knows no limits.

2. _____ The expression freaked out is slang.

3. _____ The New York Daily News has only one competitor.

4. _____ Great books like Moby-Dick and Anna Karenina occupy the mind long after we've read them.

5. _____ My Uncle Ted is on the cover of *Time* this week.

6. _____ The program includes Beethoven's Sixth Symphony and his Fidelio Overture.

7. _____ I felt much better after I spoke to my *guru*.

8. _____ The porcupine anteater belongs to the family *echidna*.

9. _____ The Transatlantic Review published Myra's first story.

10. _____ We're sailing on the *S.S. Rotterdam*.

11. _____ She worked as a *fille de chambre* [lady's maid].

12. _____ It was his last performance as Hamlet.

MISPLACED MODIFIERS

A misplaced modifier is a word, phrase, or clause that does not point clearly and directly to what it is supposed to modify. When using modifiers, be sure to place the word, phrase, or clause close to the word or words it actually modifies, for meaning changes with the placement of the modifier.

He almost had a heart attack every time he looked at his bank statement. (he almost had the attack—but not quite—every time he looked)

He had a heart attack almost every time he looked at his bank statement. (he actually had the attack—sometimes, but not every time he looked)

1. Be careful to place the adverbs *almost, even, hardly, just, merely, only, nearly*, and *scarcely* close to the words they modify. Misplacing words like *almost* and *only* occurs quite often in informal writing, but you should learn to be careful about their placement, because misplacing them can often confuse the reader badly.

Misplaced Word I *only* told the jury what I had seen. (the choices here are three: I *only*—and nobody else—told the jury; I told *only* the jury—and nobody else; or I told the jury *only* what I had seen)

Revised I told the jury *only* what I had seen.

I told *only* the jury what I had seen.

Only I told the jury what I had seen.

Misplaced   She *nearly* seemed crazy.
Revised   She seemed *nearly* crazy.

Misplaced   We *almost* decided to buy half an acre of land.
Revised   We decided to buy *almost* half an acre of land.

2. Be careful to place modifying phrases close to the word or words they modify.

Misplaced Phrase   My history professor made it clear why wars take place *on Tuesday*. (the *wars* take place on Tuesday?)
Revised   *On Tuesday*, my history professor made it clear why wars take place.

Misplaced Phrase   Airlines serve martinis to passengers *in little bottles*. (the *passengers* are in little bottles?)
Revised   Airlines serve passengers martinis *in little bottles*.

Misplaced Phrase   Environmental groups protested the oil leaks *all over the country*. (were there *oil leaks* all over the country?)
Revised   Environmental groups *all over the country* protested the oil leaks.

3. Be careful to place modifying clauses close to the word or words which they modify.

Misplaced Clause   Sid bought books for his library *that cost $19.04*. (did his *library* or his *books* cost that much?)
Revised   Sid bought books *that cost $19.04* for his library. For his library, Sid bought books *that cost $19.04*.

Misplaced Clause   The paint job looked sloppy *which was not dry yet*.
Revised   The paint job, *which was not dry yet*, looked sloppy.

A special case of the misplaced modifier is called a *squinting modifier* because it looks in two directions at the same time; that is, it "squints."

Squinting Modifier   To be beautifully dressed *often* pleases my wife. (is she *often pleased* or *often beautifully dressed*?)
Revised   It *often* pleases my wife to be beautifully dressed. It pleases my wife to be beautifully dressed *often*.

Squinting Modifier   Lucia said *when she was on her way home* she would stop and buy the vegetables. (did she say it while traveling home? or did she say that sometime on her way home she would stop?)

Revised   When she was on her way home, Lucia said that she would stop and buy the vegetables. (*said* while on her way home) Lucia said that on her way home she would stop and buy the vegetables. (she will *stop* on her way home)

TEST YOURSELF ON
Revising Misplaced and Squinting Modifiers

Some of the following sentences contain well-placed modifiers; next to these, write C. Others, however, have misplaced or squinting modifiers; correct these, even if it means recasting the sentence.

1. _____ With this calculator, I can show you how to make a million dollars in twenty seconds.

2. _____ The sick patient wanted to live happily.

3. _____ The sunset that we loved completely stunned us.

4. _____ We made plans to leave over the weekend.

5. _____ Professors who teach rarely get rich.

6. _____ Subconsciously, Kathy wanted to become famous.

7. _____ Caesar was stabbed in the heyday of his glory.

8. _____ He just left for a minute.

9. _____ For Christopher's sake, I decided to go to California.

10. _____ The state penalizes those who commit murder for good reason.

11. _____ Robert DeNiro just arrived here last week.

12. _____ The father heard the news that his son had been born with joy.

13. _____ *True Confessions* appeals to readers with scandalous stories.

14. _____ Those who jog slowly develop heart trouble.

15. _____ The ugly face scared him that looked through the window.

16. _____ They told us at midnight the show would begin.

17. _____ I took a train to Waterbury that was going north.

18. _____ She was planting seeds in her garden that she had bought yesterday.

MODIFIERS

In Part 1, we noted that adjectives and adverbs act to modify or further describe members of other word classes: nouns and verbs. Adjectives and adverbs, as well as determiners, are called modifiers. But the question of modification is a bit more complicated than you may have imagined from reading about it in Part 1. Here we shall discuss the complications by discussing other words that can act as adjectives and adverbs. These other words are called *adjectivals* and *adverbials*.

Other Words Used as Adjectives: Adjectivals

Some words are nearly always used as adjectives: *old, young, happy, proud,* and so forth. But other words, ordinarily belonging to other parts of speech, can also act as adjectives. So, of course, can phrases. All are entitled to be called adjectivals.

1. Nouns used as adjectives

We looked into the *bear* cage. (modifies *cage*)
She was wearing her *party* dress. (modifies *dress*)
We went to the *baseball* game. (modifies *game*)

2. Verbs used as adjectives

A whole class of verbs can be commonly used as adjectives. These are the participles: the *ing* forms (present participles), the *-d* or *-ed* forms (past participles), and the irregular past participles (*gone, broken, kept,* and so forth).

The *fleeing* suspect was caught by the police. (modifies *suspect,* the subject)
The *broken* arrow was useless. (modifies *arrow,* the subject)
He seemed *defeated.* (acts as predicate adjective)
The job was *finished.* (acts as predicate adjective)

3. Adverbs used as adjectives

The apartment *below* is mine. (modifies *apartment*)
The road *ahead* is closed. (modifies *road*)

4. Phrases and clauses used as adjectives

Phrase The men *in the truck* were tired. (modifies *men*)

Phrase The planes *flying overhead* are bound for Europe. (modifies *planes*)

Clause The people *who rented my house* will stay until August. (modifies *people*)

Clause I bought a Toyota, *which runs like a top.* (modifies *Toyota*)

Other Words Used as Adverbs: Adverbials

Some words are nearly always used as adverbs: *often, soon, rarely,* and so forth. But other words, ordinarily belonging to other parts of speech, can also act as adverbs, as can phrases and clauses. All these are entitled to be called adverbials.

1. Nouns used as adverbs

I went *home.* (modifies *went*)
She arrived *yesterday.* (modifies *arrived*)

2. Verbs used as adverbs

Because he was in a hurry, he decided to eat *standing.* (modifies *to eat*)
Peter played *to win.* (modifies *played*)

3. Phrases and clauses used as adverbs

Phrase We are staying *at a hotel* (modifies *are staying*)

Phrase We were impatient *to leave for the theater.* (modifies *impatient*)

Clause *Although we were tired,* we couldn't fall asleep. (modifies the whole of the main clause)

Clause *When they saw the shark,* they were frightened. (modifies *were frightened*)

TEST YOURSELF ON
Recognizing Modifiers: Adjectivals and Adverbials

Identify each of the italicized words or word groups as either an adjectival or an adverbial.

1. We were going on a *holiday* trip.
2. We would arrive *in the afternoon.*
3. He went *home.*
4. *When he spoke softly,* we had to strain to listen.
5. He gave the apples to the man *in the raincoat.*
6. He was promoted to *plant* manager.
7. The books, *which cost $18,* were overpriced.
8. The man *who sent her the flowers* was in love with her.
9. He was a *broken* man.
10. They were a *defeated* team.
11. The *purring* cat likes his milk.
12. The man *in the gray flannel suit* looks like my brother.

NUMBER

See **Shifts.**

NUMERALS

Whether your writing is formal or informal, the basic guideline in handling numerals is to be consistent in your usage: either use numerals or spell the numbers out in words—do not mix the two. There are several basic rules for handling numerals in formal writing.

1. Spell out numbers that require no more than two words. In other cases, use numerals.

There were *seventy-five* cases of swine flu reported.
The population of New York City is less than *eight million*.
but
My federal tax refund amounted to *$88.37*.

Note: In business and technical writing, numbers from 10 up are often written as numerals.

2. In writing dates, addresses, percentages followed by %, page numbers, or the time of day followed by *a.m.* or *p.m.*, use numerals.

Date   October 19, 1926 *or* 19 October 1926

Address   55 East 9th Street, Apartment 7K; Room 938, Mott 4.

Percentages   Richard gets 1%, and I get the rest.
                 but
                 This bank pays five percent interest.

Page Numbers   See Chapter 3, page 112.

Time of Day   11:30 p.m. *or* 11:30 P.M. *but* three o'clock

3. Use numerals for quantities in scientific and technical writing.

The barometric pressure is *29.31*.
The specimen was *.37* centimeters in length.

4. It is appropriate to use in the same sentence a combination of words and numerals where such a combination will make your writing clear.

You may take only *six* 6-inch trout from this stream.
The cashier counted out *70 one*-dollar bills.

5. Do not begin a sentence with a numeral that is not spelled out.

Wrong   250,000,000 is the approximate population of the
           U.S.S.R.
Right   The population of the U.S.S.R. is approximately
           250,000,000.

Wrong   6 miles from here there is a gas station.
Right   Six miles from here there is a gas station.

Note: If your text includes a great many numbers or a mixture of whole numbers and decimals, it is preferable to use numerals for all the numbers.

TEST YOURSELF ON
Using Numerals Correctly

Each of the following sentences contains errors in handling numerals. Correct them.

1. 2,000 years ago, an important event took place in Palestine.
2. Including finance charges, this new car would cost you five thousand six hundred and thirty-eight dollars.
3. They live at nine-0-eight President Street, apartment three E.
4. Dennis drinks about 36 cases of wine every year.
5. The father is 40, the mother is 37, and their children are 12 and ten.
6. 3 years ago I owned a Volkswagen.
7. The average annual rainfall in the Matto Grosso district of Brazil is one hundred twelve point seven three centimeters.
8. On February second, nineteen twenty-two, he managed to publish a book of some seven hundred pages.
9. On page five, there is a good description of a corrupt man.
10. His author's royalties amounted to twelve percent of the price of the book.
11. I promised to pay him ninety-eight fifty-six on February twenty-third.
12. It's either the fourteenth of September or the seventeenth —the odds are thirty to one that I'll forget which.
13. Take your application to room thirty-two; someone will be there by four p.m.
14. He was useful to the track team because he could run the four forty and could double in the ten thousand meters.
15. 9 years ago, I had an operation and was in the hospital for 3 weeks.

ORGANIZATION AND PLANNING

Organization and planning are essential to good writing. An essay that is disorganized is incoherent, but achieving proper organization takes planning. This entry is devoted to both.

Organization

An essay is commonly organized into three parts: an introduction, a main body, and a conclusion. The main body is the most important of these parts, for in it the writer treats the main ideas of the essay. The organization of the body of the essay is treated under **Unity, Paragraph Development,** and **Coherence.**

Here we are interested in introductions and conclusions, but before we take up these important items, let us consider a whole essay—including introduction, main body, and conclusion:

My Disaster at Freshman Registration

[1] If you've ever wondered why you see so many prematurely gray-haired freshmen on this campus, this little story will answer your question.

[2] Bright and early on the first day of registration, I showed up at the Bursar's Office at 8 a.m. to pay my fees. The line at Window 1 snaked halfway around two corners to the lobby of the Administration Building. But I was patient (not to say in shock). After a half hour, I was at the promised land—the grilled window. I paid. They stamped my receipt. I was pushed out of the way.

[3] Suddenly, it dawned on me that I didn't know what to do next. I looked around, stupidly, I'm afraid. A passerby took pity on me. "Window 2 for your days and hours booklet," he snapped.

[4] So there I was, back in line. Another half hour passed. There I was, back at the grill. I showed my receipt. They gave me—a *torn* booklet. I was shoved out of the way again. But the booklet might have been ripped into shreds for all I cared; the crazy abbreviations and symbols were nearly unreadable. How would I ever figure out how to register?

[5] This problem seemed small when I arrived at the main registration area in the Gymnasium, because there it was literally a matter of survival. The physical contact here made the shoving at the Bursar's Office seem like love pats. Again, a friendly person intervened; that is, I found an adviser who explained that I needed to go to each departmental desk and register for courses one by one according to the days and hours I preferred.

[6] By this time, afternoon was crawling toward late afternoon. As I pondered my choice, I decided I'd better get cracking before dying of starvation (I'd missed lunch by now). So I ran to the English Department desk to register for Composition 101. But I was twenty yards away from that desk—without having registered—before I realized I didn't understand what they'd meant when they told me I'd been "closed out."

[7] I'll spare you the catalog of further horrors I endured that long day. You will learn whatever else you need to know about the registration experience by looking for me on campus. I'm the stooped, graying freshman male you see arriving for an 8 a.m. math class, the same one you see leaving after his 6 p.m. biology lecture.

The *introduction*, paragraph 1, opens the essay by proposing a challenge to the readers, and it does so in a humorous vein. It also tunes the readers in to the nature of what they are about to read: a little story. Further, it gives the tone of the piece and its main idea in brief.

The *main body* consists of paragraphs 2-6 and includes everything that actually happened; this portion of the paper is the centrally important part of what the writer has to say.

The *conclusion*, paragraph 7, ends the piece by returning to an idea presented in the introduction. It also gives a climactic end to the story by telling the reader the kind of schedule the poor freshman managed for himself—a long, nine-hour day.

The main body here is a little story—a piece of narration. Under **Paragraph Development,** other types of development are explained. See that entry to study more about how to handle a main body according to your specific purpose in writing a particular paper. For now, we will continue with more on introductions and conclusions and go on to planning an outline.

Introductions

Introductions are important because they are the first words of yours that readers will see. Effective introductions perform a number of different tasks. Perhaps the most important is to catch the readers' interest and attention; right behind this come the tasks of identifying the subject and setting some sort of limit on it. A good introduction also sets the tone for the rest of the piece—it advises the readers how you, the writer, intend to treat the subject.

Here are a number of introductions, each identified by the method the writer employs:

Using the Writer's Personal Experience

There was, I think, only a brief period in my life when I actually turned heads. It was the summer of my seventeenth year when, newly graduated from a private girls' school, I was in that transition stage between being an old child and a young woman, a state of half and half that men of all ages apparently find disarmingly erotic.

—Anne Taylor Fleming, "In Defense of Flirting"

Making an Unusual Statement

There are certain things an American is not permitted to hate. Americans may, without social ostracism or penalty of law, hate their partisan or ideological opposites. They may hate someone because of race or religion or class so long as they show selective decorum and speak in coded euphemisms.

—Larry L. King, "Un-American Peeves"

Offering a Strong Opinion

The current terrorist epidemic has mystified a great many people, and various explanations have been offered—most of them quite wrong.

—Walter Laqueur, "Terrorist Myths"

Stating and Illustrating the Main Idea

The dedicated baseball fan is a man who likes to kid himself. He'll get to a World Series game early, see a ballplayer yawning

and take it as a sign of nervousness. He'll see a nervelessly relaxed body leaning against a batting cage and consider it merely
feigned indifference. He'll watch an outfielder casually scratch-
ing his nose and count it as a tic. He's wrong. In fact, what looks
like boredom on behalf of the people involved in the World Series is most often just that.

—Jim Bouton, "A Few World Series Sinkers"

Opening with a Challenge to the Reader

If you want your mate to stop guessing about your feelings and
motives, you have to be prepared to reveal yourself.

—Nena and George O'Neill, "Communicating with Yourself"

Conclusions

A good conclusion to an essay leaves readers feeling
that they have enjoyed a satisfying, rounded-off reading
experience. It does this in one of the following ways:

1. By concluding with a reiteration, often in some
varied form, of your thesis statement or main idea. A
paper called "Abolish Big-Time Collegiate Sports"
might end like this:

If big-time sports on campus were abolished, as I have suggested
they should be, then perhaps some real sports enthusiasts could
begin to engage in them—myself, for example.

2. By concluding with a summary of your main
points, thus reinforcing in the readers' minds the effective things you have said. A possible ending for "Nuclear Energy versus Solar Power" might go as follows:

Nuclear energy presents us with the prospect of dangerous operation, deadly waste products, and sinister accidents, but the sun
—as we have known all along—is an endless source of pleasure,
enduring and powerful.

3. By making a climactic point. This type of conclusion is effective when you present a series of points in
ascending dramatic order and finish with a particularly
high note.

Planning

Planning an essay—or even a five-hundred-word theme—begins with note-taking, jotting down ideas as you ask questions about your subject. Say it's "freshman registration." What time did I get there? *Awful. Arrived at eight in the morning.* Then what happened? *Got on line at Bursar's Office to pay fees.* Next? *Didn't know what to do—had to get on line again to ask!* Ask enough questions, and you may wind up with a list that looks something like this:

1. Awful. Arrived at 8 in the morning.
2. Got on line at Bursar's Office Window 1 to pay fees.
3. Had to line up again—find out what to do next!
4. Closed out of English.
5. Had to ask what "closed out" means.
6. Found out I needed to go to Window 2 for days and hours booklet.
7. Days and hours booklet torn.
8. Couldn't read it, anyway.
9. Entered registration area and was shoved and pushed for five minutes before I found an adviser.
10. Lost my pack of computer cards.
11. Finally got classes that begin at 8 and end at 6, four days a week.

Outlines

The ultimate tool for planning an essay is an outline, and although the notes above do not exactly constitute an outline, you couldn't start to make an outline without them, and very little effort will enable you to make an outline from the notes. They have, embedded within them, just what you need for *controlling* and *directing* the way your theme will proceed.

For one thing, a quick glance at the notes tells you that there is a main point here—registration is a shocking, traumatic experience for an uninformed freshman. Furthermore, the fact that two areas are mentioned— the Bursar's Office and the registration area—provides

a way of dividing the essay and beginning to organize
an outline:

I. The Bursar's Office.
   A. Got on line to pay fees
   B. Got on line again for booklet
      1. booklet torn
      2. couldn't read it
II. The registration area
   A. Got pushed and shoved before finding adviser
   B. Closed out of English
      1. Found out what "closed out" means
      2. Missed lunch
   C. Got laborer's 8-6 schedule

This outline would help you to control your writing. It
is an aid in keeping your plan in mind, indicates the order in which you discuss things, and manages to suggest
the relative importance of the two places on the day of
registration, by assigning a greater proportion of space
to one (registration area) than to the other.

In order to become competent at making useful outlines, you should know something about the formal
principles of outlining and the different types of outlines
that can be used.

Types of outlines

The three types of outlines most commonly employed
are the topic outline, the sentence outline, and the paragraph outline. In a *topic outline,* each entry is a word
or a small group of words. In a *sentence outline,* which
has the same basic structural pattern as the topic outline, the words are replaced by complete sentences. In
a *paragraph outline,* there are no divisions, headings,
and subheadings, as in the others, but only a list of paragraph topic sentences. Some writers feel that the paragraph outline is most suitable for short papers, and the
others for longer papers. A writer using a sentence outline is likely to keep in closer touch with the points because of the fuller information contained in sentences.

Whatever you do, decide beforehand which kind of

outline you plan to use, and then follow its requirements systematically: use *only* sentences in the sentence outline; be sure you have topic sentences for the paragraph outline. And check your outline to be sure that it is consistent with the principles that apply to all outlines.

Here are samples of each kind of outline, for a paper on "The Energy Crisis in Oil and Two Alternate Sources of Power":

Topic Outline

I. The Arab oil embargo of 1973
   A. Shortage of oil
   B. Dwindling of resources
II. Alternative of nuclear power
   A. Expensive
   B. Dangerous
   C. Likely to run out
III. Solar power
   A. Inexpensive
   B. Not dangerous
   C. Limitless supply
   D. Needs technology

Sentence Outline

I. The Arab oil embargo of 1973 pointed up the need for America to find alternate sources of fuel.
   A. The embargo produced a shortage of oil.
   B. It reminded us that all our fossil fuel resources are limited.
II. Nuclear power as an alternative, though widely favored, is not likely to be the answer.
   A. It's very expensive—both for new plants and fuel processing.
   B. It's very dangerous.
   C. It's also likely to prove a limited resource.
III. Solar power is probably a more attractive alternative.
   A. It's relatively inexpensive except for startup costs.
   B. It's easy to handle and not dangerous.
   C. The supply is limitless.

Paragraph Outline

1. The Arab oil embargo of 1973 pointed up the need for America to find alternate sources of fuel, by creating a shortage of oil and reminding us that oil was in any case in very limited supply—a dwindling resource.

2. Nuclear energy is widely favored as an alternative source of power, but it has many serious drawbacks.

3. Solar power is probably a more attractive alternative because it is cheap, limitless in supply, and relatively inexpensive.

4. It may be that solar energy will not be adopted because of industry's resistance to high startup costs for such a program.

Testing the outline

Use the following criteria to be sure that your outline is logical and consistent:

1. Use a conventional form of notation. The following example is a useful one; it is rarely necessary to subdivide more than is shown:

```
I.  ................
    A. ................
        1. ................
            a. ................
            b. ................
        2. ................
    B. ................
II. ................
```

2. Be sure that your outline covers your subject adequately. The major headings in your outline should include enough material to stisfy the expectations provoked by your subject. For example, consider these two outlines:

The Federal Government

Inadequate Material	*Adequate Material*
I. Congress	I. Congress
II. The Executive Branch	II. The Executive Branch
	III. The Judiciary

Obviously, the outline on the left shows the writer's failure to consider the entire subject; of course this is a simple example, but checking your outline against this criterion of completeness can save you a great deal of trouble.

3. Be sure that your outline is in logical order. All the heads and subheads in your outline indicate parts. No category of head or subhead, therefore, can have only one part—if the essay or part is brief enough to be considered one part, it doesn't need to be outlined. Every outline must have at least two main headings, and wherever you divide one of these (I, II), you must divide it into at least two parts. If a I has an A, it must have a B. If an A has a 1, it must have a 2, and so forth.

Moreover, the order of your parts (the progression from I to II to II) must follow some consistent principle: chronology is one, cause and effect another. Do not mix your principles.

Consistent Time Order

Arranging a dinner party
   I. Selecting the date
  II. Inviting the guests
 III. Preparing the menu
  IV. Cooking the food
   V. Setting the table

Mixed Order

Crime
   I. Its increase since Vietnam (time order)
  II. Its causes (cause and effect order)
 III. Robbery versus rape (order by classification)

If your outline fails to meet this criterion, you are probably uncertain of your whole approach and need to re-examine your central idea or thesis statement.

4. Be sure to cast groups of headings and subheadings in parallel grammatical form. This will ensure that the parts of the outline are clearly related to one another. Notice in the sentence outline on p. 171 that I A and I B are parallel (in B, the pronoun *it* stands for *the embargo*), but that they are not parallel with II A, II B, and II C—which are parallel with one another. (*Note:* it is only due to the nature of the subject that III A, III B, and III C are parallel with the same group under II; in most cases, they need not be and will not be parallel.)

TEST YOURSELF ON
     the Principles of Outlining

A. Using one of the manageable titles given at the end of **Subjects for Essays** (p. 255), construct three outlines for it: a topic, a sentence, and a paragraph outline.

B. Choose one of the topics on p. 256, give it a manageable title, and construct a sentence outline for it.

PARAGRAPH DEVELOPMENT

Adequate development is one of the three criteria for an effectively written paragraph. (For the other two, see **Unity** and **Coherence.** Also discussed under **Unity** is the important idea of the *topic sentence:* if you are not familiar with the topic sentence, read **Unity** before reading further here.)

A paragraph that is adequately developed is one that gives reasons, details, illustrations, or examples to fully support its topic sentence. The failure to give full development to every topic sentence leads to a series of short, choppy statements—not paragraphs—and leaves readers with the impression of a hasty and ill-thought out composition.

The United Nations, which was established to maintain peace, does not do so. Since 1945, there have been many wars —Korea, the Middle East, and Vietnam, to name just a few.

Besides, the United Nations is an instrument for propaganda. The Russians use it constantly for this purpose.

(Obviously, this writer opposes the United Nations, but the first "paragraph" gives inadequate development to the topic sentence because not enough examples of the U.N.'s failure are given. Similarly, the second "paragraph" fails to be specific enough; it doesn't give examples of *how* the Russians use the U.N. for propaganda.)

With nuclear energy, there is still the possibility of accidents. One big one in Iowa in 1962 caused three deaths and a permanent shutdown.

Besides, there is also the problem of waste materials. Some of those waste materials have toxic effects for as long as 150,000 years!

(The one example given in the first paragraph is unpersuasive. Has there *been* only one? If not, how many? The emphatic exclamation point in the second fragment does not hide the fact that the fragment is undeveloped. What is being done now with waste materials? Why is it inadequate? The fragment is badly in need of development.)

TEST YOURSELF ON
Developing Fragmentary Paragraphs

Each of the following sets of sentences is badly in need of further development. Develop each.

1. The more money you make, the more money you spend. When your income is low, you yearn for more—but learn to be restrained. As soon as your salary rises, however, you begin to give in to your desires.
2. Television tends to make us passive. The reason for this is that we have nothing to *do* as television viewers. It's all done for us.
3. Woodworking is not as difficult as it appears. The first thing you need is a reliable set of tools.

Development is not a haphazard process, but one that depends upon your topic sentence; that is, it depends on the nature of the subject you are dealing with in your paragraph. Therefore, it is important to be clear about what you're writing and to try to determine the best way to express and develop your thought. Most well-constructed paragraphs follow one or another of the following basic developmental plans, chronological, spatial, or logical (also called expository).

Chronological

Use chronological order wherever time and sequence are important. Here, clarity is achieved by purposefully ordering materials in the order in which they happen or should happen.

The *Terra Nova* sailed from London 15th June 1910 and from New Zealand 26th November. She was fearfully overloaded; on deck, as well as the motor-sledges in their huge crates, there were 30 tons of coal in sacks, 2½ tons of petrol in drums, 33 dogs, and 19 ponies. She rode out a bad storm by a miracle. "Bowers and Campbell were standing upon the bridge and the ship rolled sluggishly over until the lee combings of the main hatch were under the sea . . . as a rule, if a ship goes that far over she goes down." It took her thirty-eight days to get to Mc-Murdo Sound, by which time the men were in poor shape. They had slept in their clothes, lucky if they got five hours a night, and had had no proper meals. As soon as they dropped anchor they began to unload the ship. This entailed dragging its cargo over ice floes which were in constant danger of being tipped up by killer whales, a very tricky business, specially when it came to moving ponies, motor sledges and a pianola. Then they built the Hut which was henceforward to be their home. Scott, tireless himself, always drove his men hàrd and these things were accomplished in a fortnight. The *Terra Nova* sailed away; she was to return the following summer, when it was hoped that the Polar party would be back in time to be taken off before the freezing up of the sea forced her to leave again. If not, they would be obliged to spend a second winter on McMurdo Sound. Winter, of course, in those latitudes, happens during our summer months and is perpetual night, as the summer is perpetual day. The stunning beauty of the scenery affected the men deeply. When the sun shone the snow was never white, but brilliant shades of pink, blue and lilac; in winter the aurora australis flamed across the sky and the summit of Mount Erebus glowed.

—Nancy Mitford, "A Bad Time," from *The Water Beetle**

Spatial

Use spatial order when it is necessary to describe physical reality and the spatial relationships between persons, things, or parts of things. A spatial ordering can proceed from inside to outside, top to bottom, up to down, and so forth. This description of a turtle crossing a road is a classic one.

The sun lay on the grass and warmed it, and in the shade under the grass the insects moved, ants and ant lions to set traps

*Reprinted by permission of A.D. Peters & Co., Ltd.

for them, grasshoppers to jump into the air and flick their yellow wings for a second, sow bugs like little armadillos, plodding restlessly on many tender feet. And over the grass at the roadside a land turtle crawled, turning aside for nothing, dragging his high-domed shell over the grass. His hard legs and yellow-nailed feet threshed slowly through the grass, not really walking, but boosting and dragging his shell along. The barley beards slid off his shell, and the clover burrs fell on him and rolled to the ground. His horny beak was partly open, and his fierce, humorous eyes, under brows like fingernails, stared straight ahead. He came over the grass leaving a beaten trail behind him, and the hill, which was the highway embankment, reared up ahead of him. For a moment he stopped, his head held high. He blinked and looked up and down. At last he started to climb the embankment. Front clawed feet reached forward but did not touch. The hind feet kicked his shell along, and it scraped on the grass, and on the gravel. As the embankment grew steeper and steeper, the more frantic were the efforts of the land turtle. Pushing hind legs strained and slipped, boosting the shell along, and the horny head protruded as far as the neck could stretch. Little by little the shell slid up the embankment until at last a parapet cut straight across its line of march, the shoulder of the road, a concrete wall four inches high. As though they worked independently the hind legs pushed the shell against the wall. The head upraised and peered over the wall to the broad smooth plain of cement. Now the hands, braced on top of the wall, strained and lifted, and the shell came slowly up and rested its front end on the wall. For a moment the turtle rested. A red ant ran into the shell, into the soft skin inside the shell, and suddenly head and legs snapped in, and the armored tail clamped in sideways. The red ant was crushed between body and legs. And one head of wild oats was clamped into the shell by a front leg. For a long moment the turtle lay still, and then the neck crept out and the old humorous frowning eyes looked about and the legs and tail came out. The back legs went to work, straining like elephant legs, and the shell tipped to an angle so that the front legs could not reach the level cement plain. But higher and higher the hind legs boosted it, utnil at last the center of balance was reached, the front tipped down, the front legs·scratched at the pavement, and it was up. But the head of wild oats was held by its stem around the front legs.

—John Steinbeck, *The Grapes of Wrath**

Logical or Expository

Use logical or expository order to present illustrative details, examples, or reasons in supporting a topic sentence. There are a number of methods of expository order. They are the methods by which paragraphs and whole essays are organized for their specific purposes. One of these methods will be suitable for your particular paragraph or your particular purposes. The chief methods are 1. illustrative details and examples; 2. comparison and contrast; 3. definition; 4. classification; 5. process analysis; and 6. causal analysis.

1. Illustrative details and examples

A common and sturdy way of explaining and making vivid a generalization is to offer concrete details or examples to support the topic sentence. Most of the other methods also include use of this one at one point or another.

As things now stand, the office is a slightly meaner battle-ground than the home. Male bosses seem to dominate their women underlings as they would never dominate their wives, as if women's lib has sent them a gift to make up for what they've lost at home, while women bosses must practice either a paper-thin toughness that fools nobody or a sort of crisp femininity that must be terribly hard to sustain. The male prejudice against working for women may be the last to go, and even the best women executives must sometimes feel that the men under and around them are toying with them, helping the little woman out, carrying her and tolerating her. She is there at their pleasure and could be snuffed out in an instant if they weren't such nice, well-adjusted guys with such super-secure self-images.

—Wilfrid Sheed, "Now That Men Can Cry . . ."
New York Times Magazine, October 30, 1977

The world becomes narrower as friends and family die or move away. To climb stairs, to ride in a car, to walk to the corner, to talk on the telephone; each action seems to take away from the energy needed to stay alive. Everything is limited by the strength you hoard greedily. Your needs decrease, you require less food, less sleep, and finally less human contact; yet this little bit becomes more and more difficult. You fear that one day you will be reduced to the simple acts of breathing and taking nourishment. This is the ultimate stage you dread, the period of helplessness and hopelessness, when independence will be over.

—Sharon Curtin, "Aging in the Land of the Young,"
Atlantic, July 1972

2. Comparison and contrast

Where your need is to set two items alongside each other for the purpose of noticing their similarities or differences, comparison and contrast is the developmental method of choice. By using this method, you can also isolate one of the items as being the better of the two—thus advancing an argument; or you can isolate for study the lesser known of the two items (say the British Parliament) by comparing it with the better known (say the U.S. Congress).

Fundamentally Grant was superior to Lee because in a modern total war he had a modern mind, and Lee did not. Lee looked to the past in war as the Confederacy did in spirit. The staffs of the two men illustrate their outlook. It would not be accurate to say that Lee's general staff were glorified clerks, but the statement would not be too wide of the mark. Certainly his staff was not, in the modern sense, a planning staff, which was why Lee was often a tired general. He performed labors that no general can do in a big modern army—work that should have fallen to his staff, but that Lee did because it was traditional for the commanding general to do it in older armies. Most of Lee's staff officers were lieutenant colonels. Some of the men on Grant's general staff, as well as the staffs of other Northern generals, were major and brigadier generals, officers who were capable of leading corps. Grant's staff was an organization of experts in the various phases of strategic planning. The modernity of Grant's mind was most apparent in his grasp of the concept that war was becoming total and that the destruction of the enemy's economic resources was as effective and legitimate a form of warfare as the destruction of his armies. What was realism to Grant was barbarism to Lee. Lee thought of war in the old way as a conflict between armies and refused to view it for what it had become—a struggle between societies. To him, economic war was needless cruelty to civilians. Lee was the last of the great old-fashioned generals, Grant the first of the great moderns.

—T. Harry Williams, *Lincoln and His Generals*

A century of association has inevitably acculturated both Hispanos and Anglo-Americans to some extent, but there still persist a number of culture traits that neither group has relinquished altogether. Nothing is more disquieting to an Anglo-American who believes that time is money than the time perspective of Hispanos. They usually refer to this attitude as the "ma⁻nana psychology." Actually, it is more of a "today psychology," because Hispanos cultivate the present to the exclusion of the future; because the latter has not arrived yet, it is not a reality. They are reluctant to relinquish the present, so they hold on to it until it becomes the past. To an Hispano, nine is nine until it is ten, so when he arrives at nine-thirty, he jubilantly exclaims: "¡Justo!" [right on time]. This may be why the clock is slowed down to a walk in Spanish while in English it runs. In the United States, our future-oriented civilization plans our lives so far in advance that the present loses its meaning. January magazine issues are out in December; 1973 cars have been out since October; cemetery plots and even funeral arrangements are bought on the installment plan. To a person engrossed in living today the very idea of planning his funeral sounds like the tolling of the bells.

—Arthur L. Campa, "Anglo vs. Chicano: Why?"
Intellectual Digest, January 1973

3. Definition

Essays frequently require paragraphs defining important terms or objects. Definition can be an important aid to the reader in understanding complex matters, especially where highly connotative words or terms are being employed.

The *satire* is a verbal caricature which distorts characteristic features of an individual or society by exaggeration and simplification. The features picked out for enlargement by the satirist are, of course, those of which he disapproves: "If Nature's inspiration fails," wrote Juvenal, "indignation will beget the poem." The comic effect of the satire is derived from the simultaneous presence, in the reader's mind, of the social reality with which he is familiar, and of its reflection in the distorting mirror of the satirist. It focusses attention on abuses and deformities in society of which, blunted by habit, we were no longer aware; it makes us suddenly discover the absurdity of the familiar and the familiarity of the absurd.

—Arthur Koestler, *The Act of Creation*

One mark of schizophrenia or a schizoid personality according to R. D. Laing, one of the world's experts on the subject, is that a person gets to feeling that at least part of his life and experience is somehow unreal. There's a real self and an unreal self. The real self, his actual core personality, is what he calls me. But it's the me nobody knows. The other part, the unreal, accidental, or artificial self, is the one he projects to the world. The sicker he gets the more he thinks it is the unreal self and not the real self that is acting when he acts. The him that is driving a car, listening to the radio, fighting with his wife, or robbing a bank is not the real him. However, if you have to deal with this individual the real him is the one that's doing these things. What he thinks of as the real him is what is unreal to everybody else. The individual they see walking, talking, acting one way or another, is what that individual really is as far as they are concerned. That inner him that nobody knows, nobody knows—so it is unreal to them.

—Charles Osgood, *Profile,* CBS News, November 10, 1971

4. Classification

The grouping of persons, things, or ideas according to some principle or order frequently sheds new light on those things. Thus the paragraph that classifies also explains.

Symbolic immortality is an expression of man's need for an inner sense of continuity with what has gone on before and what will go on after his own limited biological existence. The *sense* of immortality is thus more than mere denial of death, and grows out of compelling, life-enhancing imagery of one's involvement in the historical process. This sense of immortality may be expressed *biologically,* by living on through one's sons and daughters and their sons and daughters, extending out into social dimensions (of tribe, organization, people, nation, or even species); *theologically,* in the idea of a life after death or of other forms of spiritual conquest of death; *creatively,* through "works" and influences persisting beyond biological death; *naturally,* through identification with nature, with its infinite extension into time and space; or *transcendentally,* through a feeling-state so intense that time and death disappear.

—Robert Jay Lifton, "The Struggle for Cultural Rebirth," *Harper's,* April 1973

But who, then, is the desirable man—the patron who will cajole the best out of the writer's brain and bring to birth the most varied and vigorous progeny of which he is capable? Different ages have answered the question differently. The Elizabethans, to speak roughly, chose the aristocracy to write for and the playhouse public. The eighteenth-century patron was a combination of coffee-house wit and Grub Street bookseller. In the nineteenth century the great writers wrote for the half-crown magazines and the leisured classes. And looking back and applauding the splendid results of these different alliances, it all seems enviably simple, and plain as a pike-staff compared with our own predicament—for whom should we write? For the present supply of patrons is of unexampled and bewildering variety. There is the daily Press, the weekly Press, the monthly Press; the English public and the American public; the best-seller public and the worst-seller public; the high-brow public and the red-blood public; all now organised self-conscious entities capable through their various mouthpieces of making their needs known and their approval or displeasure felt. Thus the writer who has been moved by the sight of the first crocus in Kensington Gardens has, before he sets pen to paper, to choose from a crowd of competitors the particular patron who suits him best. It is futile to say, "Dismiss them all; think only of your crocus," because writing is a method of communication; and the crocus is an imperfect crocus until it has been shared. The first man or the last may write for himself alone, but he is an exception and an unenviable one at that, and the gulls are welcome to his works if the gulls can read them.

—Virginia Woolf, "The Patron and the Crocus,"
from *The Common Reader*

5. Process analysis

Process analysis is a method of separating some complex whole into its component parts—usually a mechanical process. A paragraph that explains in detail how something functions or how a machine is put together is filled with explanatory power. Process analysis is also useful in giving directions on how to do something, and paragraphs using this method of development frequently employ chronological or spatial order.

These solitary wasps are beautiful and formidable creatures. Most species are either a deep shiny blue all over, or deep blue with rusty wings. The largest have a wing span of about four inches. They live on nectar. When excited, they give off a pungent odor—a warning that they are ready to attack. The sting is much worse than that of a bee or common wasp, and the pain and swelling last longer. In the adult stage the wasp lives only a few months. The female produces but a few eggs, one at a time at intervals of two or three days. For each egg the mother must provide one adult tarantula, alive but paralyzed. The mother wasp attaches the egg to the paralyzed spider's abdomen. Upon hatching from the egg, the larva is many hundreds of times smaller than its living but helpless victim. It eats no other food and drinks no water. By the time it has finished its single Gargantuan meal and become ready for wasphood, nothing remains of the tarantula but its indigestible chitinous skeleton.

—Alexander Petrunkevich, "The Spider and the Wasp,"
Scientific American, August 1952

The three absolute acts of the tragedy are first the entry of the bull when the picadors receive the shock of his attacks and attempt to protect their horses with their lances. Then the horses go out and the second act is the planting of the banderillos. This is one of the most interesting and difficult parts but among the easiest for a new bull fight fan to appreciate in technique. The banderillos are three-foot, gaily colored darts with a small fish hook prong in the end. The man who is going to plant them walks out into the arena alone with the bull. He lifts the banderillos at arm's length and points them toward the bull. Then he calls "Toro! Toro!" The bull charges and the banderillero rises to his toes, bends in a curve forward and just as the bull is about to hit him drops the darts into the bull's hump just back of his horns.

—*By-Line: Ernest Hemingway*, ed. William White

6. Causal analysis

This method too separates something into its component parts, but here the something is some specific event or other human situation, and the aim of the writer is to suggest the causes that produced some particular result.

We are the first society in which parents expect to learn from their children. Such a topsy-turvy situation has come about at least in part because, unlike the rest of the world, ours is an immigrant society, and for immigrans the *only* hope is in the kids. In the Old Country, hope was in the father, and how much fam-

ily wealth he could accumulate and pass along to his children.
In the growth pattern of America and its ever-expanding frontier,
the young man was ever advised to Go West; the father was ever
inheriting from his son: the topsy-turviness was built-in from the
beginning. In short, a melting pot needs a spoon. Kids' Country
may be the inevitable result.

—Shana Alexander, "Kids' Country,"
Newsweek, December 1972

Now, failure to uphold the law is no less corrupt than viola-
tion of the law. And the continuing shame of this country now
is the growing number of Americans who fail to uphold and assist enforcement of the law, simply—and ignominiously—out of
fear. Fear of "involvement," fear of reprisal, fear of "trouble."
A man is beaten by hoodlums in plain daylight and in view of
bystanders. These people not only fail to help the victim, but,
like the hoodlums, flee before the police can question them. A
city official knows of a colleague's bribe but does not report it.
A pedestrian watches a car hit a woman but leaves the scene,
to avoid giving testimony. It happens every day. And if the police get cynical at this irresponsibility, they are hardly to blame.
Morale is a matter of giving support and having faith in one another; where both are lacking, "law" has become a worthless
word.

—Marya Mannes, "The Thin Grey Line,"
McCall's, January 1964

TEST YOURSELF ON
Understanding Methods of Paragraph Development

A. Which method of development would be most suitable for
making a paragraph out of each of the following topic sentences? Give reasons. Then select one topic sentence and develop it into a paragraph.

1. Marijuana is not more harmful than alcohol, though my
   parents seem to think so.
2. The Guggenheim Museum, from the outside, looks like a
   bomb shelter.
3. Unexpected things happen to freshmen on this campus.
4. Television commercials don't care what they do as long
   as they sell, sell, sell.

5. Intelligence is the capacity to face what you do not know how to handle.
6. There are three kinds of English teacher on this campus.
7. Lung cancer is a result of certain environmental pressures on the respiratory system.
8. My troubles with mathematics began in 1973.
9. The secret to finishing raw wood to look like fine furniture finishing is patience.
10. Foreign cars and American cars differ in crucial ways.

B. Write three separate paragraphs using the topic sentence below. In the first, explain *why* this change has taken place. In the second, explain *how* these attitudes have changed. Finally, in the third, compare and contrast two sets of attitudes toward teachers: the ones you had in high school and the ones you have now.

My attitudes toward teachers have changed since I came to college.

PARALLEL CONSTRUCTION

Wherever grammatical structures—words, phrases, or clauses—are repeated, we have a parallel construction.

Words   Jenny *whispered* in David's ear, *touched* his arm, *winked* at him, then *walked* away. (parallel verbs)
Impetuously, bravely, daringly, Colin drove to the hoop and stuffed the ball through. (parallel adverbs)

Phrases   *To think clearly, to act ethically, to love completely*— these were Dierdre's goals. (parallel infinitive phrases)

Clauses   *When you have learned who you are, when you have experienced the world, when you have come to respect others* —then you are entitled to be called an adult. (parallel adverbial clauses)

The advantage of parallel construction is that it binds ideas together and allows readers to grasp each point because they have been prepared for the second and third by the *form of the first*. You may not want to use parallel construction to the extent that it is used in the above examples, but ineffective writing results when you *begin* to use parallel construction and then abandon it. You must be sure to either use it or avoid it—and not use it partly, as in the following examples:

$$1 \qquad\qquad 2 \qquad\qquad 3$$

Partly Parallel   Melissa was *bright, beautiful* and *a person who had great consideration for others.* (1. single-word adjective; 2. single-word adjective; 3. noun + adjective clause)
Revised   Melissa was *bright, beautiful,* and *considerate.*

$$1$$

Partly Parallel   The Governor favored *a revised income-tax*
$$2 \qquad\qquad\qquad 3$$
schedule, simplifying the criminal code, and *less money for judges of the State Supreme Court.* (1. adjective, compound noun phrase; 2. gerund phrase; 3. adjective + noun + prepositional phrase)
Revised   The Governor favored *a revised income-tax schedule, a simplified criminal code,* and *a lowered salary for State Supreme Court judges.*

The problem with the partly parallel examples above is that they set up an expectation in the mind of the reader and then don't fulfill that expectation. The result is confusion.

In order to avoid incomplete parallels, you should make sure that whatever grammatical construction follows the word *and* (or any of the other coordinating conjunctions) in your sentence construction should also precede it. If you have a construction like . . . *and a policeman,* you would need a noun to parallel *a policeman* before the word *and* (*a doctor and a policeman*). Similarly, if one of your sentences contained . . . *and which always haunted him,* you would need the same kind of construction *before* the word *and* (*which always followed him and which always haunted him*).

TEST YOURSELF ON
Filling in the Other Side of *and, but, or* Constructions

What could go on the other side of the words *and*, *or*, and *but* in each of the following examples?

   1. . . . and snake oil.

2. . . . and whose mother came from Italy.
3. . . . and that hasn't been seen since.
4. . . . and who thinks of himself as a gentleman.
5. . . . and lovely.
6. . . . or to live longer.
7. . . . but never wanted to live there.
8. . . . but hates whiskey.
9. . . . and tries everything.
10. . . . or went alone.

TEST YOURSELF ON
Making Constructions Parallel

Now that you have had some practice in making both sides of coordinating conjunctions parallel, try your skill at whole sentences. First locate the coordinating conjunction in each of the following examples. Then, if the constructions on either side of the conjunctions are not parallel, revise the sentences to make them parallel. If the sentence is correct, write C beside it. Make sure you underline all parallel constructions, whether or not the sentence is correct.

1. _____ The purpose of this meeting is to review past procedures, recognize what we have to do in the future, and so that we can get to know each other better.

2. _____ This term I learned math, biology, and how to write a term paper.

3. _____ My mother is neat, patient, and a person who is filled with pride.

4. _____ Bob liked falling in love and to write poetry.

5. _____ She was happy but nervous.

6. _____ Whenever I visit my relatives, I'm nervous, exhausted, and I feel like I am disoriented.

7. _____ Traveling in Italy makes you aware of art and the food is wonderful for your taste buds when you eat there.

8. _____ Having a sprained ankle and then to try to walk is murder.

9. _____ Joking with my friends, swimming in the lake, and horseback riding in the woods—those are the things I like to do on my vacation.

10. _____ At the party, I spoke to a sociologist, a detective, a stockbroker, and this man who repaired television sets.

11. _____ Because of excessive welfare spending, poor ac-
counting practices, and the fact that we borrowed
and borrowed and borrowed, New York City
experienced a financial crisis.

12. _____ My professor told me to go slowly with the material rather than trying to learn all of it at once.

13. _____ It was decided by the committee that we would
hold a Memorial Day picnic and increase our
dues.

14. _____ People who don't travel widely but want to en-
large their experience need to learn about other
people in another way.

15. _____ The rules for graduate students apply neither to
you nor me.

PARENTHESES

Parentheses is the plural of the word *parenthesis*.
Parentheses signifies *both* curved marks: ( ). Parentheses are used to set off material that is not absolutely
essential to complete the meaning of the sentence pattern but that supplements or further explains a part or
parts of that sentence. We call such material *parenthetical elements;* these elements can be appositives or other
nonrestrictive phrases or clauses.

But since parentheses, commas, and dashes can all be
used to set off parenthetical material, you should first
note the difference between these marks when they are
used for this purpose.

Dashes are used either to set off material that is emphatic or to set off material you decide to emphasize.
In other words, using dashes gives emphasis; your
material should match the emphasis given.

My friend Lewis—*who drove his pickup into the lake last night*
—is a complete madman.
What happened last night—*if you believe him*—was an accident.

Commas are used to signal that the parenthetical
material is more nearly a part of the sentence than if the

material were set off by dashes or parentheses—that the material interrupts the flow of thought only slightly.

The signs of the storm, *lightning and thunder*, frightened him.
You can, *if you wish*, rent a cheaper model

Parentheses signal that the enclosed material is not emphatic and that its nature is supplemental.

Channel 4 is owned by the National Broadcasting Company (*a subsidiary of the Radio Corporation of America*).
Most students pay heavy tuition charges (*though there are a few exceptions*).

As you can see, the choice of which marks to use can be a matter of taste. Nevertheless, the following general rules are good guidelines.

1. Use parentheses to set off material that is not essential to complete the meaning of the sentence and that is unemphatic and supplemental. Such material may include words, phrases, whole sentences, or even several sentences.

1. At that time, the vice-president (Garner) had very little power.
2. At that time, the vice-president (Garner, a gruff old man from Texas) had very little power.
3. At that time, the vice-president had very little power. (Garner, a gruff old man from Texas, understood this well.)
4. At that time, the vice-president had very little power. (Garner, a gruff old man from Texas, understood this well. It was, perhaps, Garner's understanding of the situation that later prompted Lyndon Johnson, his fellow Texan, to try to raise the status of the office.) He presided over the Senate, a largely ceremonial post, and greeted visiting dignitaries from abroad.

Note that in the third example, a full sentence is enclosed within the parentheses. In such cases, *the period comes before the closing parenthesis*. Note that there *is* a space before the open parenthesis, but there *is no* space between the open parenthesis and the first word or between the period and or closing parenthesis.

Another point about punctuation with parentheses: *where the parenthetical material is a part of the sentence, the period goes outside the closing parenthesis.*

At that time, the vice-president was Garner (a gruff old man from Texas).

2. Use parentheses to set off cross-references and figures denoting life-span.

It will become clear later (*in Ch. 7*) that James Joyce (*1882–1941*) was not exactly kind to his brother.

Note: do not use parentheses for essential material.

Wrong   The men were dog-tired; the lieutenant (*therefore*) called a halt to the march.

Wrong   I'm going to keep on taking that examination (*until I pass it*).

TEST YOURSELF ON
   Using Parentheses Correctly

Some of the sentences below have parenthetic material correctly set off by dashes and commas; next to these sentences, write C. However, some of the sentences should have parentheses *instead* of the commas or dashes; change these. In addition, where you see essential material enclosed within parentheses, eliminate those parentheses.

1. _____ I think, if you don't mind, I'll take my nap now.

2. _____ Charley—a good friend of mine—left for California yesterday.

3. _____ The power of the media—with their enormous audience—is hard to overestimate.

4. _____ We whizzed along the highway, all of us on our bicycles, enjoying the breezes and the sunshine.

5. _____ The author—authors?—of Genesis spoke the stories with reverence.

6. _____ I won't go to the party (unless you come with me).

7. _____ He had (probably) a logical mind.

8. _____ The magician—a most amazing sleight-of-hand artist—had us all on the edges of our seats.

9. _____ Then it rolled through the grating, my last coin, and I was flat broke.

10. _____ He was born in 1235, or somewhat earlier, and died about forty-five years later.

PASSIVE VOICE

See **Voice.**

PERIOD

The period, which is sometimes (especially in British usage) called the *full stop*, is a mark of end punctuation. It signals the end of a *declarative* or mildly *imperative* sentence and is used in most abbreviations. (Spaced periods (. . .) also have special uses; see **Ellipsis.**)

1. Use a period to end declarative and imperative sentences. A declarative sentence makes an assertion; an imperative sentence issues a command.

I am going to see *Jaws* tonight. (declarative)
Go to see *Jaws*. (imperative—this one a very mild command)

Note: For strongly imperative sentences, consider using the exclamation point. Example: *Get out of my sight!*

2. Use a period after an abbreviation.

Mr. Buckley	Ms.
Dr. Brody	U.S.
Ph.D.	a.m.

PERSON

See **Verbs** and **Shifts.**

POSSESSIVES

See Nouns, Pronouns; **Apostrophe, Case,** and **Pronoun References.**

PRONOUN REFERENCES

A pronoun sometimes does its work by referring back to another word or group of words. What the pronoun refers back to is called its *antecedent*.

The following guidelines will be useful to you in making sure that your pronoun references are clear and consistent.

1. Pronouns must *agree* in person and number with their antecedents.

A. In referring to persons, places and things, use pronouns that agree in person and number.

I saw *John* yesterday; *he* seemed depressed.
The *dog* wagged *its* tail.
When I saw the *Smiths* yesterday, *they* were on *their* way to the movies.

B. Use a singular pronoun in referring to antecedents like the following: *any, anybody, anyone, each, every, everybody, everyone, either, neither, man, woman, person, nobody, none, someone, somebody*. In informal writing, we frequently find plural pronouns referring to some of these, but formal usage requires the singular.

Formal   *Everybody* has *his* dreams.
Informal   *Everybody* has *their* dreams.

Formal   Mathematics requires *each* of us to use *his* intellect.
Informal   Mathematics requires *each* of us to use *our* intellect.

C. In the case of a collective noun used as an antecedent, use a singular pronoun if you are thinking of the group as a unit; use a plural pronoun if you are thinking of the members separately.

The *team* raised *its* batting average by ten points.
The *team* came through when *their* fans began urging *them* on.

D. When two or more antecedents are joined by *and*, *or*, or *nor*, the following rules apply: (1) When two or more antecedents are joined by *and*, use a plural pronoun; (2) when two or more singular antecedents are joined by *or* or *nor*, use a singular pronoun; (3) when one of the antecedents joined by *or* or *nor* is singular and one plural, use a pronoun that agrees with the nearest of the two.

1. *Tom and Lisa* did *their* work together.
2. Neither *Lisa nor April* has *her* hat on.
3. Neither the *conductor nor the musicians* have held *their* rehearsal.

TEST YOURSELF ON
Pronoun Agreement

Make all the pronouns in the following sentences agree with their antecedents according to the principles of formal usage.

1. Anybody who knows their music would know the Rolling Stones.

2. The Committee did their work in private.

3. Neither the new professor nor the first-year students knew his way around the campus.

4. Anybody who likes their morning coffee cold is peculiar.

5. When the team scored a touchdown, the band raised its instruments to play.

6. Everybody has a right to their own opinion in politics.

7. If a drugstore or a supermarket opened in our neighborhood, they would do well.

8. Neither of them could do their homework in the middle of all that noise.

9. Every cook thinks their recipes are best.

10. None of the students in biology could identify the speci-

mens under their microscope.

More on pronouns

2. Do not use pronouns ambiguously. *Ambiguous* means "able to be understood in more than one way." Therefore, an ambiguous pronoun reference occurs whenever the pronoun you use can refer back to more than one antecedent.

Ambiguous   My father told my brother that *he* had to go to Boston. (who had to go? the father or the brother?)
Clear   My father said to my brother, "I have to go to Boston."
My father said to my brother, "You have to go to Boston."

Ambiguous   When Donna looked at Lisa, *she* blushed. (who blushed? Donna or Lisa?)
Clear   When she looked at Lisa, Donna blushed.
Clear   Donna blushed when she looked at Lisa.
Clear   Lisa blushed when Donna looked at her.
Clear   When Donna looked at Lisa, Lisa blushed.

3. Do not use pronouns with remote references. A pronoun that is too far away from what it refers to is said to have a remote reference (or antecedent).

Remote   As for the Concorde, we did everything we could to stop the plane from landing at Kennedy Airport, including sending people out to picket the field and writing letters to our Congressmen. *It* is obscene. (the *it*, referring to the airplane, is too far away, too remote, from its antecedent, *Concorde*)
Revised   As for the Concorde, *it* is obscene, and we did everything we could to stop the plane from landing at Kennedy Airport, including sending people out to picket the field and writing letters to our Congressmen.

Remote   Billy gave up smoking and, as a result, temporarily gained a lot of weight. *It* was very bad for his health.
Revised   Billy gave up the smoking *that* was very bad for his health and, as a result, temporarily gained a lot of weight.

4. Do not use pronouns with faulty broad reference. A pronoun used with broad reference is one that refers back to a whole idea rather than a single noun. When the pronoun refers back to more than one idea, it has a faulty broad reference. The vague use of *this, that,* and *which* most frequently results in faulty broad references.

Faulty Broad Reference   He planted a line of tall shrubbery to stop people from looking into his garden. *That* is not easy. (what is not easy? the planting or stopping the people?)

Sometimes a loosely used *this* or *that* can be made clear by converting the pronoun to a determiner and using a noun to make things clear.

Revised   He planted a line of tall shrubbery to stop people from looking into his garden. *That job* is not easy. (now the job refers clearly to the *planting*)

Faulty Broad Reference   He spent his time getting help with his income tax forms, *which* his wife considered unfair. (what does she consider unfair? that he spends his time that way? that he gets help? or does she consider the forms unfair?)

In faulty references involving a *which* clause, it is sometimes necessary to recast the sentence, getting rid of *which*.

Revised   His wife considered it unfair that he spent his time getting help with his income tax forms.

Now we can see that what the wife considers unfair is the way in which he spends his time.

Despite the fact that writers are prone to errors of broad pronoun reference, the use of the broad pronoun reference is not prohibited. Frequently, such references are perfectly appropriate—where they are perfectly clear.

I'll take the cash to the bank. *That's* the safest thing.
We need to save money. *This* is the only way to stay solvent.

5. Do not use pronouns with implied antecedents, that is, do not let the pronoun refer to a noun or a whole idea that is absent from the sentence. The vague use of *it, you, they,* and *them* most frequently causes this error.

Implied Antecedent It says in my notebook that China has the biggest population.

Revised My notebook says that China has the biggest population.

Implied Antecedent I could have supplied the answer if I had thought about *it*.

Revised I could have supplied the answer if I had thought about the question.

Implied Antecedent In some colleges, *you*'re not permitted to live off campus.

Revised In some colleges, students are not permitted to live off campus.

Implied Antecedent *They* have mostly an agricultural economy in Southeast Asia.

Revised The economy in Southeast Asia is mostly agricultural.

Implied Antecedent I go to Yankee Stadium because I like to watch *them* play.

Revised I go to Yankee Stadium because I like to watch the Yankees play.

TEST YOURSELF ON
Pronoun References

Some of the sentences below have perfectly clear pronoun references; next to these, write C. Others, however, have faulty pronoun references; correct these, even if you have to recast the sentence.

1. _____ The Montreal Canadiens were soundly beaten by the Boston Bruins on their home ice last night.

2. _____ He carried a briefcase, which looked as if it had cost him a hundred dollars.

3. _____ During the Civil War, they struggled over the question of slavery.

4. _____ The idea that Fred broached to Eddie was one that he had thought of some years earlier.

5. _____ For the first time in months, we went up to the farm last weekend; we cleaned out the barn,

pruned the apple trees, and swam in the creek. It was wonderful.

6. _____ Driving through Yellowstone, you are likely to see a bear.

7. _____ Alice's mother died when she was twenty-three.

8. _____ Arthur and Hilda came to the wedding in a horse-drawn carriage, which somewhat amused the other guests.

9. _____ Bill and Joanna are broke, but Arthur is rolling in it.

10. _____ Stuart started out to study medicine because society needed them.

11. _____ A great many service professionals do not offer their clients a touch of humanity but only a rule for efficient living. It is a great necessity.

12. _____ Lee stole things because he had no other way of earning a living, and he went to jail for it. It was a shame.

13. _____ I dropped a pebble in the gas tank and heard no splash. That proved we were out of gas.

14. _____ I never buy clothes at Barney's because they are expensive.

15. _____ Petit balanced himself 1,200 feet above the ground, which is a hard thing to do.

QUESTION MARK

The question mark is used to end a sentence that asks a direct question.

Where is Malcolm going?
He asked where Malcolm was going. (Indirect question)

Did he ask where Malcolm is going? (a direct question, indicated by the italicized phrase)

Question marks can also convert declarative sentences into questions.

Betty went to the football game? (imagine this sentence spoken with the emphasis on *football*)
Dinitia loves David? (emphasis on *David*)
Colin and Frances are getting married? (emphasis on *married*)

An imperative sentence may also be converted into a question.

Pass the sugar?
Give you the newspaper?

A question mark is used between parentheses to indicate the writer's uncertainty about some detail.

My mother was born in 1893 (?) and died in 1972.
Shakespeare was born in 1564 on April 23(?).

It is also permissible, for emphasis, to place a question mark after each question in a series.

Did you tell him you loved him? get interested in his work? try to work out your differences?

Note that this example constitutes a single sentence and that there is no mark of punctuation or capital letter following the question marks. For treatment of the question mark in quotations, see Quotation Marks.

TEST YOURSELF ON
the Use of the Question Mark

A. Convert each of the following into questions by placing a question mark in the proper place; in some, you may have to change the pronouns.

1. Marshak ran the school.
2. Give me your pen.
3. Take off your coat.
4. George likes apples.
5. Fred likes parties.

B. Some of the following sentences are properly punctuated with question marks and some are not. Next to the correct sentences, write C. Supply question marks in the others where needed.

1. _____ He asked me if I would go to the ball game with him.
2. _____ He asked me, "Would you come with me to the ball game."
3. _____ Did he take you seriously read your paper give you a tutoring session grade you fairly.
4. _____ He mentioned to me—did I understand him correctly—that he was going to Iran next summer.
5. _____ He was born in 1882 ( ) and must have been about thirty-five ( ) when the Great War began.

QUESTIONS

You may recall that in Part 1 we classified sentences according to the response they require of a listener. One kind of sentence we identified was the question. A question usually requires an answer (or an admission that one is not able to answer)—unless the question is a *rhetorical* one. (See below for the difference between a real and a rhetorical question.)

In English there are several ways of signalling that a sentence is a question.

1. When the verb is some form of *be,* simply reverse the positions of the subject and verb as they would appear in a statement.

	subj.	verb
Statement	His parents	were delighted.

	verb	subj.
Question	Were	his parents delighted?

	subj.	verb
Statement	Arthur	is an athlete.

	verb	subj.
Question	Is	Arthur an athlete?

The change of position alone signals a question.

2. When the verb is not *be* but some other verb, form the question by beginning with an auxiliary. Then the question looks something like those in 1 above—with verb and subject reversed.

subj.   verb
Statement   The men *smoke* cigars.

aux.   subj.   aux.   subj.
Questions   *Do* the men smoke cigars? *Should* the men smoke

aux.   subj.
cigars? *Will* the men smoke cigars?

subj.   verb
Statement   Fred helps out when he can.

aux.   subj.   aux.   subj.
Questions   *Does* Fred help out when he can? *Must* Fred help out when he can?

3. When the verb is a form of *have*, form the question by using either method described above.

subj.   verb
Statement   Mary *has* a cold.
Questions   *Has* Mary a cold. *Does* Mary have a cold?

The use of the first form is no longer common but is perfectly grammatical.

4. When a statement begins with the expletive *there*, reverse the positions of *there* and the verb.

Statement   There was a riot in the gym.
Question   Was there a riot in the gym?

5. Questions can be formed by using *who, whom, whose, what, which, when, where, how,* or *why.*

Who laughed?
What works?
Which was the answer?
Whose got eaten?
When is the doctor in?
How is your mother?

Note: It is also possible, with verbs other than *be,* to use these same question words and an auxiliary.

Why did he wait?
When did Charlie leave?
How could Arthur love him?
Why are the girls laughing?

Notice that when a question begins with one of these question words, it usually requires something other than a *yes* or *no* answer. To turn one of these questions into a statement, therefore, requires something like this:

Question Who is the Dean?
Statements The Dean is Dr. Gross. Dr. Gross is the Dean.

6. Questions can be formed by adding something onto a statement, either an auxiliary and a pronoun or the same verb that occurs in the statement and a pronoun.

Fred is leaving, *isn't he?*
They were here, *weren't they?*
He plays baseball, *doesn't he?*
I should go to the dance, *shouldn't I?*

Direct and indirect questions

So far we have been speaking about direct questions —questions that end with question marks because they are being asked by the speaker (or writer). When the speaker (or writer) *tells* us *about* a question, then it is *indirect* and no question mark is required.

Direct Did you see Jane?
Indirect I asked him if he had seen Jane.

Real and rhetorical questions

When you ask a real question, you expect an answer; when you ask a rhetorical question, you don't—probably you already know the answer and you're asking the rhetorical question as a way of making your point.

TEST YOURSELF ON
Distinguishing Real and Rhetorical Questions

Which of the following sentences are real and which are rhetorical?

1. Is the coffee ready yet?
2. Who came in?
3. Is that any way to treat a lady?
4. Is anybody unluckier than I am?
5. What's this country coming to?
6. Where is my book?
7. Which one is your father?
8. What more can anyone say about Picasso?
9. What's more important than the truth?
10. Have you decided on a major?

TEST YOURSELF ON
Constructing Questions

A. Turn each of the following statements into a question.

1. Charlie is giving up his scholarship.
2. Andy's mother hates Brussels sprouts.
3. Ali has beaten George Foreman.
4. I would move to Florida if I had the chance.
5. There is a bee on your nose.

B. Turn each of the following questions into a statement.

1. Must you stand so close to me?
2. Is he going to Danbury Fair?
3. Is there something you want to tell me?
4. Do you have a dime?
5. Who is your English teacher?

QUOTATION MARKS

Quotation marks (" ") always appear twice: once at the beginning of the quoted material, once at the end. *Note:* Don't forget that second pair; proofread your paper to make sure you haven't omitted the second pair, because confusion always results when you do forget.

Quotation marks are used in the following cases:

1. Use quotation marks wherever you quote directly someone's *written or spoken* words.

Declaring themselves openly in awe of that period, Quinn and Dolan wrote: "In the sixth decade of the twentieth century America entered its middle age, and discovered its youth." They conceived of this discovery as violent, radical, dangerous.

"Well," Norman said, "I wouldn't be surprised if Nancy took off for California and surprised us all."

The first example offers a quotation of someone's (in this case Quinn and Dolan's) *written* words. In the second example, a writer quotes what *Norman* has *said* about *Nancy*. Take careful note of the position of the quotation marks and the position of the other punctuation marks *in relation to the quotation marks*.

2. Although you use regular (double) quotation marks (" ") to enclose direct quotations, use single quotation marks (' ') to enclose a quote within a quote.

"Frankly," Lillian said, "Richard answered my inquiry with 'no comment, I'm busy.' "
Louise said, "The answer Donald gave was 'I don't know.' "

3. Quoting dialogue, conversation between two or more people, requires certain special conventions: 1. Use a separate paragraph when reporting each person's speech; 2. include in the same paragraph such phrases as *he said*, *she replied*, or *he answered*; 3. punctuate according to the practice in this sample passage; note especially that the first word of a quotation is always capitalized if the quoted material itself is a full sentence.

The policeman came running up to me, and I could tell he was furious.
"Do you own this robot?" he asked.
I was startled. "I never saw him before in my life!"
"Then how come," said the policeman, "he just winked at you?"
Sure enough, the robot's green-lit eye was blinking at me. "I think he's just friendly," I replied.
"He just leaked oil on my shoes," said the policeman, menacingly.
"Am I my robot's keeper?" I pleaded.

4. Use quotation marks for titles of short stories, essays, short poems, songs, articles from periodicals, book chapters, or other parts of books.

"The Cask of Amontillado" (short story by Poe)
"Soldiers Home" (short story by Hemingway)
"Politics and the English Language" (essay by Orwell)
"The Heavy Bear" (poem by Delmore Schwartz)
"Yesterday" (song by the Beatles)
"Nefarious Times We Live In" (magazine article)
In Chapter 4, "The Myth of the Poet," the author examines a
    modern dilemma.
Modern socialism is attacked in Part 2, "The Return."

5. Use quotation marks to give special emphasis to a word or a phrase or where you speak of a word *as* a word.

Johnny had a "system" for beating the dealers in Las Vegas.
He had a "hands-off" attitude.
A "bad dude" is slang for a "splendid chap." (*Note:* italics may
    also be used in cases like this one.)

6. Do *not* use quotation marks for indirect quotations. An indirect quotation is one that reports what a speaker said but not necessarily in the speaker's exact words.

David asked Dinitia why she wanted to earn a Ph.D. (indirect)
David asked Dinitia, "Why do you want to earn a Ph.D.?"
    (direct)

Paul said that he liked my book. (indirect)
Paul said, "I like your book." (direct)

Summary on Quotation Marks with Other Punctuation

1. Place commas and periods *inside* quotation marks.

With Direct Quotation   "I wanted to quit early," he said, "but
    I couldn't think of an excuse." (the only mark *outside* is the
    one used to separate *he said* from what follows those words)
With Commas Used for Emphasis   Police work is an example

of a "high-risk occupation," and policemen are paid accordingly.
He had "the common touch."

2. Place colons and semicolons *outside* quotation marks.

He had "the common touch"; consequently, people in all walks of life responded warmly to him.
Tom said that to have a good time he needed the right "equipment": congenial company, enough leisure, and peace of mind.

3. Place question marks and exclamation points inside quotation marks if they are actually part of the quote; place them outside if they are not.

She leaned out the window and shouted "Fire!"
Did you say "I don't know"?

Note that although the exclamation point in the first example applies to "Fire" and the question mark in the second applies to the whole sentence, neither sentence takes any additional punctuation marks at the end.

Misuse of Quotation Marks

Quotation marks should not be used for the following purposes:

1. Do not make a practice of overusing quotation marks for emphasis.

Inappropriate   The cowboys in the movie were strong "men."
Inappropriate   I thought Al was a "wise guy."
Inappropriate   People like Richard are a "dime a dozen."

The first example needs no quotation marks around "men" (or *strong*) to convey its message; the quotation marks in the third example just point up a tired expression which should not have been used in the first place, and the quotation marks in the second are better left out too—though the expression *wise guy* is also trite by now.

2. Do not use quotation marks as an excuse to include an unacceptable slang expression in a piece of formal writing. If the slang expression is appropriate, use it without quotation marks; if it is not, do not use it at all.

Inappropriate   At that point, President Ford simply "flipped out" and pardoned Nixon.
Inappropriate   Most of the patients at the clinic are children who have "gone ape."

Appropriate   He was displaying a common twentieth-century *hangup:* paranoia.
Appropriate   The carnival atmosphere can only be described as *raunchy.*

3. Do not use quotation marks to excuse using a word that does not say precisely what you mean.

Imprecise   My sister used to "get" me about the braces on my teeth.
Precise   My sister used to *tease* me about the braces on my teeth.

Imprecise   The cards in the library are kept in a wooden "box."
Precise   The cards in the library are kept in a *card catalog.*

TEST YOURSELF ON
the Use of Quotation Marks

A. Some of the following sentences contain direct and some indirect quotations. Change the direct quotations to indirect ones, and change the indirect quotations to direct ones.

1. The student said that he considered me one of the best professors in the English Department.
2. "Judy's ceramics are elegant," said Mark.
3. Matt said, "In my opinion, Donna's a talented actor."
4. Fred said the policeman asked him why he was speeding.
5. Marian told Jean she wanted to see her over Easter.
6. Henry reminded Mike that they were brothers.

B. Some of the following sentences have quotation marks correctly placed. Next to them, write C. The others need quotation marks in one place or another. Supply them.

1. _____ We read a short story called The Killers and our professor said that Hemingway, the author, was an adolescent loner.

2. _____ In the poem Sailing to Byzantium, what is the significance of the line The salmon-falls, the mackerel-crowded seas?

3. _____ When we say that recording has a lot of wet, we mean that it contains many echo effects.

4. _____ In a moment of frenzy, Vito wrote: Elephants can be housed in a car garage just as well as in a regular cage.

5. _____ That song Silverbird is a winner.

6. _____ Part 2 of his book is called An Analysis of Urban Problems.

C. Place quotation marks correctly in each of the following sentences.

1. You made a fool of me, Margaret said, and I won't forgive you for it. The name of my article is not Childhood Reams but Childhood Dreams.

2. She had written: I don't care for the climate in the tropics, but when I saw her in Chicago she said I'm looking forward to visiting Puerto Rico for the second time.

3. Can you lend me a hundred dollars? she asked timidly. Slapping his hand down hard on the table, he replied, I think not, madam. I never saw you before in my life.

4. Imagine, he said, that you are in a strange environment and you are surrounded by alien creatures. What thoughts go through your mind as you try to integrate yourself into this scene? he went on.

5. She said to me, He smirked, you're a loser, and I was startled, to say the least.

6. Who said so? I asked.

RESUME WRITING

A resume (pronounced *rez-uh-may*), also called a data sheet or a vita, is an abbreviated account of your career—education, work experience, personal information, and references—usually prepared for the purpose of applying for jobs.

Prospective employers appreciate a one-page typed document similar in form to the sample resume below. (If your particular career is long enough to warrant an extra page, don't hesitate to extend the resume; be sure, however, that the pages are neatly stapled together and that your name and identification are typed across the top of the second page, e.g., "John Williams. Resume. Page 2.")

Before you begin, it is wise to make a scratch sheet and systematically list everything in the course of your adult life that might be relevant; list on the scratch sheet whatever you possess by way of skills—the ability to drive a car, run various types of business or farm machinery, swim, play baseball, and so forth. You may not want to list all your skills on the resume, but you may find that some are worth listing for the particular job you intend to apply for. Don't be modest: list everything; you can always eliminate what seems insubstantial or frivolous.

Sample Resume

```
Marion Leopold
7 Eccles Street
New York, New York 10014

Home telephone: (212) 987-3794
```

PERSONAL INFORMATION

Date of birth: September 8, 1956
Marital status: single Dependents: none
Height: 5'2" Weight: 115 lbs.
Health: excellent
Physical handicaps: none

EDUCATION

B.A., New York University, June 1978, Magna Cum
Laude

> Major: Psychology (60 credits, including
>   Statistics and Psychometrics)
> Related studies: Sociology; Laboratory in
>   Social Work (20 credits)

Special skills: fluent in spoken and written
                    Spanish; play piano; hold New
                    York State Chauffeur's License;
                    familiar with FORTRAN computer
                    language

WORK EXPERIENCE

1976-present: Continuously employed part-time;
                    full-time summers

                    Washington Square Center for
                    Psychological Counseling, New York

                    Duties: administered TAT and
                    Stanford-Binet Tests; conducted
                    intake interviews; research and
                    recording of patient follow-up
                    studies.

1975-1976:   Part-time employment

                    Greenwich Village Neighborhood
                    Counseling Office, New York

                    Duties: Conducted initial interviews
                    with counseling clients, including
                    the elderly; led group sessions
                    devoted to problem solving.

1974-1975:   Full-time employment (nights)

                The Open Line Clinic, New York

    Duties: Telephone hot line counselor; night
                supervisor.

Summers, 1972, 1973, 1974: Full-time employment

                Camp Four Winds, Oronoo, Maine

                Duties: Counselor, dramatics
                counselor, waterfront supervisor.

REFERENCES

Dr. Harvey Kaplan, Director
Washington Square Center for
   Psychological Counseling
42 West 10th Street
New York, New York 10011

Professor Sarah Gage
Department of Psychology
New York University
New York, New York 10003

Professor Barbara Comen
Department of Sociology
New York University
New York, New York 10003

Dr. Frederic Tuten
Greenwich Village Neighborhood
   Counseling Office
33 Bank Street
New York, New York 10014

Education

   In this section, you have the opportunity to include
whatever honors you have earned during your school
years and to emphasize your significant skills. You may
type up several resumes, in fact, listing different skills
appropriate to particular (different) jobs you are apply-

ing for. Of course, you have the option of listing in this section neither skills nor honors.

Work experience

This section usually begins with your present employment and works its way backwards in reverse chronological order. Notice that Marion's duties on each of her jobs are carefully and clearly spelled out.

A note on the form

You may, if you prefer, vary this form somewhat by changing the order of the first three sections (*Personal Information, Education, Work Experience;* some authorities think employers prefer to see *Work Experience* before anything else); but the *References* usually come at the end.

Some job counselors think that the applicant's name and address and phone number should be centered for easier visibility. Whatever you choose to do, it is important to see that the information is separated and clearly organized for easy reading.

RUN-ON SENTENCES

A run-on sentence is the common name given to an error in punctuation where one or more periods are omitted between sentences (or independent clauses).

My Aunt Bea is a great cook,* she always provides the food at
    big family dinners.

The writer of this sentence knows that the two parts—the one to the left of the comma and the one to the right

---

*Some writers would call this an example of the *comma splice* or *comma fault* because the clauses are *spliced* together with only a comma; if there were no comma, these writers would refer to this error as a *fused sentence*. In this book, both errors are called the run-on sentence.

of it—should be separated; that is why the comma is used. But even though the writer knows that these parts are complete sentences (independent clauses), they are not separated emphatically enough. The comma is only a light pause—it is not a full stop.

There are four ways to correctly punctuate two complete sentences (independent clauses) such as this.

1. Use a period:

My Aunt Bea is a great cook. She always provides the food at big family dinners.

2. Use a comma followed by a coordinating conjunction (*and, but, or, for, nor, yet*):

My Aunt Bea is a great cook, and she always provides the food at big family dinners.

3. Use a semicolon, which would provide enough stopping power to properly separate the clauses but would also indicate that the two clauses are closely related and belong together in the same sentence:

My Aunt Bea is a great cook; she always provides the food at big family dinners.

4. Use a semicolon followed by a conjunctive adverb (*anyway, besides, consequently, finally, furthermore, however, instead, meanwhile, moreover, nevertheless, otherwise, subsequently, therefore, thus,* and so forth). The conjunctive adverb acts to relate the two clauses more precisely:

My Aunt Bea is a great cook; therefore, she always provides the food at big family dinners. (note how this additional word brings the clauses into closer relation)

Note: There is usually a comma following the conjunctive adverb, but the strong linkage is provided by the semicolon.

TEST YOURSELF ON
Linking Independent Clauses with a Coordinating Conjunction

Try linking the pairs of sentences below with a comma followed by one of the coordinating conjunctions: *and, but, or, nor, for, yet*.

1. Charles was head of the Honors Committee. He carried out his duties with high purpose.

2. He couldn't increase the speed of the car. There was a State Trooper waiting at the exit.

3. Carla couldn't type. The paper was due the next morning.

4. Foreign policy was a pressing issue. The President knew he had to attack it.

5. He could take the train to Boston. He could stay later and take the air shuttle.

TEST YOURSELF ON
Linking Independent Clauses with a Semicolon and a Conjunctive Adverb

Try linking the pairs of sentences below with a semicolon. After you have done so, look at the list of conjunctive adverbs given above and see if the addition of one of those might create a better relation between parts. *Remember:* a comma follows a conjunctive adverb, but the strong link is made by the semicolon.

1. Lucia Ann had confidence in her ability to write. She sat down and wrote a book.

2. Painters have the urge to arrange form, line, color, and mass. They paint pictures working with these principles.

3. Free speech is a precious part of our heritage. We have a whole tradition of freedom and liberty.

4. He had just changed the spark plugs and the points. The car was in good running condition.

5. Arthur's tax refund came on July 25. On August 1, he began his European vacation.

Let us return for a moment to the sentence with which we began this discussion:

My Aunt Bea is a great cook, she always provides the food at big family dinners.

A fifth way to correct this run-on sentence is to change one of the independent clauses to a dependent clause—and leave the punctuation (the comma) as is.

Because my Aunt Bea is a great cook, she always provides the food at big family dinners.

The addition of the word *because* changes the independent clause to a dependent clause and makes the comma the correct punctuation to separate it from the main (independent) clause.

TEST YOURSELF ON
Recognizing and Correcting Run-on Sentences

Some of the sentences below are run-on sentences and some are correct. Next to the correct sentences, write C. Correct the other sentences by one or another of the methods discussed in this entry.

1. _____ I love to swim, there is no better exercise.

2. _____ I had to be in California on the 18th, therefore I decided to leave New York on the 12th.

3. _____ Crime does not result from the inborn tendency of individual criminals; rather, it is a complex social

problem, having to do with social environment and economic status.

4. _____ Thurman Munson didn't get a base hit, the Yankees won the ball game.

5. _____ Because she had always been careful about money in her youth, she could look forward to a secure old age.

6. _____ The term *arson* should apply to a fire that someone has set, even if the fire isn't set deliberately the results are the same.

7. _____ Potential students are no longer flocking to colleges, the job market no longer requires so many college graduates.

8. _____ America's oil reserves are nearly depleted, what we need now is her reserves of good will if we are to solve the energy crisis.

9. _____ Marriages are not made in heaven, divorces are not made in courts.

10. _____ He looks like my brother, he talks like my enemy.

TEST YOURSELF ON
Proofreading to Catch Run-on Sentences

Read carefully the following paragraphs, and wherever you see a run-on sentence, correct it.

Hospitals can really be depressing, it's depressing seeing all those sick people in beds. Of course, some of them get well and go home with their families, but it's depressing knowing that some of them will die in those beds. It doesn't matter, hospitals are still depressing places.

The white walls are gloomy, the beds are small and narrow. Some nurses are snobbish and make your stay impossible with their aloofness, some of them are so nice you hate to leave.

But doctors are so busy that they have no time for you personally, they treat you like an experiment most of the time. As for the food, it too is depressing, it's supposed to make you healthy but it really makes you sick just to look at it, even the way it's prepared, the way it looks, causes that depressed feeling.

Some people enter the hospital with a minor illness by the time they have been there a few days, they have a major problem, remember the movie *Hospital* they had it right.

Of course, if you think your stay in the hospital is depressing, you should wait until you leave and get the bill *that's* really depressing!

SEMICOLON

The semicolon is a mark of internal punctuation that is equivalent to a period in its power to bring an independent clause to an end. (See **Run-on Sentences** and **Sentence Fragments** for more on the semicolon.) It is therefore used to separate independent clauses (with or without a conjunctive adverb); the semicolon can also be used to set off items in a series if they are very long or contain other kinds of internal punctuation.

What he objected to in her character was that she was angry, willful and stubborn; that she had no capacity to develop or sustain a professional or vocational interest that would lead to her taking or holding a job; and that she was incapable of having easy relationships with either her peers, her family, or her neighbors.

We were divided into three groups: 1. those who could sing, dance, act, or play a musical instrument; 2. those who had carpentry or other technical skills; and 3. those who had some kind of business experience or advertising and public relations skills.

Note: Where you use quotation marks, the semicolon goes outside the closing quotation marks:

He thinks of himself as "progressive"; he voted for Nixon.
Tom said, "Stagecraft is vital to any study of Shakespeare"; he meant it, too.

SENTENCE LENGTH AND VARIETY

Variation in the length and kinds of sentences we write helps to avoid giving your readers the impression of monotony. There are a number of ways to achieve this variation in sentence structure and length, but let us first consider what to avoid.

1. Avoid writing a series of short, simple sentences. Children write this way, but that is because their minds are not yet developed to the point where they can understand the relations between ideas.

Weak   We went to the movies. It was a cowboy picture. We bought popcorn. It made noise. The other people were mad. They told us to stop.

Revised   Because there was a cowboy picture playing, we went to the movies. We bought some popcorn, but we made so much noise eating it that the other patrons were angered and asked us to stop.

The series of weak sentences constitutes a simple example, of the kind a child might write, but there are occasions when more mature writers fall into the same pattern.

Weak   The house was dark. We walked up the steps. We went through the door. There was a noise. We paused and listened. We decided it was only the wind.

Revised   The house was dark as we walked up the stairs and through the door. There was a noise, and we paused to listen more carefully, but it was only the wind.

(For further information on combining short sentences into more complex structures, see **Subordination.**)

2. Avoid writing long, excessively compounded sentences. By this is meant sentences that join together, willy-nilly, a number of independent clauses using *and* or other coordinating conjunctions.

Weak   We drove up to the park, but we saw that the gate had been locked for the night, and so we changed our plans and turned around and headed for Warrensburg.

Revised   As we drove up to the park, we saw that the gate had been locked for the night. Changing our plans, we turned around and headed for Warrensburg. (first independent clause made into a subordinate clause by the use of *as*; third clause is made into a phrase; second and fourth clauses become main clauses of two separate sentences)

Weak   He was the faculty adviser of the campus newspaper, and he was a professor in the English Department, but he was never too busy with his duties to consult with students.

Revised   The faculty adviser of the campus newspaper, who was also a professor in the English Department, was never too busy with his duties to consult with students. (first clause becomes a phrase which is the subject of the new sentence; second clause becomes a subordinate clause; third clause becomes the predicate of the sentence)

The excessively simple pattern and the badly coordinated pattern have one thing in common—they both present regular independent clauses in the regular order of subject-verb and they present only one type of sentence—the declarative. To achieve variety, you must occasionally interrupt these patterns—by beginning or ending sentences with subordinate structures or by interrupting the sentence itself with an appositive.

TEST YOURSELF ON
Revising Sentences of Monotonous Length

A. Revise the following groups of short sentences.

1. TV commercials are annoying. They insult the intelligence. They waste one's time. They should be banned from the airways.

2. President Carter is from Georgia. He grew peanuts there. He was formerly Governor of Georgia. He has brought many Georgians to Washington.

3. She wanted to be a doctor. She studied chemistry. She studied biology. She worked for good grades. She put in long hours. Her senior year arrived. She applied to medical school. She was accepted.

4. The doctor came. He took my temperature. He checked my heart. He took my blood pressure. He prescribed some medicine. Then he said I'd probably recover in a few days.

5. I needed a job. I looked at the want ads. I went to employ-

ment agencies. I even visited a number of factories and of-
fices. I got very tired. But I finally landed a job.

B. Revise the following sentences: eliminate excessive join-
ing together of independent clauses by creating subordinate
clauses and phrases.

1. The train entered the station, and I got ready to board but
   then I found I'd left my bag in the checkroom and I ran
   back inside the waiting room to get it.
2. *Star Wars* was a very successful movie and broke many
   box office records and this goes to show that science fiction
   adventure movies appeal greatly to the American public.
3. There are more than seven million American college students, and most of them believe that they need this education to get better jobs, but the job market is not encourag-
   ing for the hopes of these students, and some of them might
   do better in vocational training.
4. Members of the volunteer fire company are really dedicated and they give much of their time in public service,
   but they are not appreciated enough and often feel bitter
   because of this.
5. Soccer is the fastest growing sport in America and now as
   many as 70,000 fans turn out for one game, but if Pelé
   hadn't given the sport a boost, things might not have turned
   out so well for soccer.

Achieving Sentence Variety

So far we have looked at what to avoid: a series of
short simple sentences, and a sentence composed of
many independent clauses strung together with coordinating conjunctions. Both types of sentence tend to produce monotony when used exclusively because both begin with the subject of the sentence. This is not a bad
thing to do—more than half of your sentences will likely
begin that way—but such a practice produces monotony when followed exclusively. Therefore, variety is
achieved by changing the order of words in your sentences. Variety is also achieved by occasionally depart-
ing from the declarative sentence and using the question
or the command. You should undertake these changes

with great care, however, since altering the order of words in a sentence always involves a slight alteration of meaning. Choosing the proper alteration is a matter of carefully considering your subject matter and the meaning you want to convey. Here are the principal means of achieving sentence variety.

1. Vary the beginnings of your sentences.
Suppose you had one sentence that looks like this:

The miners worked purposefully in the tunnel and they were unaware of the storm outside.

or two that look like this:

The miners worked purposefully in the tunnel. They were unaware of the storm outside.

In either case, you could produce variations looking like these:

Working purposefully in the tunnel, the miners were unaware of the storm outside. (beginning with a verbal phrase)
In the tunnel, the miners worked purposefully, unaware of the storm outside. (beginning with a prepositional phrase)
Because the miners were working purposefully in the tunnel, they were unaware of the storm outside. (beginning with an adverb clause)
There were miners working purposefully in the tunnel, unaware of the storm outside. (beginning with an expletive)
But the miners worked purposefully in the tunnel, unaware of the storm outside. (beginning with a coordinating conjunction)
And the miners worked purposefully in the tunnel, unaware of the storm outside. (beginnings with coordinating conjunctions are perfectly acceptable, but usually the meaning of the sentence depends on something that has gone before)

2. Reverse the usual order of subject-verb or subject-verb-object. But to do this is to create a distinctly emphatic order, and you should do so only where your aim is to achieve such emphasis.

Subject-Verb	*Verb-Subject*
The mouse ran up the wall.	Up the wall ran the mouse.
Mike's letter rested in the mailbox.	In the mailbox rested Mike's letter.

Subject-Verb-Object	*Object-Subject-Verb*
Joanna loves pizza.	Pizza Joanna loves.
I never saw him.	Him I never saw.

3. Occasionally use a question or a command instead of a declarative sentence, but only when it is appropriate to do so.

Imperative (command) *Imagine a fine tapestry,* interwoven with various attractively colored threads, and you will have a picture of the diversity and beauty in the fabric of American life.

Question *What is the purpose of an education?* One purpose is to train the mind to perceive fine distinctions.

TEST YOURSELF ON
Achieving Sentence Variety

Revise the following sentences by revising their beginnings.

1. The car had broken down the night before, and they had to take the bus to school.
2. The Republican Party held a fundraiser at the Holiday Inn, and it attracted a surprising number of young people.
3. His grades were poor, and his scholarship money was almost gone, and he knew he had to do something.
4. The rescue team worked all night at the site of the cave-in, and they were unable to stop for dinner.
5. Readers with lively imaginations read the *Hobbitt* and project themselves into its adventurous moments.
6. Governments are less inclined to give in to hijackers' demands these days, but hijackings continue anyway.
7. He knew he would have to save money regularly for next year's tuition, and he opened a savings account and began to make regular deposits.
8. Nobody knew where the cat had gone, but everybody began searching furiously.
9. Big-time professional sports can accommodate very few athletes, but many American youngsters still dream of a career in the big leagues.
10. Inflation has made money worth less, and it is more expensive to live in the United States than it used to be.

SHIFTS

When you begin a sentence by saying "He *begged* and *pleaded* for the loan and . . ." the reader immediately tunes in to *begged* and *pleaded* as verbs in the past tense. The reader's expectation is that if any other verb appears in the sentence, it, too, will be in the past tense. So that if the sentence is completed with ". . . *asks* the bank officer to have some sympathy" (present tense verb), the reader will be shocked, disappointed, and confused because you have *shifted* gears.

It is not easy, but it is absolutely essential, to maintain the kind of consistency that is missing in the above example. In fact, both beginning and experienced writers shift gears in a number of different ways. A writer should understand that achieving consistency requires consistent proofreading—until they are sure they are incapable of producing the various kinds of shifts.

Reread carefully the last sentence (beginning with "A writer"). Notice that the sentence begins by speaking of a *singular* subject: *writer*. Notice, too, however, that after the dash, the second and fifth words following are both *they*, the *plural* pronoun. Thus we see another kind of shift: this one is called a shift in *number*. We can also see shifts in *tense* (as in the first example in this entry), *person*, *mood*, *voice*, and *point of view*. Below are given examples of each kind of shift.

Tense

Perhaps no other shift is so annoying to a reader as this one, because a verb carries not only meaning but a sense of time, and the writer who uses verb tenses inconsistently interferes with the reader's sense of a consistent time pattern.

Inconsistent In the movie *Taxi Driver*, Robert De Niro *plays* a cab driver. He *went* around the city until he *sees* a girl (Cybill Shepherd). He *took* her to a dirty movie and she *leaves*, insulted.

Consistent   In the movie *Taxi Driver,* Robert De Niro *plays* a cab driver. He *goes* around the city until he *sees* a girl (Cybill Shepherd). He *takes* her to a dirty movie and she *leaves,* insulted.

Inconsistent   When I *go* to the seashore for my vacation, I *went* to the beach right away because I *loved* to swim. I *see* the lifeguard and I *asked* him if it *was* all right to swim. *Jaws makes* me frightened to go in the water.

Consistent   When I *went* to the seashore for my vacation, I *went* to the beach right away because I *love* to swim. I *saw* the lifeguard and I *asked* him if it *was* all right to swim. *Jaws made* me frightened to go in the water.

Person

The English verb system recognizes three *persons:* the first person (*I* refuse, *we* refuse), the second person (*you* refuse [both singular and plural]), and the third person (*he, she,* or *it* refuses, *they* refuse). Most person shifts occur because writers use the second person (*you*) carelessly. But that is not the only problem in person shifts.

Inconsistent   People shouldn't expect to be dependent all their lives. *You* have to take care of *yourself* in adult life.

Consistent   People shouldn't expect to be dependent all their lives. *They* have to take care of *themselves* in adult life.

Inconsistent   When *you* have a cold, *one* should get plenty of rest and drink fluids.

Consistent   When *you* have a cold, *you* should get plenty of rest and drink fluids.

Number

Errors in consistency can happen when writers begin with a singular noun and shift to a plural pronoun—or vice-versa.

Inconsistent   The American *medical student* abroad *has* special problems because *they* have to do *their* work in a foreign language.

Consistent   American *medical students* abroad *have* special problems because *they* have to do *their* work in a foreign language.

Inconsistent   Business is so good at the U.S. Time Company that *no one* loses *their* job there.
Consistent   Business is so good at the U.S. Time Company that *no one* loses *his* job there.

Inconsistent   *Lawyers* have an easy life, because every time *he* goes into court *he* makes a fat fee.
Consistent   *Lawyers* have an easy life, because every time *they* go into court *they* make fat fees.

Voice

Once you have begun to use the active voice in a sentence, do not shift to the passive voice, and vice-versa. (See also **Voice**.)

Inconsistent   We *leave* for the beach at 8 o'clock, *swim* from 9:30 to 11, and lunch *is eaten* at 12.
Consistent   We *leave* for the beach at 8 o'clock, *swim* from 9:30 to 11, and *eat* lunch at 12.

Inconsistent   *Dig* a hole for the seeds, *drop* them in and *cover* them with loose soil, and then the ground *is lightly watered.*
Consistent   *Dig* a hole for the seeds, *drop* them in and *cover* them with loose soil, and then *water* the ground lightly.

Mood

Do not shift from the indicative to the subjunctive mood—or vice-versa. Maintain consistency by sticking with one or the other, bearing in mind that in formal writing the subjunctive is preferred where it is called for. The indicative mood is used for statements of fact or other kinds of assertions or questions; the subjunctive mood is used for statements contrary to fact or those expressing possibility or potential.

Inconsistent   If I *were* a rock star and I *was* making a lot of money, I'd give a lot of free concerts.
Consistent   If I *were* a rock star and I *were* making a lot of money, I'd give a lot of free concerts.

Inconsistent The Red Cross representative prefers that the do-
nations *be* given by check and that the amounts *are* entered
on their special form.
Consistent The Red Cross representative prefers that the dona-
tions *be* given by check and that the amounts *be* entered on
their special form.

Point of View

A point of view is a position from which an observation is made; it is also the place from which an idea
springs. You should be consistent in making your observations from the same place (point of view) and
should be sure the reader knows whose ideas belong to
whom—i.e., that the place the ideas come from is consistently named.

Inconsistent Observation

Lying face down on the pavement, I could see the collected de-
bris of the day—cigarette butts, candy wrappers, odd bits of
paper—*and then came the sound of the ambulance and I
could see it approach.* (obviously, the writer could not *see* the
ambulance if he were lying face down on the pavement)

Consistent Observation

Lying face down on the pavement, I could see the collected de-
bris of the day—cigarette butts, candy wrappers, odd bits of
paper—*and then came the sound of the ambulance and I
knew it was getting closer.*

Inconsistent Assignment of Ideas

Most people understand that animals need space in which to
live. Malin Himes, the anthropologist, says that the acquisi-
tion of such space is connected to the amount of power the
animal has. How we fight for space—and thus gain the necessary power to get it—is determined by our cultural training.
For example, the current conflict between Russia and the
United States over outer space exemplifies this idea. (the
reader does not know to whom the ideas in the third and
fourth sentences belong)

Consistent Assignment of Ideas

Most people understand that animals need space in which to
live. Malin Himes, the anthropologist, says that the acquisi-
tion of such space is connected to the amount of power the

animal has. *Himes asserts* that how we fight for space—and thuu gain the necessary power to get it—is determined by our cultural training. *Hines offers as an example of this notion* the current conflict between Russia and the United States over outer space.

TEST YOURSELF ON
Correcting Shifts

Correct all the unnecessary shifts you find in the sentences below. Some are correct as they stand; next to these, write C.

1. _____ People need to be praised when we work hard and accomplish our goals.

2. _____ Tommy argued with his counsellor about the curfew and asks him to make an exception.

3. _____ He goes up to the cashier's window and asked for three tickets.

4. _____ Anybody who cares about his health can have themselves examined by a doctor twice a year.

5. _____ According to Quinn, Shakespeare is the greatest writer in English. Shakespeare takes in all points of view.

6. _____ My wife said she was thirsty and would I please get her a glass of water.

7. _____ We arrive in London on Tuesday, leave for Paris on Thursday, and then the rest of the week is spent in Rome.

8. _____ Johnny Carson is known to all because he sparkles on television every night.

9. _____ Every basketball player has their own way of driving to the hoop.

10. _____ He went to the movies, sees *King Kong,* is terribly frightened, and was afraid to go home.

11. _____ Finally, we added the icing, and then it was baked for fifty minutes.

12. _____ Barry said that he liked Lorna and would she care to have dinner with him.

13. _____ From the top of the Empire State Building, the people looked like toy figures, strutting mechanically along, smoking their cigars.

14. _____ I was told that cigarette smoking would ruin my lungs and that you should give it up if you wanted to avoid heart trouble, too.

15. _____ Wagner recommended that admissions standards be raised and students warned about their poor preparation for college.

SPECIFIC/GENERAL

See **Diction.**

SPELLING

There is no evidence to support the idea that writers who spell poorly are unintelligent. Nevertheless, writers whose spelling is poor communicate to the reader that they are a little backward. Poor spelling also communicates—when it manages to communicate at all—that the writer is either sloppy, lazy, badly educated, or all three at once. But the capacity to spell words correctly is not a God-given talent; it is, like most things, learned, and those who spell poorly and say "I'm just not good at spelling" are not facing the problem. The "problem" can be divided into two parts: you and English spelling.

1. You

If your education had gone along as it ideally should have gone along, you would not have reached college with a spelling problem. What this means is that some people of college age have learned to spell more or less painlessly, but for others the learning—because it comes along now—must involve some rather painful hard work. If you are willing to undertake this hard work and if you have the capacity to endure the pain that comes with such work, you *can* become a competent speller. (The reason that the emphasis is on *you* here is that instruction from another person, your teacher, cannot count for much in *your* learning to spell.)

To begin to undertake the work necessary to improve your spelling, you should bear in mind the following suggestions on how to proceed:

1. Be aware when you are in doubt about the spelling of a word and consult a good dictionary for the correct spelling. One of the most important things you can do for yourself is to admit when you are in doubt; that way, you can do away with the doubt by consulting the dictionary. The doubt can be your most useful tool.

2. When you have looked up the word, don't try to simply memorize it. Use the word in five or six sentences, *immediately* after you've looked it up. This will give you brain-hand practice; it will tend to reinforce your grasp of the correct spelling by permitting your hand and eye the practice of seeing and making the correct letters.

3. Keep tabs on the words you misspell; make a list of them and keep the list handy. Notice if there are types of words that you consistently misspell and learn, memorize, and make use of the rule that applies to the special group you misspell. *Remember:* rule memorizing is only one thing to do: writing out the misspelled word and giving yourself practice is more important than memorizing the rule.

4. Don't reserve certain words for writing and certain words for speaking. Try to use your whole vocabulary in both speaking and writing. This is useful in improving your spelling because the correct pronounciation of words often helps you to "see" the correct spelling—but not always. See below for remarks on how pronounciation can mislead you.

5. Proofread everything you write at least once for spelling errors alone.

6. Develop your own special "tricks" to help you in this process. Some students write down on a separate card every word that gives them difficulty and then take the pack of cards with them wherever they go, flipping through the deck at odd moments to help reinforce in their minds what they have to learn.

If you work hard enough, your creative juices will start to flow and you will conceive of other aids to help you learn.

2. English spelling

English spelling, unlike the spelling of other languages, is relatively eccentric. That is, there are only a few rules to help you along and there are a number of exceptions to these rules. There is, in short, no logical pattern to English spelling that holds good in all cases. For example, pronunciation is not always a reliable guide to spelling.

through = thrOO	sew = sO
threw = thrOO	so = sO

There are literally hundreds of examples of words spelled similarly and pronounced differently. In fact, as Professors Waldhorn and Zeiger have pointed out (following George Bernard Shaw), in the sentence

We had *ghoti* on *phraideigh*.

the word *ghoti* is really *fish* and the word *phraideigh* is really *Friday*. They explain the pronunciation-spelling confusion as follows:

gh = f as in the word cou*gh*   ph = f as in *ph*iloso*ph*y
o = i as in w*o*men   ai = i as in *ai*sle
ti = sh as in vaca*ti*on   eigh = a as in n*eigh*bor

The reasons English spelling is in such confusion are many and need not trouble us here. The place for our work to begin is with the rules.

Rule 1: *ie* and *ei*

When the word is pronounced *ee*, as in *seek* or *peek*, *i* is followed by *e*, except after *c*. After *c*, place *e* before i.

ie Pronounced as ee

achieve	chief	niece	siege
belief	field	piece	thief
believe	fiend	pierce	tier
bier	fierce	reprieve	wield
brief	frieze	shield	yield
cashier	grief	shriek	

Some Exceptions   either, neither, seizure, sheik, leisure, weird

ei, Pronounced ee, *After* c

ceiling	conceit	deceit	receive
conceive	deceive	receipt	perceive

Some Exceptions   financier, species

ei, Pronounced ā, *as in* neighbor *and* weigh

feint	vein	weigh	heinous
skein	sleigh	freight	deign
reign	neighbor	veil	neigh

ei If Pronounced i *as in* hit

counterfeit	forfeit	foreign
surfeit	sovereign	

Some Exceptions   sieve, mischievous

ei If Pronounced i *as in* ice

sleight	height	eider

In all other combinations of sounds, the order is *ie:* friend, lieutenant.

TEST YOURSELF ON
ie and ei

Complete the spelling of the following words by using either *ie* or *ei* to fill in the blank spaces.

1. fr_____nd

2. conc_____ve

3. bel_____f

4. ach_____vment

5. exper_____nce

6. rec_____ving

7. th_____r

8. f_____ld

9. effic_____ncy

10. conven_____nce

11. aud_____nce

12. dec_____t

13. misch_____f

14. p_____ce

15. y_____ld

16. sl_____gh

17. w_____ght

18. forf_____t

19. v_____n

20. h_____nous

Rule 2: Final Silent e

1. Final silent *e* is usually dropped before adding a suffix (ending) that begins with a vowel.

argue—arguing   dare—daring
baste—basting   give—giving
charge—charging   assure—assurance

2. Final silent *e* is usually retained when adding an ending that begins with a consonant.

arrange—arrange*ment*   love—lovely
sure—sure*ly*   hate—hateful
like—like*ness*   sore—soreness

Note the following exceptions:

a. The final silent *e* is retained after soft *c* (as in *dance*—as opposed to hard c, as in *color*) and soft *g* (as in *rage*—as opposed to hard *g* as in *gave*) when adding endings (suffixes) beginning with *a* or *o*. Because *c* and *g* are generally hard before *a, o* and *u,* we keep the silent *e* in order to keep the consonants soft.

charge—charging—chargeable
stage—staging—stageable
slice—slicing—sliceable

b. In some words, the final silent *e* must be retained before the suffix *-ing* in order to prevent either mispronunciation or ambiguity.

singe—singeing (to scorch; to prevent confusion and mispronunciation with *sing—singing*)
dye—dyeing (to tint; to prevent confusion with *die—dying*)

c. Final silent *e* is retained when the endings (suffixes) *ye, oe,* or *ee* precede the suffix *-ing*.

free—freeing	hoe—hoeing
see—seeing	shoe—shoeing
tree—treeing	eye—eyeing

TEST YOURSELF ON
Final Silent e

Complete the spelling of the following words by using an *e* to fill in the blank space in each. If no *e* is needed, leave the space blank.

1. mov____ing	11. receiv____ing
2. prov____ing	12. bor____ing
3. mov____ment	13. bor____dom
4. peac____able	14. car____ing
5. chang____able	15. car____ful
6. liv____ly	16. dy____ing (to tint)
7. manag____ment	17. rang____ing
8. sens____ible	18. rag____ing
9. realiz____ation	19. troubl____some
10. ton____al	20. bar____ness.

Rule 3: Final *y*

1. When preceded by a consonant and followed by a suffix other than one beginning with *i*, final *y* changes to *i*.

beauty—beautiful	marry—marriage
busy—business	mercy—merciful
duty—dutiful	pretty—prettiness
easy—easily	rely—reliance

However, where the initial letter of the suffix is *i*, retain the final *y*.

parry—parrying	hurry—hurrying
parry—parried	hurry—hurries
fly—flying	dry—drying
fly—flies	dry—dries

2. If the final *y* is preceded by a vowel, it is usually retained.

boy—boys	monkey—monkeys
toy—toys	chimney—chimneys
play—plays	attorney—attorneys
flay—flays	

Some exceptions day—daily; lay—laid; pay—paid; say—said

3. Before suffixes like *-ness, -ous, -ment*, and *-ful*, final *y* is retained

dry—dryness	play—playful
joy—joyous	enjoy—enjoyment

3. Before the suffix *-ly*, the final *y* of monosyllabic adjectives is sometimes dropped and sometimes changed to *i*. Either form is correct, although the change to *i* is generally preferred.

dry—drily or dryly
shy—shily or shyly
gay—gaily or gayly

TEST YOURSELF ON
Final *y*

Complete the spelling of the following words by using either
y or *i* or *ie* to fill in the blank spaces.

1. occup_____ing

2. lonel_____ness

3. anno_____ing

4. pl_____s

5. turke_____s

6. fr_____s

7. plo_____s

8. repl_____ing

9. cr_____s

10. pra_____s

11. theor_____s

12. stor_____s

13. bur_____ing

14. histor_____s

15. histor_____s   (belonging
to history)

16. accompan_____ing

17. opportunit_____s

18. happ_____ness

19. modif_____ing

20. def_____ance

Rule 4: Final Consonants

This is the most complicated rule we will deal with.

1. A final single consonant is doubled under the following conditions:
   a. when it is preceded by a single vowel, as in *rot*,
   b. when it appears in a monosyllabic word, as in *bat*
or *run*,
   c. when it is followed by a suffix beginning with a
vowel, such as *-ing*,
   d. when it appears in a word that is stressed on the
last syllable, as in the word *preFER*.

ho*p*—ho*pp*ing (fulfills conditions a, b, and c)
(Note the difference in sound between *hoping* and *hopping*)
omi*t*—omi*tt*ing (fulfills conditions a, c, and d)

Here is a list of some other words whose final consonants are doubled:

Monosyllables		Polysyllables	
beg	ship	begin	equip
lag	slip	forget	transfer
drop	slap	compel	confer
crop	trap	dispel	extol
stop	trip	occur	repel
swim	whip	permit	submit
trim	cop	defer	omit

2. The final single consonant is *not* doubled under the following conditions:

a. when the accent (or stress) is shifted to a preceding syllable when the suffix is added, as in con*fer*—*CON*ference,

b. when there are already two final consonants, as in pa*rt*—pa*rting,*

c. when the final consonant is preceded by two vowels, as in s*ail*—s*ailing.*

de*fer*—de*fer*ence (meets condition a)
trans*fer*—trans*fer*ence (meets condition a)
rela*x*—rela*xing* (the *x* is really *ks*—two consonants—so that this case meets condition b)
trai*l*—tra*iling* (meets condition c)

Note on -cede, -ceed, -sede

Learning four special words can help you to eliminate a whole host of errors.

Word 1: supersede is the only word in the English language that ends in *-sede.*

Words 2, 3, 4: exceed, proceed, and *succeed* are the only words in English that end in *-ceed.*

Thus all other words in English having the same sound end in *-cede.*

accede	recede	precede
concede	intercede	secede

Note on the sound of words ending in c

To preserve the hard sound of *c*, words ending in *c* add a *k* before adding a suffix ending in *e, i,* or *y.*

panic—panicked—panicky
mimic—mimicked—mimicking
traffic—trafficked—trafficking

Note on forming the plurals of words ending in *o*

The plural of some nouns ending in *o* preceded by a consonant is formed by adding -*es:*

echoes	tomatoes	vetoes
heroes	tornadoes	torpedoes
potatoes	mosquitoes	innuendoes

Exceptions

albinos	ghettos	solos
altos	halos	provisos
banjos	lassos	quartos
cantos	pianos	tobaccos
dynamos	piccolos	zeros

TEST YOURSELF ON
Spelling Rules 1–4

Complete the spelling of the words with blanks in the example below by filling in the blank spaces according to one or another of the rules or notes explained in this section. Some blanks do not need filling in.

1. she is occasional_____y absent

2. the Sh_____k of Araby

3. a sens_____ible commit_____ment

4. pro_____ to jail; do not pass go; do not collect 200 dollars.

5. he perc_____ved a sunset

6. cake top_____ing

7. I like the ic_____ing

8. the c_____ling is cracking

9. the professor counsel_____ed me

10. the water is boil_____ing

11. a terrible argu_____ment

12. he stud_____ed hard

13. he went swim_____ing

14. he was stop_____ing me from drop_____ing my p_____ce of cake

15. the lovel_____ness of the flowers

16. it is occur_____ing often

17. a bus_____ness appoint_____ment

18. standing around ey_____ing girls

19. attorn_____s work in courthouses

20. my brother is dy_____ing

Word Lists

One or both of the following lists of words may be useful to you in working on your spelling problem.

Words that sound alike but mean different things (homophones)

The following pairs of words sound alike or look somewhat alike, but are spelled differently. Of course, their meanings are different, too. To master this list, you should write out sentences, using each word correctly in a number of different ways.

After each word is an abbreviation indicating the part of speech to which it belongs (*n.* for *noun; v.* for *verb;*

adj. for *adjective; adv.* for *adverb; prep.* for *preposition; conj.* for *conjunction; pro.* for *pronoun; poss.* for *possessive; contr.* for *contraction*). This is followed by a definition.

accept *v.* to receive
except *prep.* not included
except *v.* to leave out

access *n.* means of approach; admission
excess *n.* too much; lack of moderation

adapt *v.* to adjust to some situation or condition
adopt *v.* to choose; to follow a course of action

advice *n.* counsel; information offered
advise *v.* to give advice or counsel

affect *v.* to have an effect on; to influence
effect *n.* the result of some action
effect *v.* to accomplish or execute

aisle *n.* a corridor or passageway
isle *n.* an island

all ready *pro. + adj.* all are prepared
already *adv.* at or before this time

all together *pro. + adj.* all in the same place
altogether *adv.* entirely

allude *v.* to refer to
elude *v.* to escape or evade

allusion *n.* a reference
elusion *n.* escape, avoidance
illusion *n.* a false impression

aloud *adv.* audibly or loudly
allowed *v.* permitted

altar *n.* a special place for religious ceremony
alter *v.* to change

always *adv.* constantly; at all times
all ways *determiner + n.* in every manner

anecdote *n.* a little story
antidote *n.* something that counteracts poison

angel   *n.* a heavenly figure
angle   *n.* geometric entity formed by the divergence of two lines from a single point

arc   *n.* part of a circle
arch   *n.* a curved architectural form

ascend   *v.* to rise or go up
ascent   *n.* a movement upward
assent   *n.* an agreement
assent   *v.* to agree

assistance   *n.* help given
assistants   *n.pl.* helpers

band   *n.* a group or a strip
banned   *v.* forbidden or excluded

bare   *adj.* naked or uncovered
bare   *v.* to uncover or make known
bear   *v.* to put up with or to give birth to
bear   *n.* a wild animal

beside   *prep.* by the side of
besides   *prep. and adv.* in addition to

boar   *n.* a wild hog
bore   *n.* someone most uninteresting and tiresome

boarder   *n.* a person paying for subsistence in someone's house
border   *n.* a boundary

born   *v. always passive* given birth to
borne   *v. always active* carried; given birth to

brake   *n.* a mechanism to stop a vehicle
brake   *v.* to stop a moving vehicle
break   *v.* to cause damage to something

breath   *n.* air inhaled or exhaled
breathe   *v.* to inhale and exhale

canvas   *n.* a heavy, coarse cloth
canvass   *v.* to search for, examine or solicit

capital   *n.* a city that is a seat of government; an upper-case letter; money
capital   *adj.* principal; first-rate; upper-case
capitol   *n.* a building used by a legislature

censer *n.* a vessel for burning incense
censor *v.* to prohibit publication or performance in whole or part
censor *n.* one who prohibits publication; one who decides on suitability
censure *v.* to reprimand
censure *n.* disapproval
sensor *n.* a device that responds to physical stimulus—heat, light, etc.—and then sends an impulse to measure the stimulus

choose *v.* to select
chose *v. past tense of choose;* selected
chosen *v. past participle of choose;* selected

cite *v.* to quote; to charge with an offense
site *n.* a place or location
sight *n.* the faculty of seeing
sight *v.* to see or spot

coarse *adj.* rough; not refined
course *n.* school subject; a way or a path

complement *n.* something that completes
compliment *n.* praise

conscience *n.* part of the mind that rules on moral questions
conscious *adj.* awake or alert

council *n.* a deliberative body
counsel *n.* advice given; a lawyer
counsel *v.* to give advice
consul *n.* representative of one country residing in another

descent *n.* a downward movement
dissent *n.* disagreement
dissent *v.* to disagree

desert *n.* a dry, barren area of land
desert *v.* to abandon
dessert *n.* final course of a meal

device *n.* something contrived
devise *v.* to prepare, originate or make a contrivance

dining *v.* eating
dinning *v.* making a loud noise

do   v. to perform
due   adj. with *to* specifies the cause of something; owing

dual   adj. twofold
duel   n. a formal fight between two people

dyeing   v. giving a color to
dying   v. losing life

eminent   adj. famous
imminent   adj. about to happen

envelop   v. to enclose
envelope   n. a paper container used for mailing

extant   adj. still existing
extent   n. the degree of something

fair   adj. pleasing; just, impartial
fair   n. public sale or exhibition
fare   n. price charged for transportation

farther   adv. and adj. usually refers to distance
further   adv. and adj. usually refers to time, quantity, or degree

formally   adv. in a formal manner
formerly   adv. at an earlier time

forth   adv. forward; onward; out
fourth   adj. or adv. the one following the third

hear   v. to perceive with the ear
here   adv. in or at this place

human   adj. pertaining to people
humane   adj. compassionate or kindly

idol   n. a likeness of something, usually a god, for worship
idle   adj. not occupied or employed; v. to spend time in idleness
idyll   n. a peaceful, country scene; a carefree episode; a poem emphasizing this mood

ingenious   adj. resourceful, clever
ingenuous   adj. showing innocent or childlike simplicity

its   poss. pro. belonging to it
it's   contr. it is

know *v.* to understand, recognize, have experience of
no *adv.* expressing the negative
now *adv.* at the present time

later *adj.* following a specified time
latter *n.* the second of two things mentioned
ladder *n.* a structure for climbing up and down

lead *v. pronounced leed;* to show the way, to conduct
lead *n. pronounced led;* the metal
led *v.* past tense of *lead;* showed the way; conducted

loose *adj.* not tight
lose *v.* to misplace; to be defeated

marital *adj.* pertaining to marriage
martial *adj.* pertaining to military; warlike

maybe *adv.* perhaps
may be *v.* possibly may exist or happen

moral *adj.* relating to right or wrong
morale *n.* the mental or emotional condition of a person or
group

passed *v.* past tense and past participle of pass
past *n.* an earlier time
past *prep.* at the farther side of

patience *n.* the capacity to endure calmly
patients *n.pl.* people under medical care

peace *n.* not war
piece *n.* a part of

personal *adj.* relating privately
personnel *n.pl.* a group of persons employed

pore *v.* to study closely (takes prep *over* + indirect obj.)
pour *v.* to make stream or flow, esp. a liquid (takes direct obj.)

principal *n.* chief; head of a school; capital owned
principal *adj.* most important
principle *n.* rule or doctrine

prophecy *n.* a prediction
prophesy *v.* to predict

quiet *adj.* not noisy
quite *adv.* rather; almost completely
quit *v.* to depart from or out; resign

respectfully *adj.* showing deference
respectively *adv.* each in the order given

right *adj.* correct or suitable
rite *n.* a ceremony or ritual

sense *n.* ability to think properly; meaning
since *prep. and conj.* before this time; because

shone *v.* past tense of shine
shown *v.* past participle of show

sole *adj.* being the only one
soul *n.* immaterial essence of a person

stationary *adj.* fixed, or immobile
stationery *n.* paper for writing or typing

than *conj.* a comparative term
then *n. or adv.* indicates time

their *poss. pro.* belonging to them
there *adv.* a place; also used as expletive at beginning of
  sentences
they're *contr.* they are

to *prep.* indicates direction
too *adv.* excessively; overly much
two *n.* the number

trail *n.* a path, as through woods
trail *v.* to follow furtively
trial *n.* an experimental action or a courtroom procedure

vice *n.* immorality
vise *n.* a mechanical object used to hold things firmly in place

weather *n.* climate
whether *conj.* expresses alternatives

were *v.* past tense plural of to be; also subjunctive form
where *adv. or pro.* indicates place or position
we're *contr.* we are

whose *poss. pro.* belonging to whom?
who's *contr.* who is or who has?

your *poss. pro.* belonging to you
you're *contr.* you are

2. Words that are troublesome to spell

The following list consists of words that are habitually troublesome to spell. The part or parts of each that are the sources of the trouble are printed in bold face or noted in parentheses, or both. The best way to use this list is to write sentences using each of the words; write as many as five sentences for each word, and in that way embed in your hand, eye, and brain the correct spelling of each word. Proceed gradually. If you do a mere five words a day, you will master the whole list by the end of the semester.

a lot of
absence
abundance
abundant
academic
academically
academy
acceptable
acceptance
accessible
accidental
accidentally
acclaim
accommodate
accompaniment
accompanying
accomplish
accumulate
accuracy
accurate (one r)
accuser
accuses
accustom
achievement
acquaintance
acquire
across (one c)
actuality
actually
adequately

admission
admittance
adolescence
adolescent
advantageous
advertisement
advertiser
advertising (no e after s)
advice/advise
affect/effect
afraid
against
aggravate
aggressive
all right (2 words)
alleviate
allotted
allotment (one t)
allowed
allows
already (one l)
altar/alter
all together (2 words)
altogether (1 word; 1 l)
amateur
among (no u after o)
amount (one m)
analysis
analyze
and

another
annually
anticipated
apologetically
apologized
apology
apparatus
apparent
appearance
applies
applying
appreciate
appreciation
approaches
appropriate
approximate
arctic
area
argument (no e after u)
arguing (no e)
arise
arising
arouse
arousing (no e after s)
arrangement
article
atheist
athlete (no e after h)
athletic
attack (no t after k)
attempts
attendance
attendant
attended
attitude
audience
authoritative
authority
autumn
available

bargain
basically
basis

beauteous
beautified
beautiful (one l)
beauty
become
becoming (no e)
before
began/begin/begun
beginner
beginning
behavior
belief
believe
beneficial
benefited (one t)
bigger
biggest
boundary
breath (no final e)
breathe
brilliance
brilliant
Britain
burial
buried
bury
business
busing, bussing
busy

calendar
candidate
capitalism
career
careful (one l)
careless
carried
carrier
carrying
category
cemetery
certainly
challenge
changeable

changing
characteristic
characterized
chief
children
Christian
Christianity
choice
choose (double o)
chose
cigarette
cite/sight/site
clothes
coming (no e after m)
commercial
commission
committee
communist
companies
comparative
compatible
competition
competitive
competitor
completely
concede
conceivable
conceive
concentrate
concern
condemn
confuse
confusion
connotation
connote
conscience
conscientious
conscious
consequently
considerably
consistency
consistent
contemporary
continuously

controlled
controlling
controversy
controversial
convenience
convenient
correlate
council
counsel
counselor
countries
create
criticism
criticize
cruelly
cruelty
curiosity
curious
curriculum

dealt
deceive
decided
decision
definitely
definition
define
dependent
describe
description
desirability (no e after r)
desire
despair
destruction
detriment
devastating
device/devise
difference
different
difficult
dilemma
diligence
dining/dinning
disappoint

disastrous (no e after t)
disciple
discipline
discrimination
discussion
disease
disgusted
disillusioned
dissatisfied
divide
divine
doesn't
dominant
dropped
due
during (no e after r)

eager
easily
effect/affect
efficiency
efficient
eighth
eliminate
embarrass
emperor
emphasize
encourage
endeavor
enjoy
enough
enterprise
entertain
entertainment
entirely
entrance
environment
equipment (no e)
equipped
escapade
escape (no x)
especially
everything
evidently

exaggerate
excellence
excellent
except
excitable
exercise
existence
existent
expense
experience
experiment
explanation
extremely

fallacy
familiar
families
fantasies
fantasy
fascinate
fashions
favorite
February
fictitious
field
finally
financially
financier
foreigners
forty (no u after o)
forward/foreword
fourth
friendliness
fulfill
fundamentally
further

gaiety
generally
genius
government
governor
grammar
grammatically

group
guaranteed
guidance
guiding (no e after d)

handled
happened
happiness
harass
hear/here
height (no h after t)
heroes
heroic
heroine/heroin
hindrance (no e after d)
hopeless
hoping (no e)
hospitalization
huge
humorist
humorous
hundred
hunger
hungrily
hungry
hypocrisy
hypocrite

ideally
idyll/idol/idle
ignorance
ignorant
imaginary
imagination
imagine
immediately
immense
importance
incidentally
increase
indefinite
independence
independent
indispensable

individually
industries
industrious
inevitable
influence
influential
ingenious/ingenuous
ingredient
initiative
intellect
intelligence
intelligent
interest
interference
interpretation
interrupt
introduce
involve
irrelevant
irresistible
irritable
its/it's

jealousy
judgment (no e after g)

know/no/now
knowledge

laboratory
laborer
laboriously
laid
later/latter
led/lead
leisurely
lengthening
liable
library
license
lieutenant
lightning (no e)
likelihood
likely

likeness
listener
literary
literature
liveliest
livelihood
liveliness
lives
loneliness
lonely
loose/lose
losing (no e)
loss
luxury

magazine
magnificence
magnificent
maintenance
management
maneuver
manner
manufacturers
marriage
material
mathematics
matter
maybe/may be
meant
mechanics
medical
medicine
medieval
melancholy
mere
methods
miniature
minutes
mischief
mischievous (no i after v)
moral/morale
morally
mysterious

narrative
naturally
necessary
Negroes
ninety
noble
noticeable
noticing (no e)
numerous

obstacle
occasion
occasionally
occurred
occurrence
occurring
off/of
omit
operate
opinion
opportunity
opponent
oppose
opposite
optimism
organization
original

paid
pamphlets
parallel
parliament
paralyzed
particular
passed/past
peace
peculiar
perceive
performance
permanent
permit
persistently
personal/personnel
persuade

pertain
phase/faze
phenomenon
philosophy
physical
piece
planned
plausible
playwright
pleasant
politician
political
pore/pour
possession
possible
practical
practice
precede
predominant
preferred
prejudice (no *d* before or after *j*)
prepare
preparation
presence
prestige
prevalent
primitive
principle/principal
prisoners
privilege
probably
proceed
procedure
professor (one *f*)
profession (one *f*)
prominent
pronounce
pronunciation (no *o* after *n*)
propaganda
propagate
prophecy/prophesy
psychoanalysis

psychology
psychopathic
psychosomatic
pursue

quantity (one *t*)
quiet/quite

realize
really
rebel
receive
receiving
recognize
recommend
referring
regard
relative
relieve
religion
remember
remembrance
reminisce
repetition
represent
representative
resources
response
revealed
rhythm
ridicule
ridiculous
roommate

sacrifice
safety
satire
satisfied
satisfy
scene
schedule
seize
sense/since

sentence
separate
separation
sergeant
several
shepherd
shining
significance
similar
simile
simple
simply
sincerely
sociology
sophomore
source
speaking
speech
sponsor
stabilization
stepped
stories
story
straight
strength
stretch
strict/strictly
stubborn
studying
substantial
subtle
subtly (no e)
succeed
succession
sufficient
summary
summed
suppose
suppress
surprise
susceptible
suspense
swimming

symbol
synonym
synonymous

technique
temperament
temporary
tendency
than/then
their/there/they're
themselves
theories
theory
therefore
thorough/through
those
thought
to/too/two
together
tomorrow
tragedy
transferred
tremendous
tried
tries
tyranny

undoubtedly
unnecessary
unusually
useful
useless
using

vacuum
valuable
varies
various
vengeance
veteran
view
villain
visual

warrant
weather/whether
weird
where/were
whole/hole
wholly/holy
whose/who's

woman/women
write
writing

yield
your/you're

SUBJECTS FOR ESSAYS: CHOOSING AND LIMITING A TOPIC

Choosing a Topic

The only time selecting a subject may become a problem for you is when you are asked to select one. (If you are assigned a subject, the problem doesn't come up.) Your best course of action then is to choose a subject that interests you, one that captures your imagination and that you either know or want to learn more about.

The place to begin is in your personal experience—in the things that have happened to you, the things you have done, the beliefs you hold, the skills and special interests you have nurtured.

Student writers who think they have nothing to say are much mistaken. *Everybody has something to say.* In fact, we might define being human as the state of having something to say. The trouble is that we are not always aware of what we have to say until we've begun to look for it. That is why you should begin with experience; there is the great repository of writing materials, and questions are the entree to this great storehouse.

What do I like and dislike? Whom have I known that would be of interest to others? What interesting places have I seen? What books and articles have I read that have provoked me? What movies and TV shows have impressed me—one way or another? What do I do in my spare time? About what aspects of life in my community, town, or country am I passionately concerned?

Are there wrongs that I think should be righted? Social inequities that stick in my craw?

Questions like these will generate subject matter for essays, and if you generate the concrete details that make these subjects come alive, the essays will be interesting.

Sometimes these questions, this examination of the range of your personal experience, will lead you directly to a usable specific subject. But often the result will be a wide generalization. For example, the answer to one of the questions above ("What do I like?") might be "television comedy." Television comedy is simply too wide a generalization on which to base a 300-to-500-word essay. In any case, you would have to give specific examples of television comedy in your essay in order for it to be an effective piece of writing. Your task, then, when your experience suggests a widely general topic, is to narrow it down to a manageable, specific one. Instead of "television comedy," you would have to come up with an essay topic like "The Humor of Edith Bunker in *All in the Family*."

TEST YOURSELF ON
Generating Subject Matter

A. Examine your taste in television fare. Are there specific types of shows you like and watch consistently? Make a list of them. Now see if they are related. Make a list of five essay titles—possible writing assignments—suggested by the list. Examples might be such titles as "The Basic Plot of the Situation Comedy," "Why Rhoda Will Never Marry," and "The Amount of Violence in Five Episodes of *Hawaii Five-O*."

B. Make a list of places or buildings you've seen and been impressed by recently—or even during the past few years. Ask yourself what features of these natural or man-made environments appeal to you most or interest you most. Now make a list of five essay titles, possible writing assignments, suggested by those places. Examples might be such titles as "A Barn with a Gambrel Roof" or "A Campsite in Glacier National Park."

Limiting a Topic

Subjects should "fit" the size of the paper or essay for which they are intended. If you were assigned to write a three-volume book, you might very well choose "The Life of George Washington" as your subject. Since you are unlikely to be given such an assignment, better forego that subject. In fact, for the size of the assignment you are likely to be given—say a paper 300 to 500 words—better forego all subjects on that massive scale. You can't possibly do a creditable job in 500 words of writing on topics such as "The Causes of the Civil War" or "The Drug Culture in America." Short papers on subjects such as these can only wind up being filled with windy judgments and vague generalities.

To limit yourself, it is necessary to continually pare down a topic until it is manageable. It is not enough to go from "The Drug Culture in America" to "Marijuana Use in Chicago"—you must go further, for "Marijuana Use in Chicago" is quite as unmanageable in 500 words as is "The Drug Culture in America." Another problem with large topics like these is that they probably go beyond your own experience and would require considerable research before you could plausibly do a good job on them.

The process of limiting a topic involves successive narrowings from a general topic to a usable subject for a short theme.

Suppose you have chosen the general topic of "Sports Cars." Since you probably have no knowledge of the history of sports cars—and therefore wouldn't be able to talk about Bugattis and Reos—your first narrowing would take you to "Contemporary American Sports Cars." This may strike you as exactly right until you realize that it would be folly to try to try to talk about the dizzying number of makes and models available from American manufacturers nowadays.

Then you get a brainstorm: you decide to talk about your own sports car. This is a shrewd decision, but you realize further that "My Sports Car" is a subject that would certainly require more than the assigned 500 words, because of the complexity of the piece of machinery you own. Try talking about a '68 Thunderbird —about its basic specifications, size, equipment, road handling characteristics, and so forth, all in 500 words. Not possible. At this point, you see that *one* of the aspects of your own car would really do nicely, and you finally (and correctly) decide on "Acceleration and Deceleration in My Thunderbird."

This subject is not only the right size, it is also well within the bounds of your experience—so far within, in fact, that you are a great authority on the subject, probably the *only* authority.

You may find that your method of narrowing down a general topic requires less deliberation than the process above. Perhaps you will be able to proceed more quickly. Whatever the case, limiting a topic requires a disciplined effort to proceed toward the specific and manageable from the wide generalization.

TEST YOURSELF ON
Limiting a Topic

A. Below are listed five general topics and the manageable subjects derived from each. Provide the intermediate steps between them. Use the analysis given above as a model in arriving at each stage.

1. Clothing fashions . . . . The Role of Blue Jeans on Campus
2. Education . . . . My Troubles at the Beginning of Biology (or some other subject) 101
3. Television . . . . What Archie Bunker Hates Most
4. Student self-government . . . . . . The Duties of the Student Senator at My School
5. Urban decay . . . . Why My Family Left the City (the South Side of Chicago)

B. Write specific, manageable titles for five of the topics listed below.

1. Political parties	6. Kurt Vonnegut
2. The United Nations	7. Race prejudice in the U.S.
3. Basketball	8. The energy crisis
4. Vacations	9. Television commercials
5. Water pollution	10. Farm-price supports

SUBJECT-VERB AGREEMENT

In English, the problem of subject-verb agreement arises mainly in the present tense. To understand what it means, consider the verb *to play* and the forms of *play* in the present tense:

Subject	Verb	Subject	Verb
I	play	we	play
you	play	you	play
he, she, it	plays	they	play

The subjects in the left-hand column are all *singular;* the subjects in the right-hand column are all *plural*. All the verb forms are the same—except the third one in the left-hand column. It is a feature of the English language that whenever the subject is *he, she* or *it,* in the present tense, indicative mood, the verb form that goes with it must end in -s.

He considers me his friend.
She tells me when to pick her up.
It seems like a nice day.

Most of us have no trouble when the subject is *he, she,* or *it*. The trouble starts when the subject gets more complicated.

My Aunt Vicky plays basketball on Friday nights.
My Uncle Joe and my cousin Lewis *think* she's a good player.

In these cases, once you have decided whether the subject is singular or plural, you can make the right choice. In the first sentence, you can think of Aunt Vicky as *she;* in the second, there is what we call a compound (and therefore plural) subject; therefore, the first sentence requires a verb with an *-s* at the end, and the second does not. In the first sentence, there is a singular subject and a singular verb in the third person. In the second sentence, there is a plural (compound) subject and a plural verb form.

When the subject *agrees* with the verb in *number* (singular verb/singular subject, or plural verb/plural subject), there is no subject-verb agreement problem.

TEST YOURSELF ON
Subject-Verb Agreement

A. Change each of the sentences below following the procedure of the example.

Example: Joanna's best *feature is* her eyes.
    Her *eyes are* Joanna's best feature.

1. His main interest is guns.
2. Rock and roll records are my only hobby.
3. Our greatest need is dollars.
4. Many days of nonstop studying were the cause of his breakdown.
5. Too many drinks on an empty stomach were the cause of his drunkenness.

B. Change each of the sentences below following the procedure of the example.

Example: They let me know when they want to take a break.
    She lets me know when she wants to take a break.

1. They amuse themselves when they have no toys to play with.

    He _____

2. This turns me off.

    These _____

3. It seems to like being fed by the children.

    They _____

4. That forces the argument in another direction.

Those _____

5. They happen a lot more often than you think.

It _____

6. She frightens me when she talks like that.

They _____

7. She seems to profit from the time she spends in the biology
lab.

They _____

The Subject: How to Determine Number

You can begin to clear up the problem of subject-verb
agreement by gaining an understanding of what number
(singular or plural) to assign to certain subjects.

Compound subjects

A compound subject consists of more than one noun
or pronoun connected by *and* and therefore requires a
plural verb.

Rocco, Vito, and Danny are brothers.
My *sister* Lucia *and I* are starting a rock band.

The use of *neither . . . nor* or *either . . . or* with a
compound subject produces a singular subject when
both individual subjects are singular.

Neither my father nor my mother *is* a Democrat.
Either biology or astronomy *is* required.

When one of the subjects is plural, use the verb that
agrees with the closest one.

Neither my uncle nor my *aunts play* pool.
Either fruits or *cereal is* all right for breakfast.

When a compound subject consists of two items that are considered one unit, the subject can be thought of as singular.

Ham and eggs is my favorite dish.
Stormin' Norman and Suzy is my favorite rock group.

TEST YOURSELF ON
Subject-Verb Agreement with Compound Subjects and *either/or, neither/nor* Subjects

In some of the sentences below, the subject and verb agree. Next to these, write C. For the others, underline the complete subject and the verb and decide whether these are singular or plural. Correct the lack of agreement between subject and verb by changing one or the other.

1. _____ Either your father or your mother are responsible for the financial aid repayment.

2. _____ Charlie and Dick open their new bookstore next month.

3. _____ The professional and the rich man decides their own fates in the labor market.

4. _____ Coffee and donuts is fine for breakfast.

5. _____ Was the sofa and chair on sale?

6. _____ Either lung cancer or heart disease is the chief killer in the United States.

7. _____ Public transportation and welfare is the items needing reform in American cities.

8. _____ Neither Margaret nor Maureen think their kid brother is a failure.

9. _____ Air, water, the earth, and people are all being polluted.

10. _____ Neither George nor the Joneses plays bridge.

Collective nouns as subjects

Such collective nouns as *army, audience, class, faculty, committee, team,* and *public* indicate a number of people, but they usually take singular verbs because they are thought of as units.

The *team is* in first place. (the team as one whole; not the separate players)
The crowd *was* on its feet.

Such collective nouns as *plurality, minority, mass,* and *majority* may take either singular or plural verbs, depending on how you use them.

A minority of students *are* Greek majors. (the minority consists of separate Greek majors—a plural number).
A minority of students is a force to be reckoned with. (the minority is a political unit—a singular number)

TEST YOURSELF ON
Subject-Verb Agreement with Collective Nouns as Subjects

In each of the following sentences, determine whether the collective noun subject refers to a single unit or a plural number of individuals. Then cross out the incorrect verb in parentheses.

1. In this course, the class (decide, decides) whether to have a final exam.

2. The jury (render, renders) a verdict of *not guilty.*

3. The majority of my stamp collection (is, are) valuable.

4. The majority of my stamps (is, are) valuable.

5. The Congress (vote, votes) into law a thousand bills every year.

6. A plurality of Democrats (vote, votes) for liberal candidates.

7. The Appointments Committee (settle, settles) the fate of the faculty.

8. The staff (organize, organizes) the summer program.

9. The mass of men (leads, lead) lives of quiet desperation.

10. The audience (applaud, applauds) the performance vigorously.

Subjects modified by phrases and clauses

Sometimes the full subject of a verb is a whole string of words, consisting of the simple subject and its modifiers; these modifiers are frequently phrases, clauses, or both. But regardless of how many or what kinds of words intervene between the simple subject and the verb, the basic rule still holds: the verb must agree with the simple subject.

Subject Modified by a Phrase
Living alone in college dormitories seems to encourage students' maturity.

The full subject is the italicized portion of the example. But the headword, *living,* is the simple subject; it is singular and agrees with the singular verb *seems.*

Subject Modified by a Clause
Students who butter up their professors earn better grades than those who don't.

The full subject is the italicized portion of the example, but the headword, *students,* is the simple subject; it is plural and agrees with the plural verb *earn.*

We could take either of these examples and make the full subject longer and longer by adding more and more phrases and clauses, but the fact is that these long strings of words accompanying the simple subject are *modifiers;* and the verb never agrees with a word or words in the modifier—only with the simple subject.

The *music is* beautiful. (*music* is singular; therefore *is* is also singular)

The *music* of the *strings is* beautiful. (*strings* is plural, but *strings* is part of the modifying phrase *of the strings;* the correct verb remains singular *is* because singular *music* is still the subject)

TEST YOURSELF ON
Choosing the Correct Verb for Subjects Modified by Phrases and Clauses

Underline the simple subject of each of the following sentences. Then, ignoring the phrase or clause that modifies it, read the sentence to determine which of the verbs in parentheses agrees with that subject. Cross out the incorrect verb.

Example: Actors ~~who look like other actors~~ (hate, hates) to be reminded of the fact.

Actors who look like other actors (hate, ~~hates~~) to be reminded of the fact.

1. The passenger with a cowboy hat and boots in the aisle seat (look, looks) like my brother.

2. The patrons who are waiting in line behind the ropes (want, wants) desperately to be seated.

3. The purpose of the rules (is, are) to assure order.

4. The catch-22 in the examinations given by the Biology Department (lie, lies) in the large numbers of choices you are given.

5. The guard who stands at the doors of the museum (punch, punches) the tickets.

6. The difference between you and your cousins (appear, appears) to be that you are more comfortable away from home.

7. The smell of those fresh pastries (make, makes) my mouth water.

8. The progress of Jim's achievements in college (please, pleases) his parents.

9. Classes that meet late in the day (is, are) poorly attended.

10. Ed's affection for politics (distract, distracts) him from his real work.

Special cases

1. Pronouns as subjects. All of the following are singular and take singular verbs:

anybody	each	everyone	nobody
anything	either	everything	none
anyone	everybody	neither	no one
somebody	someone	something	one

Everyone with an interest in ecology *opposes* offshore oil drilling.
Each writes well.
Neither writes brilliantly.

2. Words ending in *-ics* as subjects. Words like *mathematics, economics, politics,* and *dialectics* are singular when you are speaking of the subject as a whole—as *one* thing.

Mathematics offers us a way of looking at the world.
Economics has no solution to the problem of inflation.

Where these terms refer to a number or collection of ideas rather than a singular, academic subject, they take a plural verb.

Marx's *economics do* not apply in all societies.
Since 1968, my *politics have* changed considerably.

3. *One of those which/who.* Where you find this structure, the first verb you use must be plural, the second singular.

One of those who *sing* in the choir *is* my brother. (*sing* agrees with the subject of the relative clause *who—which* agrees with *those* (plural)—and *is* agrees with *one,* the main subject)

4. *There is, there are. There* is not usually a subject. That's the trouble. Whether you use *is* or *are* depends on what follows the word *there.*

There is something I want to discuss with you. (the subject here is *something,* which agrees with the singular *is*)

There are reasons that I can't see you tonight. (*reasons* is the plural subject here—agreeing with the plural verb *are*)

5. *A number of, the number of.* The *number of* always takes a singular verb; *a number of* always takes a plural verb.

A *number of* dogs are playing in the garden.
The *number of* dogs playing in the garden is small.

6. *Part* and *portion.* These words, though they indicate a quantity, always take a singular verb, because each signifies a single unit or fraction.

Part of my time *is* spent loafing
Part of my work *is* boring.
A *portion* of my salary *goes* into savings bonds.
A *portion* of cherries *is* fine for dessert.

7. Expressions such as *together with, as well as, in addition to, including.* A parenthetical expression introduced by phrases such as these does not affect the agreement of the subject and the verb.

The *truck cab* and the *trailer* are barreling down the highway. (the compound subject—*truck cab and trailer*—requires the plural verb *are*)
The *truck cab,* together with the trailer, *is* barreling down the highway. (the subject is now *truck cab*—the parenthetical expression introduced by *together with* doesn't count—and the verb is therefore the singular *is*)

TEST YOURSELF ON
Subject-Verb Agreement in Special Cases

For each of the sentences below, cross out the verb in the parentheses that does not agree with the italicized subject.

1. *Billiards* (is, are) a difficult game to learn.
2. *Economics* (involve, involves) a lot of statistics.
3. Joanna noticed that Bill's *trousers* (was, were) dirty.
4. *Gymnastics* (require, requires) a high degree of agility.
5. The *news* these days (depress, depresses) me.
6. Now that I have graduated, a *part* of my life's tasks (is, are) over.
7. A *portion* of these marbles (is, are) yours.
8. A *portion* of blueberry pancakes (is, are) served with butter and syrup.

9. The *number* of people waiting to see the movie (is, are) promising.
10. *One* of these radios (is, are) perfect for my room.
11. A number of stray dogs (goes, go) to the pound every day.
12. *One* of those boys who hang around the schoolyard (is, are) my brother.
13. There (happen, happens) to be a *fly* in my soup.
14. There (was, were) unidentified flying *objects* in the sky.
15. There (don't, doesn't) seem to be *raisins* in this rice pudding.
16. The *teacher*, as well as the students, (display, displays) a great interest in the subject.
17. At the beginning of the semester, there (is, are) *orientation and registration*.
18. The *stereo* set, including the speakers, (cost, costs) $300.
19. *Anybody* who agrees with my viewpoints (is, are) intelligent.
20. *Franny*, as well as her mother Vera, (make, makes) all her own clothes.

SUBJUNCTIVE MOOD

See **Verbs** and Part 1, Verbs.

SUBORDINATION

Subordination is the technique of indicating that one idea is not as important as another. Consider these two ideas:

Jimmy Carter was virtually unknown to the American people in January 1976.
He was elected President in November.

Both ideas are interesting, but the second is clearly more important than the first, and, in looking over an essay that contained the two sentences, you should be able to indicate their relative importance by rewriting them as follows:

Although Jimmy Carter was virtually unknown to the American people in January 1976, he was elected President in November.

Note: It is possible that an essay could be dealing with Jimmy Carter's anonymity. In that case, the proper way to rewrite the two sentences would be as follows:

Although Jimmy Carter was elected President in November 1976, he was virtually unknown to the American people in January of that year.

Presumably, then, the essay would go on to speak of his being unknown.

In either case, however, it is important that you learn the technique of subordination and then go on to use it habitually in your writing.

Subordinate ideas may be expressed, as we did above, by putting them in the form of a dependent (subordinate) clause. They may also be put in the form of phrases or even single words.

Included in my wardrobe is a summer suit, *which is made of cotton.* (subordinate idea cast in the form of a dependent, subordinate clause)
Included in my wardrobe is a summer suit *made of cotton.* (subordinate idea cast in the form of a participial phrase)
Included in my wardrobe is a *cotton* summer suit. (subordinate idea made into an adjective)

Probably the most important technique of subordination is the capacity to cast subordinate ideas into the form of subordinate clauses. Otherwise your prose can sound like the following childish and monotonous passage:

I went to the movies. I ran into my friend Charlie. The movie ran two hours. I hated it. Charlie wanted to sit up front. I wanted to smoke in the balcony. We sat in the third row.

Because these seven ideas are presented as seven separate sentences, they appear to be of equal importance. But of course they are not. Nor would it be much help to string them together with *and* or *but* or other coordinating conjunctions. In fact, you should avoid such strings at all costs. What is needed is subordination—reducing the less important ideas and highlighting the more important ones. One possible way of revising the passage is this:

> I went to the movies, where I ran into my friend Charlie. The movie, which I hated, ran for two hours. Although I wanted to smoke in the balcony, Charlie wanted to sit up front and we sat in the third row.

You might disagree over whether this is the best way to revise the passage, but you would surely agree that this change is for the better.

In practicing subordination, you should be wary of two errors that are likely to crop up.

1. Don't subordinate the more important idea. Where you have two ideas and want to subordinate one of them, do not haphazardly make your choice. That is, do not subordinate one of the ideas without thinking through the problem and deciding what you want to stress. What you want to stress will, of course, go into the main clause.

Ali won the fight.
Ali was tiring at the end.
Although Ali won the fight, he was tiring at the end. (are you just subordinating the first of the two ideas because it is the first one your eye fell on, or do you really want to stress the fact that Ali was tiring rather than that he won the fight?)

I break out in hives.
I eat strawberries.
Whenever I break out in hives, I eat strawberries. (in this case, subordinating the first of the two ideas because your eye fell on it first results in an absurdity)
Whenever I eat strawberries, I break out in hives. (of course, this is in keeping with the more probable sequence of events)

2. Don't use the wrong subordinating conjunctions.
Be sure to use the correct subordinating conjunction whenever you *do* subordinate.

Poor   *While* my English professor is not Woody Allen, he does have a good sense of humor.

Better   *Although* my English professor is not Woody Allen, he does have a good sense of humor.

Poor   I read in the paper *where* the Beatles are making a comeback.
Better   I read in the paper *that* the Beatles are making a comeback.

Poor   My final exams, *what* I have to take next week, have me scared.
Better   My final exams, *which* I have to take next week, have me scared.

TEST YOURSELF ON
Subordination

A. Combine each of the following groups of sentences into one or two effective ones using the techniques of subordination.

Examples: 1.   I ran into the water.
It was cold.

When I ran into the water, it was cold.

2.   James Joyce was an Irish novelist.
He wrote all his books in exile in Europe.
He wrote five books.
Dubliners was a book he wrote.

James Joyce, an Irish novelist who wrote all his books in exile in Europe, wrote five books, including *Dubliners*.

Note: Not every student will combine the groups in exactly the same way. Several ways are possible.

1. Marylea has a lovely blue shirt.
The shirt is cotton.
She likes to take it to the beach.
She likes to walk around with it.
2. My television set is broken again.
I paid four hundred dollars for it.
It happens.
I get furious.
3. Air pollution is a problem.
The problem affects us all.

The problem affects us if we live in the country.
The problem affects us if we live in the city.
4. We left Cleveland.
  It was raining there.
  We arrived in Chicago.
  Chicago surprised us with its sunlit beauty.
5. My friend's name is Chris.
  He is English.
  He loves the United States.
  He occasionally longs to return to London.
6. Some crimes are against the person.
  These crimes are increasing.
  These crimes must be dealt with.
  These crimes must be dealt with firmly.
7. It was early.
  It was a Sunday.
  It was morning.
  The streets were deadly quiet.
8. Promises are made.
  These promises are sincere.
  Promises can be broken.
  The breaking is easy.
9. It rains.
  My roof leaks.
  The roof tiles are loose.
  They were never repaired by the former owner.
10. Paul Klee was a painter.
  He was a Swiss.
  His paintings look like drawings.
  The drawings are made by children.

B. Revise the following sentences through the effective use of subordination.

1. My hair is drying. I'll read a book.
2. I eat too much pastry and I gain a lot of weight.
3. A whole set of encyclopedias came in the mail and I didn't order them.
4. You see a rainbow across the meadow and you know there's been a recent rainstorm.
5. Jerry was unpacking but Noella was cooking supper.
6. She was frightened of air travel and she got on the plane for Paris.
7. Her exams were over, so she could afford to relax.

8. She had enough money and she had enough time and she needed a change of scenery, so she went out to California to visit Craig.

9. The car is a symbol of his virility, so he spends a lot of time polishing it to a high luster.

10. He likes working in the darkroom, so he does his own printing.

THESIS STATEMENT

Thesis statement is the name given to a central idea when it is written out as a sentence. A thesis, or theme, is simply the stand you take on an issue or the main point you want to make about a subject.

The Decline of American Cities is not a thesis statement but a title. In fact, it isn't a sentence, and a thesis statement must be a complete sentence. "My subject is the decline of American cities" is not a thesis statement, either, but an announcement to the reader of what your subject will be—a job done better by a title. (Notice that it is not an improvement to write "My *thesis* is the decline of American cities.") "The decline of American cities is deplorable" is also not a thesis statement, because it needs no essay to support it; it is a fairly obvious statement of fact. A reader would be as interested in reading an essay about it as he would be in reading one that supports the statement, "Hank Aaron holds the major league home run record."

You need an effective thesis statement in order to control your writing. A poorly worded thesis statement guarantees a poorly constructed, badly focused, and uninteresting piece of writing. In order to be sure that you have a thesis statement that will help control your writing, you should pay attention to the following criteria of a good thesis statement:

1. An effective thesis statement is limited or narrowed down from a larger statement. The idea is to give yourself a manageable, *limited* piece of territory to cover. "College teachers go too fast for the average col-

lege student" is a very broad statement that would take you into too large a territory. For example, you would have to talk about more than one college teacher and would also have to deal with whatever is an "average college student." The territory can be scaled down considerably if this topic is changed to "Professor Lucia John goes too fast for her math students." You can see how this limits the territory to one professor in just one class and how it provides real material in the form of actual students. Here are two more examples of large and narrower statements:

Large   Our tax burdens are too great.
Narrower   Federal tax rates penalize people for being single.

Large   Baseball is fun.
Narrower   Nothing matches the excitement of a low-scoring baseball game between evenly matched teams.

2. An effective thesis statement is singular. More than one major idea in an essay is too many. If you have too many major ideas, you will write diffusely, your essay will wander all over the territory, and the reader loses track of what he or she is supposed to be following. "The United Nations has not fulfilled its original purpose of keeping world peace; it's used for narrow political purposes instead, and many countries neglect to pay their share of its unkeep—which is quite expensive." This is a mouthful—enough for at least two and probably three essays. Better would be either "The UN has not fulfilled its original peace-keeping purpose" or "The UN is used for narrow political purposes." Here are two more examples:

Multiple   The social life of a freshman at this college is very limited, the place is so big that you can get lost looking for a classroom, and besides, the professors are an unfriendly bunch.
Singular   A freshman at this college has a number of difficult adjustments to make
The social life of a freshman at this college is very limited.
The professors at this college are an unfriendly bunch.

Multiple   Our ecological problems are mounting, a situation
that is not helped by the energy crunch, the increasing population, and the plans for modern industrial development by
the Third World countries.

Singular   The energy crisis is contributing to our mounting ecological problems.

Plans for industrial development by Third World countries will
contribute to our ecology problems.

Rapid increases in world population will contribute to our ecology problems.

3. An effective thesis statement is concrete. A thesis
statement that is limited and singular must also be concrete. An abstract or vague expression can ruin it. "The
Olympic Games are a great spectacle" is too vague. "A
great spectacle" of futility? "A great spectacle" of athletic prowess? Better would be "The Olympic Games
are a great spectacle of people's capacity for friendly
competition." Another example: "My mother is some
kind of cook" doesn't say *what* kind. Better: "My
mother is a versatile cook."

TEST YOURSELF ON
Recognizing an Appropriate Thesis Statement

Place a check next to any of the following that seem to be
strong and effective thesis statements. Rework the others.

1. Diabetes is a leading killer of Americans.
2. American movies are hung up on nostalgia for the fifties.
3. My Aunt Rose is a stylish dresser.
4. Punk Rock is for punks.
5. Mathematics is an engineering student's most useful basic
   subject.
6. The difference between newspaper coverage and TV coverage of the fire on 29th Street illustrates an important media principle.
7. *Hamlet* is a better play than *Macbeth*.
8. The rules for getting a candidate on the ballot for mayor
   in this town are unfair to those without funds.
9. Utilities in this country make a fortune in profit.
10. The life of a pro athlete is a poor model for youth.
11. Science and art have nothing to say to one another.
12. A person's hobby is the key to that person's character.

TOPIC SENTENCE   See **Unity.**

TRANSITIONS

Transition is the relating of one idea to the next as your essay proceeds from start to finish. Smooth transition contributes to the coherence of sentences, paragraphs, and essays. A tight organizational pattern is usually the best guarantee that you will achieve coherence. (For more on **Coherence,** see that entry.)

The necessity for coherence is based on the readers' need to be led from point to point in the writing by some familiar principle of order. In other words, readers need a solid bridge to get from sentence to sentence, paragraph, idea to idea. When such bridges are absent, readers lose confidence in the writing and distractedly wander away from what they are reading.

Thus unless the organizational pattern is so powerful that the writing has exceptionally smooth flow from part to part, it is a good idea to use what are called *transitional devices* to establish points of reference, bridges for the readers' eyes and minds. These devices are also useful in that they establish the exact relationship between succeeding parts. In that sense they are useful in *saying* more, and saying is the essential function of expository writing.

The major transitional devices, sometimes used in combination, are the following.

Repetition

Repeating a word or a phrase is a most common device. Sometimes a pronoun, referring back to a subject, will also do the trick, as will repeating a reference to an idea.

The whole sentence or brief paragraph

A sentence can be used as a transition between different ideas following and preceding it. A brief paragraph can also serve as a transition between two longer paragraphs.

Standard transitional words or phrases

All of these are good bridges and most are also useful in indicating relationships. A few of the large number available are listed below:

soon, later, at the same time, afterward, meanwhile, simultaneously, in a little while, subsequently
nearby, close by, there, here, at the other end
therefore, thus, hence, consequently
similarly, likewise, in the same way
on the other hand, however, but, nevertheless, still, yet, by contrast
moreover, furthermore, finally, also, in addition
indeed, in fact, in other words

TEST YOURSELF ON
Making Effective Transitions

Each of the groups of sentences below could be made more coherent by the use of one or more transitional devices. Use either repetition (which will require a little rewriting) or standard transitional words and phrases.

1. He had given Tom a handsome wedding gift. He had offered him a well-paying job with the firm.
2. He stood in a small ravine. There was a running brook.
3. The country is running out of oil. Our coal supply is low. Research and development for new energy sources are at a standstill.
4. He received a receipt for his tuition. He was able to register.
5. She wanted to go to the seashore. He preferred the mountains.
6. Reading stimulated his taste for mulling over in his mind the writer's great ideas. The notions gave him a sense of participating in some great enterprise. He was always reading.
7. Among his possessions were a sports car, a motorcycle, a boat, and a bicycle. He had no need to use public transportation.
8. Sam made his way through his classes by impressing on his teacher what a bright, personable young man he was. He made contacts with girls and impressed them, too.

9. After walking around downtown for an hour, she stopped and had dinner. She went to the movies.
10. He was graduated *summa cum laude*. He was able to pick and choose from a number of high-paying jobs.
11. She treated him shabbily, never letting him know from one minute to the next how she felt about him, breaking appointments, speaking rudely to him in public. He could find things about her to love.
12. She said she had known him in Chicago. He had never been to Chicago.

UNITY

Effective paragraphs possess a quality called *unity*. All the sentences in a unified paragraph are directed toward a single purpose: they supply specific details to illustrate, explain, or define a single generalization made somewhere in, but usually at the beginning of, that paragraph. This generalization is called the *topic sentence*, and it states what the paragraph is *about*.

Thus every unified paragraph is about one thing and pursues the one thing by organizing itself about its topic sentence. The three ways of placing the topic sentence are illustrated by the following sample paragraphs.

1. The topic sentence can be the opening sentence of the paragraph. Such a paragraph follows the deductive method of stating the generalization and then adding illustrative or supporting details.

In the folklore of the country, numerous superstitions relate to winter weather. Back-country farmers examine their corn husks —the thicker the husk, the colder the winter. They watch the acorn crop—the more acorns, the more severe the season. They observe where white-faced hornets place their paper nests—the higher they are, the deeper will be the snow. They examine the size and shape and color of the spleens of butchered hogs for clues to the severity of the season. They keep track of the blooming of dogwood in the spring—the more abundant the blooms, the more bitter the cold in January. When chipmunks carry their tails high and squirrels have heavier fur and mice come into country houses early in the fall, the superstitious gird themselves for a long, hard winter. Without any scientific basis, a wider-than-usual black band on a woolly-bear caterpillar is accepted as a sign that winter will arrive early and stay late. Even the way a cat sits beside the stove carries its message to the credulous. According to a belief once widely held in the Ozarks, a cat sitting with its tail to the fire indicates very cold weather is on the way.

—Edwin Way Teale, *Wandering Through Winter*

Observations indicate that the different clusters of galaxies are constantly moving apart from each other. To illustrate by a homely analogy, think of a raisin cake baking in an oven. Suppose the cake swells uniformly as it cooks, but the raisins themselves remain of the same size. Let each raisin represent a cluster of galaxies, and imagine yourself inside one of them. As the cake swells, you will observe that all the other raisins move away from you. Moreover, the farther away the raisin, the faster it will seem to move. When the cake has swollen to twice its initial dimensions, the distance between all the raisins will have doubled itself—two raisins that were initially an inch apart will now be two inches apart; two raisins that were a foot apart will have moved two feet apart. Since the entire action takes place within the same time interval, obviously the more distant raisins must move apart faster than those close at hand. So it happens with the clusters of galaxies.

—Fred Hoyle, "When Time Began"

2. The topic sentence can be the final sentence of the paragraph. Such a paragraph follows the inductive method by giving details first and allowing these details to lead up to the concluding general statement.

Television sells cars as if they were sex objects. It tells one-hour stories that wind up with all the pieces in the right places, the heroines and heroes clearly marked. It pictures the news only in pictures—as if there were nothing else newsworthy. It relegates "educational" programs to a special channel—as if educational material did not belong with the other material. And it's right to do so, because commercial television does everything it can to sell us illusions.

The sports pages have columns telling us how to hit a tennis ball and how to flog a golf ball. The slick magazines give us expert advice on how to sew, build furniture, repair cars, use tools, and redecorate our houses. Stirring books are printed every day with titles bearing the words "How To . . ." and television talk shows consistently feature people who are *experts,* people who have *accomplished* something. Thus it is easy to see that Americans value nothing so much as competence.

3. The topic sentence can be unstated but implied. This is a frequent tactic of narrative and descriptive paragraphs. In the example given below, the implied topic is *a description of the plant life at the edge of a concrete highway.*

The concrete highway was edged with a mat of tangled, broken, dry grass, and the grass heads were heavy with oat beards to catch on a dog's coat, and foxtails to tangle in a horse's fetlocks, and clover burrs to fasten in sheep's wool; sleeping life waiting to be spread and dispersed, every seed armed with an appliance of dispersal, twisting darts and parachutes for the wind, little spears and balls of tiny thorns, and all waiting for animals and for the wind, for a man's trouser cuff or the hem of a woman's skirt, all passive but armed with appliances of activity, still, but each possessed of the anlage of movement.

—John Steinbeck, *The Grapes of Wrath**

TEST YOURSELF ON
Identifying Topic Sentences

What are the topic sentences in the paragraphs below? If you cannot find one expressed directly, consider the possibility that it may be implied.

1. While the relationship between loving and being loved is an intimate one, this is not to say that love is automatically reciprocated. Indeed, it may lead to feelings of revulsion if the individual's self-image is already irretrievably low: "Anyone who says he loves *me* must be either a fool or a fraud." Still a person is relatively likely to love someone who loves him. Indirect support for this generalization comes from a number of experiments in which persons are falsely informed that they are liked (or disliked) by other members of their group. This misinformation is enough to elicit congruent feelings in most of the deceived subjects. A similar kind of feedback often operates in the elaborate American game of dating. The young woman, for any of several

reasons, may pretend to like her escort more than is actually the
case. The man, hungry for precisely this kind of response, responds favorably and in kind. And the woman, gratified by this
expression of affection, now feels the fondness she had formerly
feigned. Falling in love may be regarded, in cases such as these,
as a snowball with a hollow core.

—Lawrence Casler, "This Thing Called Love Is Pathological"

2. The gallows stood in a small yard, separate from the main
grounds of the prison, and overgrown with tall prickly weeds.
It was a brick erection like three sides of a shed, with planking
on top, and above that two beams and a crossbar with the rope
dangling. The hangman, a greyhaired convict in the white uniform of the prison, was waiting beside his machine. He greeted
us with a servile crouch as we entered. At a word from Francis
the two warders, gripping the prisoner more closely than ever,
half led, half pushed him to the gallows and helped him clumsily
up the ladder. Then the hangman climbed up and fixed the rope
round the prisoner's neck.

—George Orwell, "A Hanging," from *Shooting an Elephant*

3. Money in England is august. What a fine, scrolled document an English banknote is, and how carefully one thinks before one parts with it. How noble and weighty is the English
penny, compared with the equivalent American coin, which is
a mere scrap of metal. Try and get hold of an English penny;
weigh it in your hand; savor its medallion-like quality, and think
how painful it is to spend it on a mere bus ticket or a visit to
the lavatory. And then think of the flimsiness of American cash,
and how glad one is, really, to get rid of it. It doesn't confer
status on a man, the way cash does in England. Indeed, one dis-
cerns a strange sense of abasement in American financial quar-
ters. The last thing an American banker would like you to think
of him is that he might *deal* in cash. He deals in bonds, and he
finances things, but he doesn't touch money.

—Malcolm Bradbury, "Can We Bring Back the
Old Fashioned Bank Robber?"

4. Anyone who has worked on a committee preparing a document to be signed by all fellowwriters knows some of the difficulties. Disagreements of opinion and emphasis can produce a
voice that is hardly a voice at all. Constant qualification makes
for weakness. The various writers, all too aware of their audience as real people, may try to anticipate hopelessly conflicting
prejudices and objections. Everybody has a point he wants in-

cluded, but what is worse, no one feels any personal responsibility for the tone of the whole. Nobody cares, really. Contrast the situation of the single writer alone at his desk, who can establish a single speaking voice and an ideal assumed reader to listen to it. Yet a great deal of modern prose is written, or at any rate rewritten, not at a lonely desk but around a table where everybody talks at once. The loss of personality almost inevitable under such circumstances should cause us anguish whenever, as so often happens, we have to read or write the prose of organization life. When we speak of official prose as *stuffy*, we are referring, I think, directly to this loss of personality. (Not that you need a committee to produce stuffiness. . . .) Stuffiness may imply, by way of the stuffed shirt, that the speaker has no insides, no humanity. It is scarecrow prose. Other familiar metaphors also seem to recognize an emptiness within; thus we speak of the "inflated" language of officialese, the speaker in that case being filled with gas, or hot air.

—Walker Gibson, *Tough, Sweet, and Stuffy*

5. The running styles were as different as the physical characteristics. Dick Crompton, a small Texan scatback, ran with sharp exhalations when he had the ball, *ah-ah-ah*, like piston strokes —a habit he had picked up in high school which he felt gave power to his run. He could be heard across the width of a field. The "Gasper" some of the players called him, and he was also nicknamed "Roadrunner"—after the quick-running desert bird of his home state.

Jake Greer also had a distinctive run—moving his spindly body in leaps like a high jumper moving for the crossbar, high, bouncy steps, and then he stretched out fast, and when he got to the defending back he feinted with his small high-boned head, sometimes with a tiny bit of toothpick working in it. Then he'd fly on past or off at an angle, his hands splayed out wide, looking back for the ball honing in to intercept his line of flight, and then he'd *miss* it—good moves but bad hands in those early training sessions, they said—and the shouts would go up, "Squeeze that thing, baby," "Hands, man, hands." Greer would circle back, stricken, staring into his big hands as if they had betrayed him as he bent down to pick up the ball. His face would remain long and melancholy, and when his signal came up again, Scooter McLean would shout: "Look like you want it, Al, come *on*, baby."

—George Plimpton, *Paper Lion*

TEST YOURSELF ON
  Achieving Unity in Paragraphs

Each of the three topic sentences printed below is accompanied by a set of statements. Each topic sentence together with its accompanying statements could be made into an effective paragraph were it not for one problem: some of the statements in each set are irrelevant to the topic sentences. In each set, eliminate the potential hurdles to unity and organize the rest into an effective paragraph. Slight alterations in the statements are permissible.

I. Basketball is a game requiring great physical skills and coordination.

1. Basketball players must be able to run backward as well as forward.
2. They must have good peripheral vision in order to see their teammates and their opponents.
3. In order to leap for the ball off the backboard, players must have excellent timing.
4. Timing is also important in passing and shooting—the exact moment counts in basketball.
5. In football, such skills and coordination are not necessary; there you need brute strength.
6. Basketball can be played anywhere.
7. The speed at which the game is played seems to be the factor that requires these skills.

II. Your chances of getting a summer job are best if you make a systematic search and present yourself as a useful worker.

1. Explore all the relevant sources for jobs: want ads, school placement agency, friends and relatives, and signs hanging in the windows of businesses in your home town.
2. Begin your campaign early.
3. If you get the right summer job, you can earn as much as $2,500 over the summer.
4. If you are applying to a large corporation, show your professionalism by presenting a resume.
5. The resume should not be modest; it should list all the skills you possess.
6. Then decide on what kind of job you want and go after it.
7. In appearing for an interview, be on time and present a neat and business-like appearance.

8. The vigorous job-seeker will appear vigorous to an employer.
9. A summer job is not so tiring that you will not be able to have fun and work at the same time.

III. There are a number of reasons why it is difficult for most high school seniors to adjust to college life.
1. For one thing, they usually come to a large campus from a much smaller high school setting, and this change alone is unsettling.
2. College administators should be forced to go to freshman registration and see what's involved.
3. Not only a big school, but big classes contribute to the freshman's unease.
4. Crowded together in a large lecture hall with hundreds of students, they miss the old high-school intimacy.
5. Where they were once friendly with a small number of "teachers," they are now subject to the alienating presence of the "professor."
6. Moreover, going to college often involves a change of residence—from home with the family to a college dorm in another town—and this factor requires some adjustment.
7. Colleges should try to make this transition easier.

VERBS

A verb is a part of speech that expresses either action or some state of existence or condition of being.

Dr. J. *sank* a jumper.
The Rolling Stones *played* a concert.
My Uncle Gene *eats* like a whole platoon of Marines.
The typewriter *sits* waiting.

After a while, I *felt* better.
Eddie *seemed* depressed today.
She *is* a princess.
They *were* startled.

The verbs italicized in the second set of examples above are called *linking verbs*. (See Part 1, Verbs, for more information about them.) The verbs italicized in the first set of examples above denote some kind of action. (See Part 1, Verbs, under the headings *transitive* and *intransitive* for information about them.)

What all these verbs have in common is the fact that each one not only carries a meaning but also indicates *time*.

1. I *begin* work at eight o'clock. (present tense)
2. I *am beginning* work at eight o'clock. (continuous or progressive present tense)
3. I *was beginning* work at eight o'clock. (continuous past tense)
4. Yesterday, I *began* work at nine o'clock. (past tense)
5. Everyday this week, I *have begun* work before ten o'clock. (perfect tense)
6. Before that, I *had begun* work at eleven o'clock. (past perfect tense)
7. Tomorrow, I *will begin* work at twelve o'clock. (future tense)
8. I *will have begun* work by twelve noon. (future perfect tense)

Sentence 1 indicates action taking place in the present or action that is typical and ongoing (something like "I *always* begin work at eight o'clock—I have done so and I will do so in the future"). Sentence 2 says much the same, perhaps with a bit more urgency—the statement could be read as a kind of warning, i.e., "You'd better say what you have to say to me now because I'll be too busy after eight: I am beginning work at eight o'clock." Sentence 3 might answer the question, "What time were you beginning work last week?" Sentence 4, the simple past tense, indicates that the action took place in the past and was completed then. Sentence 5 suggests that the action was begun in the past and has continued on up to the present. Sentence 6 tells us that the action specified took place and was completed *prior* to some other time in the past, perhaps prior to the week spoken of in sentence 5. Sentence 7 indicates future time, and sentence 8 indicates an action that *will be* completed at or by some specific time in the future.

There are other important things to notice about these examples. First, you should notice that a verb can consist of more than one word. Second, you should notice that in all the examples there appear only four forms of the verb *begin:*

begin (stem, or present tense form)
began (past tense)
begun (past participle)
beginning (present participle)

These are called the *principal parts* of the verb. Knowing the principal parts of a verb and knowing the forms of the auxiliary (helping) verbs *be* and *have* will enable you to form any tense or form of that verb.

Conjugation of *Be* and *Have*

The *conjugation* of a verb is a listing of its forms.

Be		*Have*	
present tense		*present tense*	
I am	we are	I have	we have
you are	you are	you have	you have
he, she, it is	they are	he, she, it has	they have
past tense		*past tense*	
I was	we were	I had	we had
you were	you were	you had	you had
he, she, it was	we were	he, she it had	they had

perfect tense: have been
past perfect tense: had been
future tense: will be
future perfect tense: will have been

perfect tense: have had
past perfect tense: had had
future tense: will have
future perfect tense: will have had

Regular and Irregular Verbs: Principal Parts

Notice these principal parts:

Present (stem)	Past	Present Participle	Past Participle
talk	talked	talking	talked
play	played	playing	played
freeze	froze	freezing	frozen
catch	caught	catching	caught

Notice that in the case of the first two verbs, the past and the past participle simply add *-ed* (the two forms are the same). These are called regular verbs. The last two are *irregular*.

Irregular verbs in English do not form the past and past participle with -ed. The irregularities of these verbs must be studied and memorized; here is a list of some of the main irregular verbs, together with their principal parts.

Present (stem)	Past	Present Participle	Past Participle
arise	arose	arising	arisen
bear	bore	bearing	borne
begin	began	beginning	begun
bind	bound	binding	bound
blow	blew	blowing	blown
break	broke	breaking	broken
bring	brought	bringing	brought
buy	bought	buying	bought
catch	caught	catching	caught
choose	chose	choosing	chosen
come	came	coming	come
creep	crept	creeping	crept
deal	dealt	dealing	dealt
do	did	doing	done
draw	drew	drawing	drawn
drink	drank	drinking	drunk
drive	drove	driving	driven
eat	ate	eating	eaten
fall	fell	falling	fallen
flee	fled	fleeing	fled
fly	flew	flying	flown
forbid	forbade	forbidding	forbidden
forget	forgot	forgetting	forgotten
freeze	froze	freezing	frozen
get	got	getting	gotten
give	gave	giving	given
go	went	going	gone
grind	ground	grinding	ground
grow	grew	growing	grown
hang	hung*	hanging	hung*
hold	held	holding	held
hurt	hurt	hurting	hurt
know	knew	knowing	known

*The past and past participle forms are *hanged* when the word is used in the sense of *executed*.

Present (stem)	Past	Present Participle	Past Participle
lay	laid	laying	laid
lead	led	leading	led
lend	lent	lending	lent
lie	lay	lying	lain
lose	lost	losing	lost
mean	meant	meaning	meant
mistake	mistook	mistaking	mistaken
ride	rode	riding	ridden
ring	rang	ringing	rung
rise	rose	rising	risen
run	run	running	run
see	saw	seeing	seen
seek	sought	seeking	sought
send	sent	sending	sent
shake	shook	shaking	shaken
shine	shone/ shined	shining	shone/ shined
sing	sang	singing	sung
sleep	slept	sleeping	slept
slide	slid	sliding	slid
speak	spoke	speaking	spoken
spin	spun	spinning	spun
spill	spilt/ spilled	spilling	spilled
spit	spat	spitting	spat
spread	spread	spreading	spread
spring	sprang	springing	sprung
steal	stole	stealing	stolen
sting	stung	stinging	stung
stink	stank	stinking	stunk
strike	struck	striking	stricken/ struck
swear	swore	swearing	sworn
swim	swam	swimming	swum
swing	swung	swinging	swum
take	took	taking	taken
teach	taught	teaching	taught
tear	tore	tearing	torn
thrive	throve/ thrived	thriving	thrived/ thriven
throw	threw	throwing	thrown

Present (stem)	Past	Present Participle	Past Participle
wear	wore	wearing	worn
weep	wept	weeping	wept
win	won	winning	won
write	wrote	writing	written

TEST YOURSELF ON
Forming Principal Parts

In the boxes below, some principal parts are given; others are not. Fill in the blank spaces with the appropriate principal part. Find the part you need by looking at the forms already filled in.

	Stem	Past	Present Participle	Past Participle
1		kept		kept
2	lose			
3		played		
4	tell			told
5	pursue			
6	love	loved		
7			growing	grown
8	answer			
9		dreamt/dreamed	dreaming	
10		tried	trying	
11			asking	asked
12		wanted		
13	shave		shaving	
14	walk	walked		

	Stem	Past	Present Participle	Past Participle
15		sewed		
16			smoking	
17		went		
18		hit		
19			having	
20	build			
21			breaking	
22				seen
23				become
24		rode		
25	prove			

TEST YOURSELF ON
Forming Tenses

Circle the form or forms appropriate to complete each of the phrases given.

Example: 1. I will have   *went, (played,) doing, (grown,) build*

    I will have played and *I will have grown* are correct

1. I will have   *went, played, doing, grown, build*

2. She was   *giving, lose, wrote, prepared, saw*

3. They could have   *became, run, saw, operated, driven*

4. We had   *travel, happened, dreaming, walk, wish*

5. They will   *going, believed, decided, grown, punish*

6. We are not   *became, laughed, dance, jumping, buying*

7. They could be   *want, follow, requested, teach, guess*

8. This property might have been *change, appraise, divide, rent, sold*

9. Complications could not have been *rule, testing, know, avoided, saw*

10. Many men should have *telephone, speaking, singing, talked, known*

11. The ordinary problem is *say, use, suggested, going, called*

12. My son John might have been *named, charge, singing, swearing, known*

Using Verb Tenses Correctly

Present tense

The present tense indicates action taking place at the present moment:

I *suggest* you go later.
He *suggests** we take a walk.
They *suggest* dinner and a movie.

The present tense is also used to indicate an action that is habitual or ongoing:

This dog *bites* people.
My mother *hates* bananas.
Lucia *loves* beautiful plates.

Another form of the present tense is called the progressive present tense. Used with forms of the verb *to be*, it denotes action that is *continuing:*

I *am suggesting* Reading, Writing, and Rhetoric for my freshman students.
He *is draining* the water out of the boat.

---

*Note the *-s* ending on this verb. See **Subject-Verb Agreement** for information about this ending.

Note: Substitute *suggest* for the first verb and *drains* for the second in these sentences. Can you see what is gained or lost by the changes?

Past tense

The past tense consists of a single form—the simple past:

I *suggested* the book.
I *wrote* my paper.

You should be careful to use the proper form of the past. This is not a problem with regular verbs (which end in *-ed* in both the past and the past participle) but it *is* a problem with irregular verbs:

Wrong   I *rung* the bell.
Right   I *rang* the bell.

Wrong   He *torn* his pants.
Right   He *tore* his pants.

Perfect tense

The perfect tense uses the past participle with a form of the auxiliary verb *have*. This tense denotes action begun some time in the past and continuing up to and including the present moment:

I *have written* a letter.
He *has played* basketball every day this week.

The problem in using this tense is that writers frequently use the auxiliary with the *past tense* instead of the auxiliary with the *past participle*. Again, there is no problem when the verb involved is a regular verb; there *is* a problem where the verb is irregular:

Wrong   She *has wrote* her term paper.
Right   She *has written* her term paper.

Wrong   He *has rode* horses since he was a boy.
Right   He *has ridden* horses since he was a boy.

Past perfect tense

The past perfect tense is used to denote the earlier of two actions, both of which have taken place in the past:

Dana *discovered* (simple past tense) that he *had taken* the wrong road (past perfect tense for earlier action)
Bill *saw* that Joanna *had rearranged* the furniture. (the *seeing* is later than the *rearranging*)

Future tense

Few problems are presented by the future tense. It is formed by using the words *will* or *shall* with the infinitive (leaving out the word *to*):

I *will go* tomorrow.
We *shall begin* Wednesday.

Note: In formal English, *shall* in the first person and *will* in the second and third person are used to express simple future:

I shall go to the library tomorrow.
Mary will go with me.

To express more forceful intentions, such as command, promise, or prediction, just the opposite is used: *will* in the first person, *shall* in the second and third.

I will not allow you to borrow my car again.
You shall pay for the repairs.

Future perfect tense

The future perfect tense is used to express the *earlier* of two actions, both of which will be completed in the future:

By the time I *arrive* in Oneonta, she *will have risen*. (*arrive* here is used to denote the *future; will have risen* denotes the earlier of the two actions)
Before I *leave* for the airport, he *will have packed* my bag. (the *leaving* must take place *after* the *packing*)

TEST YOURSELF ON
the Correct Use of Tenses

Underline the verbs in parentheses that make the sentences correct.

1. The tournament will end soon and our team (will lose, will have lost) its chance for the championship.

2. By the time the police get here, the burglar (will be, will have been) gone for half an hour.

3. When Bill (entered, had entered) the room, he saw that Joanna (rearranged, had rearranged) the furniture.

4. I (learned, have learned) quite a lot about Shakespeare this year, and I am hoping to learn even more next year.

5. Fred was terrified that his dog (bit, had bitten) the policeman.

6. By my next birthday, I (will live, will have lived) for half a century.

7. Once I (finished, had finished) writing Volume 1, I (began, had begun) to worry about Volume 2.

8. The people we saw in the restaurant (acted, had acted) like clowns.

9. Lasagna (was, had been) my favorite pasta before I discovered macaroni.

10. When the game (ended, had ended), the stadium (closed, had closed).

11. The chairman (left, had left) the meeting before it (adjourned, had adjourned).

12. He (was brought up, had been brought up) on charges after we (discovered, had discovered) his misconduct.

Some Problems with Verbs

1. Final *-d* or *-ed*

Some writers make the error of omitting a final *-d* or *-ed* from past tense or past participle verb forms. It is especially important that you beware of the problem in one-syllable words, where the *-ed* ending is not likely to be sounded (as in *blamed, dreamed, missed,* and so forth). The *-ed* ending is not so frequently forgotten in words of more than one syllable, such as *completed* or *departed,* but the error is occasionally made in two-syllable words. *Supposed* and *used* (as in *I used to go to church regularly* and *I was supposed to see my analyst today*) are especially likely to be pronounced or written incorrectly.

TEST YOURSELF ON
the Final-*d* Sound

A. Pronounce the following underlined words so that the sound of the final *-d* is clearly heard by other students in the room:

1. I am *tired.*
2. He is *prejudiced.*
3. After he *arrived.*
4. The store he *owned.*
5. The lesson she *learned.*
6. He *blamed* me.
7. The meat is *weighed.*
8. Vegetables are *preferred.*
9. The defendant is *judged.*
10. Students are *graded.*
11. The army *surrendered.*
12. My song was *played.*
13. The crowd *cheered.*
14. Drowning man *saved.*
15. My pay increased.
16. Food is *provided.*
17. Choice is *offered.*
18. Package is *received.*
19. My heart was *deceived.*
20. I am *relieved.*

B. In the passage below, some words have had *-ed* endings removed and some are spelled correctly. Read the passage aloud and notice how the fact that you pronounce some endings (the ones that are there) influences your pronunciation of others (ones that are *not* there). Write in endings wherever they are needed.

Something was needed to cheer me up. I was tire and hadn't been to bed in two days. I thought I would never be rescue and I was worried that even my best friends would not have notice me gone. My foot hurt a lot from when I had slip down the side of the gully and I would have given anything for a little sip of water.

A bird start to chirp. I wish I was as happy as he was. I wish I had his wings!

The accident must have happen because I wasn't as young as I use to be. Still, I was only 23! Are people suppose to lose all their agility after the age of nineteen? It all weighed on my heart. Suddenly, I notice that the sky was getting very dark. If anybody look for me now, they would have a hard time seeing me. I try to move a little, to see if I could climb to the crest of the hill and make myself more visible. But it was no use. I wish I had climbed up there earlier, when I had more strength.

2. Sequence of tenses

If you are using two or more verbs in a sequence, either within a single sentence or in sentences that follow each other, it is important that you indicate precise time to the reader.

A. *Finite verbs* (forms expressing tense, person, number, and mood)

When the Judge *banged* his gavel, the courtroom *grew* silent. (both verbs in the past—both actions took place at the same time in the past)

Although I *have complained,* I *have received* no satisfaction. (two perfect tenses: time started in the past and continuing up to the present, in both cases)

He *said* that he *was* a Martian. (indirect discourse; both tenses should match: here, the past)

By the time I *hand in* my papers, I *will have finished* the term's work. (correct sequence for use of future perfect)

B. *Infinitives* (*to* forms)

Use the present infinitive to indicate action that happens at the same time as or later than the main verb, and use the present perfect infinitive (*to* + *have* + past participle) for action prior to that of the main verb.

Bill *needed* (past tense) *to forget* (present infinitive). Bill needs (present tense) *to forget* (present infinitive)

He would love *to have charged* his purchase. (present perfect infinitive used for time prior to main verb)

C. *Participles*

To denote action happening at the same time as the action of the main verb, use the present participle. To denote action that happened prior to that of the main verb, use the present perfect participle (present participle of *have* + past participle of verb).

Jogging along the main road, he *noticed* many other joggers. (the *noticing* and the *jogging* take place at the same time)

Having mastered geometry, he *knew* he could tackle calculus. (first came the *mastering,* then the *knowing; having mastered* is the present perfect participle)

TEST YOURSELF ON
Sequence of Tenses

Underline the correct verb form in the parentheses for the sequence of tenses in each of the sentences below.

1. Because the patient's heart has begun beating, the doctors believe that the danger to his life (diminished, has diminished).
2. (Having finished, Finishing) the painting, Edward walked away from the easel.
3. They had not expected (to go, to have gone) to California last summer.
4. Pamela plans (to publish, to have published) her novel next year.
5. Arthur thought William missed the point, that he (neglected, had neglected) important issues.

6. (Having been taught, Being taught) good manners by my parents, I did not yawn when he began to speak.
7. (Reaching, Having reached) Chicago, she knew she could drive to Montana.
8. When they (visited, have visited) Italy, they never ate a poor meal.
9. Allan regretted (being born, having been born) handsome instead of rich.
10. Beth wanted (to read, to have read) the books in sequence.
11. Dan insisted that he (once saw, had once seen) a drunken Irishman.
12. (Teaching English, Having taught English), she thought she knew grammar.

3. Could of, being that, would have/had

Never use the expression *could of*. It is an approximation of what some writers hear when they say *could have*.

Wrong He *could of* gone with me to the movies.
Right He *could have* gone with me to the movies.

The same holds true for the forms *would of* and *should of* and any other *of*.

Never use the expression *being that* for *since* or *because*.

Wrong *Being that* he was just a kid, I helped him across the street.
Right *Because* he was just a kid, I helped him across the street.

Never use the expression *would have* in place of *had*.

Wrong If he *would have* done well on his GRE's, he would have been admitted to graduate school.
Right If he *had* done well on his GRE's, he would have been admitted to graduate school.

4. The subjunctive mood

The subjunctive mood expresses actions or states of being that are contrary to fact, wishful, imaginary, or not yet actualities. Current English usage has found substitute expressions for virtually all uses of the subjunctive:

If he *were* to leave ....If he leaves
I imagine he *be* young ....I imagine he *is* young.
I wish I *were* finished ....I wish I *was* finished.

Nevertheless, there are a few circumstances in which the subjunctive is required usage.

A. In contrary-to-fact propositions:

He was eating the pizza as if there *were* nothing else on his mind.
I wish you *were* here.

B. Where clarity is urgently needed:

I insist that the barn *be* painted red. (substituting *is* for *be* makes the sentence say something entirely different, i.e., that the speaker insists the color of the barn *is already* red)

C. In certain *that* clauses.

He moved that the meeting *be* adjourned.
The student asked that he *be* given an oral examination.
Is it right that a woman *suffer* just because she is a woman?
It is necessary that justice *be* done.

The subjunctive also persists in certain idiomatic expressions:

Peace *be* with you.
Be that as it may.
Be it ever so humble, there's no place like home.

TEST YOURSELF ON
the Correct Use of Verb Forms

A. In each of the sentences below, some form of *could, should, would,* or *being* is misused. Correct them.

1. If he would have gone earlier, he would have seen the pre-game show.
2. Being that it had the best psychology program she could find, she went to Jefferson College.

3. I could of been a star.
4. She wasn't as alert as she should of been.
5. If he had gone earlier, he would of seen the pre-game show.

B. For each italicized verb form in the sentences that follow, supply the correct subjunctive form.

1. It is necessary that justice *is* done.
2. He was eating as if there *was* no tomorrow.
3. He suggested that their lunch date *is* postponed until the following week.
4. Is it right that a man *suffers* for someone else's crime?
5. My brother asked that he *is* given the car tomorrow.

UNDERLINING

See **Italics**.

VOICE

Most verbs can be used in either the active or the passive voice.

Active Voice   John *saw* his son yesterday.

Passive Voice   John *was seen* by his son yesterday.

The subject of both sentences is *John*. In the first (active voice) sentence, *John* is performing the action; in the second sentence, *John* is undergoing the action.

In English, the active voice is more vigorous and more emphatic than the passive voice. Beginning writers frequently find their sentences slipping into the passive voice because they are not quite sure what they want to emphasize.

Passive   These fancy jeans *were bought* by me at the Clothes Barn.

Active   I *bought* these fancy jeans at the Clothes Barn.

These sentences convey the same information, but each emphasizes a different thing. The passive emphasizes the *fancy jeans* (because *jeans* is in the subject position in the sentence) and the active emphasizes *I*. The passive sentence also requires two more words to say the same thing that the active sentence says. The passive sentence is also made awkward because of the *by me* phrase.

We emphasize that the active voice is the stronger and therefore the preferred choice because beginning writers, as well as more experienced ones, are frequently evasive in their use of the passive voice. The use of the active voice corrects this tendency.

Evasion by a Beginning Writer

Tutoring help in algebra *is needed* by Al. (the sentence reads as if the writer were a little reluctant to mention Al's name, so he has delayed saying that name as long as possible)

Evasiveness Corrected by Using the Active Voice

Al *needs* tutoring in algebra.

Evasion by a More Experienced Writer

It *has been decided* that your application *will not be considered* at this time. (the evasion here is that no decision-maker is named)

Evasiveness Corrected by Using the Active Voice

We *have decided* not to consider your application.

Of course, there are circumstances where the use of the passive voice is appropriate.

1. Use of the passive voice when the doer of the action is not known.

The making of bronze *was begun* in Southwest Asia around 2500 B.C.

A fire *was set* in an abandoned warehouse on Pier 88 this morning.

It is easy to see why the specific doer in the first of these examples—the person who began to make bronze —is not known. In the second, the opening sentence of a newspaper story, it is clear that the person who set the fire is unknown. Nor would this sentence be improved if the author had written something like "Somebody set a fire . . ." or "A person or persons unknown set a fire. . . ."

2. Use the passive voice when it is more important to emphasize the receiver than the doer of the action.

The vote on the Equal Rights Amendment *was* not *taken* until midnight.

My vegetable garden *was ruined* by the heavy rainstorm in April, but it *was replanted* in time to give us enough vegetables to last the summer.

In the first sentence, the vote on the amendment is much more important than those who voted. In the second, the rainstorm is unimportant compared to the garden (in the first clause), and the people who replanted it less important than the garden itself (referred to by the pronoun *it* in the second clause).

Nevertheless, you should beware of using weakly or evasively passive sentences in a consistent pattern in your work. Sentences such as "This class *was taken* by me last semester" and "My car *was smashed into* by a truck" can only make your writing weak and uninteresting.

TEST YOURSELF ON
the Appropriate Use of the Active Voice

A. Change each of the following passive sentences into an active one.

1. I was bored by the book.
2. Dr. Waldorn is respected by his patients.
3. Everyone on my block is annoyed by Joe's dog.
4. The rich and the famous are admired by most people.
5. The police are angered by disrespect.
6. Financial aid is hoped for by all students.
7. Milk cows are given special care by dairy farmers.
8. Paying bills in an inflationary economy is disliked by everybody.
9. Help is urgently needed by the earthquake victims.
10. Subway riders are exhausted by rush hour traffic.

B. Some of the sentences below use the passive voice appropriately. Next to these, write C. Where the passive voice is either weak or evasive, recast the sentence into the active voice.

1. _____ It is thought by my mother that I'm too young to drive.

2. _____ The Montreal Canadiens were badly beaten by the Boston Bruins at the Montreal Forum last night.

3. _____ Freedom was given to us by God.

4. _____ The ring was given to me for Christmas by my brother.

5. _____ Television is watched by more and more people in this country.

6. _____ Crime is feared more by people in the cities than people in the country.

7. _____ The labels on canned foods are not read by shoppers in supermarkets.

8. _____ While the kids were being filled with Cokes at the fountain, the car was being filled with gas.

9. _____ It is forbidden to feed the animals.

10. _____ The victims of the two-car crash were taken to the hospital by ambulance.

11. _____ The fuse was ignited.

12. _____ Hot cereal was eaten for breakfast by Jake.

WORDINESS

Direct expression is best. Wordiness, the use of more words than necessary, defeats directness. A good rule is to use as few words as possible but as many as necessary to say what you mean. Below are listed some of the writing faults that cause wordiness; discussed under each heading are ways of making your writing more economical.

Redundancy: The Elimination of Deadwood

Redundancy means "needless repetition." Examine your writing carefully to make sure you are not being redundant.

1. Transform your clauses into phrases and your phrases into single words wherever possible. What you eliminate is called *deadwood*.

Unnecessary Clause   The professor, *who teaches mathematics,* was angry.
Revised   The professor *of mathematics* was angry.
Revised   The *mathematics* professor was angry.

Unnecessary Phrase   She was lovely *in appearance.*
Revised   She was lovely.

Deadwood   After the concert had come to a close, we went to dinner.
Revised   After the concert, we went to dinner.

Deadwood   I am learning the skill of how to do the work of the job.
Revised   I am learning how to do the job.

Deadwood   The driver of the truck was angry.
Revised   The truck driver was angry.

2. Eliminate *twofers* from your writing. A *twofer* is the use of two words that mean virtually the same imprecise thing where a single more accurate word, or one of the pair, will do.

Twofer   He was a *real* and *true* friend.
Revised   He was a *genuine* friend.

Twofer   The *light* and the *brightness* were dazzling.
Revised   The *sun* was dazzling.

Twofer   I had a lot of *love* and *regard* for her.
Revised   I *cared* for her very much.

Twofer   She gave me a *warm* and *friendly* smile.
Revised   She gave me a *friendly* smile.

3. Eliminate words that needlessly repeat what you have already said. *He made revised changes in his book* has a needless repetition. The sentence should read either *He made changes in his book* or *He revised his book*.

Repetitious   A hermit is someone who is isolated by himself.
Revised   A hermit is someone who is isolated.

Repetitious   The animals' roars were audible to the ear.
Revised   The animals' roars were audible.

Repetitious   Her shawl was a deep red in color.
Revised   Her shawl was deep red.

Repetitious   The assignments he gave were several in number.
Revised   He gave several assignments.

4. Do not use several words where one will do. Eliminate from your writing such long-winded (and by now hackneyed) expressions as *in this day and age* or *in this modern world* (*today* will do); *it should be noticed* (*notice* will do); and *as far as* _____ *is concerned* (where your subject fits in the blank space; eliminate this construction and just use the noun).

TEST YOURSELF ON
Eliminating Redundancies

The following sentences all contain some kind of redundancy. Correct each one by eliminating the redundancy.

1. John is an expert in the field of urban government.
2. Professor Buckley referred back to the Civil War.
3. The snow which fell yesterday is melting into water today.
4. At 9 a.m. in the morning, the driver started to drive toward Cincinnati.
5. As soon as he started to look for a job, he connected up with a large corporation.
6. I'm going to repeat again what I said a moment ago.
7. As far as reading is concerned, I would say that it is a difficult thing for me to do.
8. Most students spend the majority of the hours in each school day attending classes for which they are registered.
9. Although he seemed to be a warm and friendly man, I didn't care for him or like him for some reason.
10. It was not exactly a meaningful or worthwhile experience.

Awkward Repetition

Effective repetition of words can make for emphasis; awkward repetition is merely wordy: it makes for dullness.

Awkward   The *driver drove* steadily; his *driving* made us feel safe.
Revised   The driver was steady; his skill made us feel safe.

Awkward   My *membership* application was accepted by the club and I was made a *member.*
Revised   The club accepted my membership application.

Awkward   If *one examines* the *case, one can* see that it is one of those *cases* that *cannot* stand close *examination.*
Revised   The case cannot stand close examination.

Effective Repetition   The average politician has a *sinister* past, a *sinister* attitude, and a *sinister plan* for the future.
Effective Repetition   *New* mouthwash, *new* deodorant, *new* toothpaste, *new* teeth—television sells them all with equal enthusiasm.

Wordy Formulas

Eliminate from your writing phrases such as *to be, there is, it is, the type of, of the fact that, the use of.* These can just as well be left out of most sentences.

Wordy   She seems *to be* sad this morning. (read the sentence without the italicized portion and notice that nothing is lost)
Wordy   Higher mathematics appears *to be* difficult.
Wordy   The cowboy was considered *to be* a hero.

Wordy   *There is* something I have to say.
Revised   I have to say something.

Wordy   *It is* the truth that is important.
Revised   The truth is important.

Wordy   I got *the type of* job I wanted.
Revised   I got the job I wanted.

Wordy   Because *of the fact that* it was raining, we couldn't play the game.
Revised   Because it was raining, we couldn't play the game.

Wordy His *use of* English is bad.
Revised His English is bad.

Passive Voice

By using the active instead of the passive voice, you can eliminate words and create a more vigorous style.

Passive Anxiety about examinations *is felt* by some students.
Active Some students *feel* anxious about examinations.

Passive The holiday *was enjoyed* by everybody.
Active Everybody *enjoyed* the holiday.

Complicated Diction

Eliminate complicated diction from your writing. Invariably, the fancy way to say something requires more words than the plain way and is not more effective.

Fancy It is my intention to make a careful scrutiny of the record.
Plain I plan to look closely at the record.

Fancy I observed that his behavior was somewhat less than intelligent.
Plain I told him he was silly.

TEST YOURSELF ON
Eliminating Wordiness

Each of the following sentences contains awkward repetitions, wordy formulas, wordy passive voice constructions, or complicated diction. Correct each by using straightforward, active language.
  1. The important subject of my speech will be a subject important to students, educators, and others to whom the subject is of professional interest.
  2. It should be made clear to everyone that utmost silence is necessary while working in the library.
  3. Whenever he's in trouble, he makes use of rationalization.
  4. There is a special beach I'd like to take you to.
  5. It is a terrible thing to be chronically sick.
  6. That point was made by Darwin.

7. He is the type of person unaware of the fact that people in this modern day and age are unhappy.
8. Because of the fact that we used logic, we solved the problem and came up with the solution.
9. George is known to be moody.
10. Some of the best times we had were when we were on vacation.

The Research Paper Part 3

THE NATURE OF THE RESEARCH PAPER

If you were assigned to write a brief, biographical sketch of your life and your family situation, it would present no problem. You would simply reach into your memory for the necessary information. If the assignment asked that you write on your vocational plans, you would speculate on these, gathering together thoughts and ideas you have had on this subject—again, from the resources of your mind. Even if you were asked to write on, say, the physical and social conditions of your neighborhood or community, you could probably do so from the facts and opinions stored in your mind, buttressed perhaps by things you recall having read about the subject. The research paper differs from these assignments in that you are asked to go outside the resources currently in your mind: for the library research paper, the kind we are interested in here,* you will be asked to gather material available in the library and weave that material into a coherent paper.

Thus the research paper asks you to acquire knowledge that is new to you and come to some conclusion about it. This process is analagous to the course of ordinary experience: as our lives go on, we acquire new knowledge (experience) and we act on (by making conclusions about) that experience or knowledge.

At the outset, it is important to understand that an interesting research paper, and an acceptable one, does not exclude your own opinions and conclusions. A research paper that did so would not only be dull and uninteresting, it would also be a waste of time; you can learn nothing by merely compiling data. Only by thinking deeply about the facts can you learn anything; and the net result of this thought must be a conclusion, an idea, a thesis. For example, a paper entitled "The Use of Acupuncture in Limited Surgery" might present facts about where and under what circumstances surgeons are using acupuncture instead of the standard an-

---

*There are, of course, other kinds of research papers, based on laboratory experiments or other kinds of original investigation.

esthetics, but it would be dry reading, indeed, if you failed to conclude (for example) that *acupuncture for minor surgery is rapidly replacing standard drugs,* or, *acupuncture for minor surgery is reducing the side effects commonly associated with standard drugs.*

Such possible theses not only enliven the research paper, they are also absolutely essential for controlling what you have to say, for organizing your material properly and thus preventing your writing from wandering from the subject.

At this point, you might feel the cold hand of fear: *what do I know about coming to a judgment on such matters?* Do not fear. You know, or, rather, *will know* plenty when you have concluded your research, probably more than most of your readers know about the limited topic you have selected, and therefore you will be quite capable of declaring and defending a thesis about the topic. In writing your library research paper you become an expert—you follow the path of all professional researchers in many fields. You follow, in fact, the pathway that every intelligent human being follows in evaluating experience and coming to general ideas about that experience. From such a pursuit, you have nothing to fear.

FINDING AND NARROWING A TOPIC

Three general limitations govern the selection of a topic for your paper. First, certain topics are eliminated because they are *subjective.* For example, it would be futile to undertake to find out whether the Beatles are better musicians than the Rolling Stones or Whitman a better poet than T. S. Eliot, because such judgments depend on personal taste and no amount of research can possibly decide them.

Second, you must eliminate topics that can be based on a single source, such as an explanation of the process of photosynthesis. For a library paper that will provide you with enough practice in using sources of recorded knowledge—an important goal in writing the paper—

you must consult a number of different sources: eight to ten, depending on how far you and your instructor think you need to go.

Finally, there is the limitation of length. College research papers are usually 1,500 to 2,000 words long, and your paper should *fit* whatever length is decided upon. By *fit* is meant "occupy comfortably." That is, your paper should actually exhaust the topic you are writing about; it should be "worth" the length it is, no more and no less. It's no use trying to write an account of the Women's Liberation Movement in the 1960s in twelve manuscript pages (about 3,000 words), because such an account must surely occupy at least one long book. Similarly, "Naval Battles of World War II" *should* occupy comfortably a dozen large volumes—not sixteen manuscript pages. However, "The Turning Point in the Battle of Midway" (a single naval engagement in the Pacific Ocean in World War II) might be exactly right for the size of the paper you aim to write.

In the light of these preliminary considerations, how should you proceed to find and limit a topic?

First, you should understand that the best topic for your research paper is one that interests you. This interest usually asserts itself in one of two ways. Either you are curious about something and have a question in mind, such as *Why are they fighting in Northern Ireland?* or *Why did Truman drop the atomic bomb instead of demonstrating its power first?* Or you have simply always had an interest in communications or music or computers or literature or China. If you are curious about something and already have a question, you are well on your way toward a manageable research topic. The answers to the two questions above, for example, could very well be theses for two papers—one on the Irish question, the other on the atomic bomb. A student who pursues questions like these by doing introductory reading on the subjects can arrive fairly soon at a topic, either "The Basic Issues in the Conflict in Northern Ireland" or "The Decision to Drop the First Atomic Bomb."

The student with the more general interest, an interest in, say, communications, would need to narrow that topic considerably *before* finding some question that the paper could address. The way to do this is to qualify the word that describes your interest—and to keep on qualifying what you've qualified until you have a string of words that adds up to a topic. Look at these examples:

communications—communication through the mass media— communication through one of the mass media (television)— programing in television—violence in television programing —the effects of violence in television programing—*what is known about the effects of violence in television programing*

John F. Kennedy—the Presidency of John F. Kennedy—foreign policy during the Presidency of John F. Kennedy—foreign policy toward Communist countries during the Presidency of John F. Kennedy—*President Kennedy's decision in the Cuban missile crisis of 1962*

Notice that only the last groups of words in these examples seem suitable for the size of the research paper we are discussing here. Notice, too, that at each step, the narrowing process involves a qualification of the preceding term in the series. You will probably *not* be able to do this in your head; it will require preliminary reading, during which you acquaint yourself further with the single subject (i.e., Communications or John F. Kennedy) that interests you, and find more and more specific aspects of the subject that can be used. (See Preliminary Reading, below.)

The question that can be answered in the television violence paper might be something like *has anyone found a direct connection between watching violence on television and violent behavior in real life?* The Kennedy paper might answer the question *what major considerations went into Kennedy's decision to institute the Cuban missile blockade?*

Another way to think of the ''questions'' that a paper can answer is to regard them as constituting a statement of purpose. That is, you might preface your paper with a statement of purpose in which you pose the question you propose to answer. In fact, If you can formulate this question (or questions) early enough, it will help to guide you more accurately in your research.

If you simply cannot "find" a topic, you must work harder at the search. You need to be continually *active* in your search for a topic by undertaking such inquiries as these:

1. Go over notes for other courses. What issues, people, events puzzle you or excite your interest? Are there problems in anthropology, history, sociology that stick in your memory?

2. Look at your neighborhood or community: what aspects of these places are you curious about? Is there a problem on the streets or on the farm or in the town that you notice and care about?

3. Read a newspaper from cover to cover every day for as long as it takes you to uncover some group, person, or event that excites or interests you. Begin to work with one of those.

4. Ask for an appointment with one of your instructors. Explain your problem and see if the instructor can suggest a broad area of interest.

Finally, let us repeat, only your *active* search can land you a topic—and the sooner the better.

TEST YOURSELF ON
Identifying or Narrowing a Suitable Topic

Listed below are a number of possible topics for the research paper. If you think the topic is suitable, place a checkmark next to it and be prepared to explain why you think so. If it is not suitable, explain why. If it can be successfully narrowed down to make a good topic, do some preliminary reading, after consulting both the list of texts given in this chapter and your instructor, and make it into a useful topic.

1. How to manufacture steel
2. The energy crisis in the United States
3. Abraham Lincoln's military service
4. Norman Lear's situation comedies: what they have in common
5. Mohammed and Jesus

6. The Mormon Settlement of Salt Lake City
7. Symbolism in dreams
8. Gas rationing during World War II
9. The significance of agribusiness to American farming
10. The job market in America for 1979 college graduates

PRELIMINARY READING

At this stage, you may have a topic in hand, or you may still be working toward narrowing down a larger interest or question. Whatever the case, you would do well to begin your work slowly by reading very general material about your topic in one or more of the general reference works listed in this section. The purposes of this preliminary reading, other than to help you narrow down your topic, are to make you broadly acquainted with the field you have chosen to explore and to suggest possible sources for further reading (most, if not all, the works listed here refer the reader to more specific and detailed reading matter). What you read at this stage will probably not appear in your paper, so it is not entirely necessary to take notes while you do it.

A List of Reference Works for Preliminary Reading

One of the glories of modern culture and technology is the systematic collection of information. One of the not inconsiderable pleasures awaiting the student of research techniques is to become aware of this collection —and its dimensions. Below are listed a number of works in one or more of which you may begin your preliminary reading. The great majority of the works listed are encyclopedias and dictionaries with short general articles. Some, however, are bibliographies—books listing sources for further reading. Yet even these bibliographies are valuable for preliminary reading.

You should also know that books entitled "Dictionary of . . ." and "Encyclopedia of . . ." are available about virtually any subject a researcher is likely to be interested in, so if the book you need is not here, do not despair. Ask either your instructor or your librarian to point you to the proper reference work, or consult the standard work on references, Constance M. Winchell, *Guide to Reference Books*, 8th ed.* Your need will be answered.

Agriculture

Cyclopedia of American Agriculture. 4 vols. A popular survey of agriculture in the United States and Canada, covering such topics as crops, livestock, machinery, statistics on productivity.

Arts (Architecture, Dance, Drama, Film, and Music)

American Architecture Since 1780: A Guide to the Styles. Exhaustive descriptions of American architectural styles; arranged chronologically.

Art Dictionary. A compendium of terms used in painting, sculpture, architecture, heraldry, etc. Many of the definitions are accompanied by illustrations.

City Planning: A Basic Bibliography of Sources and Trends. Gives annotations of books and articles on this subject.

Dance Encyclopedia. Revised and enlarged edition. Numerous articles on all phases of the dance, from the so-called primitive to the most sophisticated modern and ballet.

Dictionary of Architecture and Building: Biographical, Historical and Descriptive. 3 vols. Many specialists write on all aspects of these subjects; covers the United States and foreign countries; profusely illustrated.

Dictionary of Films. Lists casts, plots, production information, and critical status of more than 1,300 important American and foreign films.

Dictionary of Filmmakers. Biographical sketches and filmographies of important film artists (actors, directors, producers, cameramen) from the beginnings of the art to 1971.

Encyclopedia of Folk, Country and Western Music. Covers the development and aesthetics of these branches of popular music.

Encyclopedia of Jazz. Biographies of over 2,000 jazz performers from the beginnings through 1959; history of jazz on records; discography and bibliography.

*Many of the annotations of these reference works are based on details given in Winchell.

Encyclopedia of Painting: Painters and Painting of the World from Prehistoric Times to the Present Day. Illustrated one-volume encyclopedia of art, artists, styles, etc.

Encyclopedia of World Art, 15 vols. Long and detailed articles on every aspect of art, every country, period, genre, etc. Many bibliographies.

Grove's Dictionary of Music and Musicians. 5th ed. 10 vols. Articles on music, forms, styles, instruments—and musicians of all periods.

Harvard Dictionary of Music. 2nd ed. rev. and enl. Omits biographies of musicians, but in its historical emphasis covers virtually all other aspects of music.

New Oxford History of Music. 11 vols. A survey of music from ancient times to 1960. Covers every aspect of the art. However, biographical material is not detailed. Many short excerpts from musical scores are given as examples of particular styles and forms.

New York Times Film Reviews. Collects all this newspaper's film reviews from 1913 to 1970; contains index of titles, names of people associated with films, and awards.

Oxford Companion to the Theatre. Complete coverage of all aspects of theater in all countries of the world—plays, theatres, actors, scenery, etc.

The Reader's Encyclopedia of World Drama. Gives historical accounts of various developments in theatre and of theatres all over the world, and includes titles of plays and biographies of playwrights.

Banking and Finance

Economic Almanac. An annual published between 1940 and 1968-9. Provides every significant statistic related to housing, finance, trade, industry, etc. in the United States. Several chapters deal with international finance. A glossary defines frequently used economics terms.

Encyclopedia of Banking and Finance. 6th ed. Also defines terms; also has articles on money, commodities, banking practices, and much else in the field.

McGraw-Hill Dictionary of Modern Economics. A handbook of terms and economic institutions and organizations.

Biography

Chambers's Biographical Dictionary. Gives brief biographies of the more famous people who have ever lived in the world—includes kings, queens, princes, etc.

Current Biography. 37 vols. and supplements. Valuable source of biographical data on people who have recently made some achievement.

Dictionary of American Biography. 20 vols. and supplements. Biographies of noted Americans no longer living.

Dictionary of National Biography. 22 vols. and supplements. The British equivalent of the preceding work.

New Century Cyclopedia of Names. 3 vols. Includes names of literary characters and names from myth and legend.

Notable American Women: 1607–1950. 3 vols. Biographies of women, prominent or important members of American society.

Webster's Biographical Dictionary. Contains brief biographies of people of all nationalities and all time periods.

Who's Who. Annual list of prominent British citizens, giving biographical data supplied by those listed. *Who Was Who* is the companion volume listing those no longer living.

Who's Who in America. The equivalent to the preceding, appearing biennially. The companion is *Who Was Who in America.*

Note: There are a number of volumes that begin with the words *Who's Who in . . .* that are useful to locate information on people in special fields (*Who's Who in France, Who's Who in Australia,* etc.). These may be supplemented by such works as *The Directory of American Scholars, American Men and Women of Science* (11 vols.), etc.

Current Events

Americana Annual. Annual supplement to the *Encyclopedia Americana.** Contains signed essays on the past year's events and longer articles dealing with topics of public interest; profusely illustrated.

Britannica Book of the Year. Alphabetically arranged review of the past year. Contains detailed articles on a cross-section of topics, written by specialists; many charts, tables, photographs.

Facts on File. A weekly digest of world news, with annual index; useful compendium of events in politics, science, sports, education, etc.

Statesman's Yearbook. Gives current information—including statistics and some historical data—about all the countries of the world.

Statistical Abstract of the United States. Statistics of every imag-

*For fuller information about general encyclopedias, see Preparing a Bibliography.

inable kind on the status and activities of United States citizens.

World Almanac and Book of Facts. A one-volume work that reports international statistical information. Also contains short essays on various topics and biographical sketches of important people. Arranged by subject.

Note: "Almanacs," of which the above is only one, compile statistics and lists of notable events—records, appointments to important posts, etc.—over the year, year by year. "Yearbooks," do approximately the same—sometimes in greater detail, sometimes by signed articles on various subjects, such as politics, foreign affairs, etc.

Ecology

Advances in Ecological Research. A periodical first published in 1962. Articles on all aspects of the field.

An Ecological Glossary. Terms defined; bibliographies.

Ecology and Environmental Quality: A Selected and Annotated Bibliography. A good index of the literature.

The Ecology Action Guide. Discusses man's influence on nature and the accretion of pollutants and suggests courses of action.

Ecology of Populations. A discussion of biotic communities and studies in population.

The Environment Index. An annual published since 1971; gives references to the literature.

Environmental Conservation. 3rd ed. Discussions of natural resources and the principles involved in their conservation.

A Geography of Plants and Animals. World-wide distribution of plants and animals and their places in the ecosystem.

A Guide to the Study of Terrestrial Ecology. Articles on the environment and experimental work in ecosystems.

Man's Impact on Terrestrial and Oceanic Ecosystems. Articles on various aspects of these subjects; includes bibliographies.

Who's Who in Ecology. Biographical sketches of the leading workers in the field and their affiliations.

Wildlife in Danger. Contains short, detailed articles about endangered species and some on the verge of extinction. Discusses natural habitats, physical characteristics, ecological status of the animals; includes many photographs and illustrations.

Education

Dictionary of Education. Gives definitions of technical and professional terms. It defines common foreign terms; cross-referenced.

Educator's Complete ERIC Handbook. A valuable set of abstracts of articles and reports of research on the education of disadvantaged and culturally deprived children.

Encyclopedia of Education. 10 vols. More than 1,000 signed articles dealing with various aspects of education: history, institutions, theory, philosophy, etc.

Encyclopedia of Educational Research. Contains articles by educators on the latest developments in the field of education.

World Survey of Education. 4 vols. A publication of UNESCO; covers all levels of education, arranged by countries of the world.

Ethnic Studies

American Indian Almanac. Gives complete data on Native Americans of the United States. Arranged by geographical area.

Black Studies: A Bibliography. A guide to the literature.

Directory of Afro-American Resources. Gives a list of primary sources—documents, diaries, papers, narratives—available through organizations and institutions in the United States.

Ethnic Studies in Higher Education: State of the Art and Bibliography. Gives general information, sources, research issues on Blacks, Chicanos, Asian-Americans, Native Americans, Puerto Rican and other Spanish-speaking peoples, and various white ethnic groups.

The Mexican American: A Selected and Annotated Bibliography. Gives excellent annotations for materials available through 1968.

Mexican Americans: A Research Bibliography. 2 vols. A computer-assisted bibliography that covers the whole subject by theme and topic.

Minority Studies: A Selective Annotated Bibliography. Gives select materials available through 1974 on a rich selection of American minorities, including Hawaiians, Filipinos, Japanese, Chinese, Blacks, Spanish-Americans, and Native Americans.

The Negro in America: A Bibliography. 2nd ed., rev. and enl. Arranged by topics such as health, intergroup relations, art, literature.

The Puerto Ricans: An Annotated Bibliography. Arranged by topic, covers history, geography, current status.

Reference Encyclopedia of the American Indian. 2nd ed. 2 vols. A guide to sources of information about Native Americans. Includes a who's who and bibliographies.

History

Cambridge Ancient History. 12 vols. Immensely detailed history of the Western World from the beginnings through the middle of the 4th century A.D.

Cambridge Medieval History. 8 vols. The same for the Medieval period, to the beginning of the Renaissance.

Dictionary of American History. 7 vols. plus supplement. Consists of short articles on all aspects of American history.

Chronology of the Modern World, 1763 to the Present Time. This and a companion volume, *Chronology of the Expanding World, 1492-1762,* cover the history of all areas from Columbus onward.

Documents of American History. 8th ed. Gives documents of importance in the Western world since the time of Columbus.

An Encyclopedia of World History. 5th ed., rev. and enl. A one-volume treatment of world events.

A Guide to the History of Science. A beginning guide to the history of science, with introductory essays on science and tradition.

Harper Encyclopedia of the Modern World, 1760 to the Present. One-volume history arranged by periods, subjects and geographical areas. Ends at 1970.

Harvard Guide to American History. rev. ed. 2 vols. A guide to research; methods and resources; contains valuable bibliographies arranged by periods.

New Cambridge Modern History. 14 vols. A detailed history from the Renaissance onwards.

Literature and Mythology

Cambridge History of American Literature. 4 vols. From the Colonial through the modern periods, ending in the 1930s.

Cambridge History of English Literature. 15 vols. From the Anglo-Saxon beginnings through the modern period, ending in the 1930s.

Cassell's Encyclopaedia of World Literature. 2nd ed., 3 vols. rev. Articles on world authors, with biographies and bibliographies.

Columbia Dictionary of Modern European Literature. Begins at the end of the 19th century and gives critical commentary on many works of the modern period.

Dictionary of Mythology, Mainly Classical. Emphasizes Greek and Roman mythological characters.

Everyman's Dictionary of Non-Classical Mythology. Emphasizes non-Western mythology.

Funk & Wagnall's Standard Dictionary of Folklore, Mythology and Legend. 2 vols. Covers the mythologies of the world. (1972 ed. is 1 vol.; it is a reissue of the 1949-50 ed. with minor corrections.)

The Golden Bough. 12 vols. (Also available in one-volume edition.) An exhaustive study of mythology.

Harper's Dictionary of Classical Literature and Antiquities. Covers not only literature but the other arts and historical objects and events as well.

New Larousse Encyclopedia of Mythology. Essays on world mythologies.

A Library of Literary Criticism: Modern American Literature. 3rd ed. Gives samples of literary criticism of the works of twentieth-century American authors.

Literary History of England. 2nd ed. 4 vols. Also available in one-volume edition. Complete literary history from the Anglo-Saxon through the modern periods.

Literary History of the United States. 4th ed. rev. 2 vols. The second volume is a bibliography; the first, a history of American literature from the Colonial through the modern periods.

Mythology of all Races. 13 vols. Mythologies in very great detail.

New Century Classical Handbook. Includes the most recent information on archaeological findings. Well illustrated.

Oxford Classical Dictionary. 2nd ed. Good brief articles on classical subjects.

Oxford Companion to American Literature. 4th ed., rev. and enl. Excellent source for brief articles on all aspects of American literature.

Philosophy

The Concise Encyclopedia of Western Philosophy and Philosophers. Concise articles, by scholars, on the main figures and ideas.

Encyclopedia of Philosophy. 8 vols. Contains entries on both Western and Eastern philosophers and philosophies.

History of Western Philosophy. An excellent overview by a noted philosopher, Bertrand Russell.

How to Find Out in Philosophy and Psychology. A guide, for undergraduates, to research methods in these fields.

Political Science

Cyclopedia of American Government. 3 vols. Brief articles on all aspects of government in the United States from the founding to the early twentieth century.

Dictionary of American Politics. A one-volume compendium of aspects and figures of American politics.

International Encyclopedia of the Social Sciences. 17 vols. Longer articles on political movements and ideas—as well as on comprehensive subjects in the social sciences.

Palgrave's Dictionary of Political Economy. 3 vols. Reprints of classic articles on economics as it relates to politics.

Religion

Book of Saints. 5th ed. A dictionary of canonized saints, together with a calendar of their days and brief biographies.

Concise Encyclopedia of Living Faiths. Detailed articles on all world religions.

A Dictionary of Angels, Including the Fallen Angels. Information about all the angels and angelology.

Dictionary of the Bible. Entries on people and places mentioned in the Bible.

Encyclopedia of the Jewish Religion. A compendium of information on theology and history of Jewish religion.

Encyclopaedia of Religion and Ethics. 13 vols. Very detailed articles on all aspects.

History of Religions. 2 vols. Detailed accounts of the rise of religions in Europe, Asia, and the Near East.

Interpreter's Bible . . . 12 vols. Contains the King James and Revised Standard Versions along with extended commentaries.

New Catholic Encyclopedia . . . 15 vols. Treats every aspect of Catholicism in great detail.

New Schaff-Herzog Encyclopedia of Religious Knowledge . . . 13 vols. plus supplements. An encyclopedic work.

Sacred Books of the East. 50 vols. Contains translations of the major works of the seven non-Christian religions that have influenced Asian culture. The *Concise Dictionary of Eastern Religion* is an index to these volumes.

Science

Britannica Yearbook of Science and the Future. Annual; gives the latest scientific developments—with illustrations.

The Dictionary of the Biological Sciences and *Encyclopedia of the Biological Sciences.* 2nd ed. Together, these cover all aspects of the field.

A Dictionary of Genetics. 2nd ed. Gives a chronology of developments in this field, a bibliography, and a list of laboratories working in the field.

Famous First Facts. 3rd ed. A record of discoveries and inventions in the United States, with dates and descriptions.

Harper Encyclopedia of Science. rev. ed. 4 vols. (Also available in one-volume edition.) A very complete work, covering all aspects of science.

History of Magic and Experimental Science. 8 vols. Details the history and development of the experimental sciences and ideas of magic which at one time or another served a scientific function.

McGraw-Hill Encyclopedia of Science and Technology: An International Reference Work. 15 vols. Supplemented by the *McGraw-Hill Yearbook of Comprehensive Science and Technology.* Contains general and specific essays dealing with every branch of science and technology. Biographical and historical material is not included. Psychology and medicine are treated only in their preprofessional aspects.

Van Nostrand's Scientific Encyclopedia 5th ed. A one-volume compendium of inclusive scientific knowledge.

Social Sciences

American Labor Unions: What They Are and How They Work. A standard reference work in this field.

Anthropology Today: An Encyclopedic Inventory. Extensive bibliographies of work in this field up to 1952; gives the range and extent of the whole field.

Dictionary of Psychology. rev. ed. Defines terms and gives foreign equivalents.

Handbook for Social Research in Urban Areas. A guide to research on urban sociological themes; bibliographies.

Harvard List of Books on Psychology. 3rd ed. A selected bibliography with supplements.

History of Psychiatry: An Evaluation of Psychiatric Thought and Practice from Prehistoric Times to the Present. A comprehensive review of ideas and developments in the field.

How to Find Out in Philosophy and Psychology. A guide for undergraduates to research methods in these fields.

International Encyclopedia of the Social Sciences. 17 vols. A comprehensive set of articles on all aspects of the social sciences.

Professional Problems in Psychology. A sourcebook for information on the field and information on the profession.

Women's Studies

American Women: The Official Who's Who Among the Women of the Nation. 3 vols. Published from 1935-1940. A valuable source of biographies of accomplished women of the period.

The Book of Women's Achievements. A list of these achievements and notes on the achievers, arranged by area of work.

The Changing Role of Women: A Select Bibliography. A bibliography of literature on this subject.

Female Studies. 6 vols. College syllabi for study; reading lists; a review of women's studies.

Index to Women of the World from Ancient to Modern Times. A list; brief biographies, bibliographies.

Library on the History of Women in America. 3 vols. Manuscript inventories and the catalogs of manuscripts, books, and pictures in the library of Radcliffe College. A useful sourcebook.

Professional Women and Minorities: A Manpower Resource Service. A comprehensive set of statistics on the professional status of these groups.

Research Guide in Women's Studies. A valuable guide to writing research papers in this field.

Who's Who and Where in Women's Studies. Courses, colleges, teachers, researchers.

Women and Society: A Critical Review of the Literature with a Selected Annotated Bibliography. The title is accurate.

Women's Organizations and Leaders Directory. Rev. ed. 1975. Gives names and addresses of organizations useful to women and the leaders of the women's movement.

Women's Rights Almanac. State-by-state lists giving information sources and other resources of interest to women; discussions of legal issues important to women.

The World Who's Who of Women. Published from time to time; gives brief biographies of prominent women of the world.

Women and Sport. Bibliography of research involving female subjects.

Note: There are numerous books beginning with the words "Women and" and ending in the name of some specialized field of work.

Other General Reference Works

Two other types of general reference works should be mentioned here.

General encyclopedias

For preliminary reading as well as for bibliographic references, the most useful general encyclopedias are the *Encyclopaedia Britannica* and the *Encyclopedia Americana*. Good one-volume works are the *Columbia Encyclopedia* and the *Random House Encyclopedia*.

Dictionaries

These rarely contain bibliographies, but the student working in the field of language should know about these useful sources:

General

A Dictionary of American English on Historical Principles. 4 vols.

The Oxford English Dictionary. 12 vols. and supplement. Also issued in a two-volume Compact Edition, complete but photographically reduced.

Webster's Third New International Dictionary

Special

Dictionary of Afro-American Slang
Dictionary of Word and Phrase Origins
Oxford Dictionary of English Etymology
Dictionary of Slang and Unconventional English. 7th ed.
Dictionary of American Slang. 2nd ed.

TEST YOURSELF ON
Using Reference Works

In order to gain practice in using general reference works in the library, find at least five general reference works in which you can find information on:

1. your research paper topic,
or
2. a sample topic assigned by your instructor,
or
3. one of the following topics: a. the development of computers; b. Napoleon Bonaparte (1769–1821); c. the Iroquois

Indians; d. gas rationing in the U.S.; e. the drug *laetrile;* f. the origins of the Democratic party in the U.S.; g. dolphins.

PREPARING A BIBLIOGRAPHY

After your preliminary reading has been completed, you are ready to prepare a bibliography. For our purposes, it is useful to distinguish between a *working bibliography* and a *final bibliography*. The working bibliography is a list of books, articles, pamphlets and other reference materials—*the* list from which your paper will be written; it is kept on a series of index cards, one card for each publication (see below for a discussion of how to set up a working bibliography on index cards). The final bibliography is a typed list of those publications actually used in the preparation of your paper; it is appended to the final draft. Thus it is possible to end up with a final bibliography that is not identical with the working bibliography; along the way, you may drop some items from the working bibliography and, of course, add others. For now, however, your task is to begin to put together a manageable list of publications with which you can begin to do research.

Naturally, every researcher's project is different, and each writer will have to look in different places in order to compile a list. But a familiarity with the principal sources for locating materials on any topic is a crucial asset in your search, and you should become acquainted with these.

The card catalog

Probably your most important source will be the library's card catalog, which lists alphabetically on 3″×5″ index cards every piece of printed or filmed material the library owns. For each book, there are usually three cards: an author card, a title card, and a subject card (see p. 327 for samples of all three kinds). Some books have additional subject cards and/or additional author cards if there are two or more authors. The author card is always the basic card; all other cards are duplicates

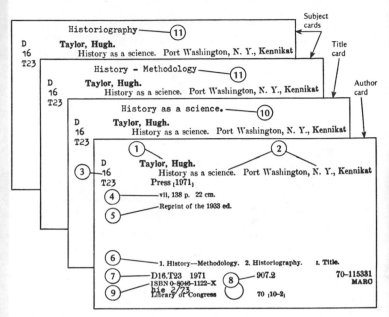

1—Author's name; following name, author's dates often are given.
2—Title of book, place of publication, name of publisher, edition, date of publication or copyright (brackets around year indicate that date is not printed on title page).
3—Call number in the library being used.
4—Number of pages (roman numerals indicate 7 pages of introductory matter); illustrations, if present; height of book in centimeters. (As this book is a little under 9″ high, it would normally be found in its regular shelf place; large books often are shelved on a separate large-size shelf.)
5—Explanatory notes; description of special features, if present.
6—Other places in the card catalog where cards for this book are filed. These other cards are shown here.
7—Call number under the Library of Congress System.
8—Call number under the Dewey Decimal System.
9—International Standard Book Number.
10—Title.
11—Subject.

of this card, with the title or subject heading typed at the top.

The different kinds of cards are there to help you in your research. You may, for example, remember that a particular author writes well on a subject that interests

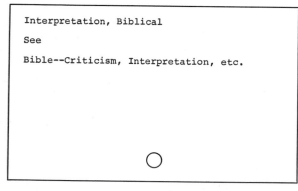

```
 Culture Conflict

     See also

Marriage, mixed

Miscegenation

Race problems
```

This card appears at the head of the subject "Culture Conflict"

```
Interpretation, Biblical

See

Bible--Criticism, Interpretation, etc.
```

you. Finding that author's name in the catalog will lead you to the books you want. Or you may remember a title but not the author; the title card will be most useful to you in that case. Finally, if you know neither author nor title but have only a subject in mind, the card catalog lists books under numerous subject headings.

Moreover, the card catalog also includes cross-reference cards. A cross-reference card will give a subject heading not used in the library and then go on to tell you what related subject heading you should look for (see samples above). These cross-reference cards also suggest additional subject headings to look under—even when the subject heading you sought is actually used.

It is useful to read the explanatory key printed with the sample cards on p. 327, because knowing what the card symbols mean can help you to select books on your topic that are especially valuable rather than just general. For example, a card may offer information on the book's contents, whether or not it contains a bibliography (and if so, how long), illustrations, maps, graphs, etc. When you can quickly assimilate this information, you can make a much shrewder choice of books to add to your working bibliography than a researcher who cannot. Take another example: paying attention to dates of publication and information on the edition of the book (how many times it has been revised and reissued) can also be useful. As a researcher, you may be making a good choice by consulting a recently published work on your topic, but you should also consult a book whose first edition was published, say, ten years ago but whose latest edition is marked "4th ed." This information would suggest that the book may be on its way to achieving status close to that of a standard in its field—by virtue of its having been reissued so often over so short a period of time.

The card catalog is probably the first place to go and a place to return to often.

Lists of periodicals

Researchers who want to locate a periodical should consult one of the following:

Ayer Directory of Publications. A standard source of information about newspapers and magazines published in the United States, Canada, Bermuda, Panama, and the Phillipines.
Ulrich's International Periodicals Directory. Periodicals of the whole world, arranged by subject.
Union List of Serials in Libraries of the United States and Canada

Indexes to periodical literature

Articles in newspapers and magazines are an important source for research material, but they are not listed in the library's card catalog and must be sought in the various indexes to periodical literature. The major index for articles on a wide variety of subjects published in nonspecialized magazines is the *Readers' Guide to Periodical Literature*. This is published twice a month and then cumulated in annual volumes. Articles are indexed by subject and author and by titles of certain creative works (including films). Here is a sample set of entries from the *Readers' Guide:*

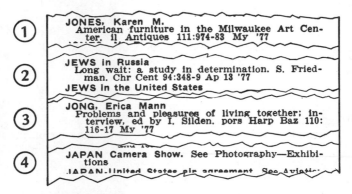

①
JONES, Karen M.
    American furniture in the Milwaukee Art Center. il Antiques 111:974-83 My '77

②
JEWS in Russia
    Long wait: a study in determination. S. Friedman. Chr Cent 94:348-9 Ap 13 '77
JEWS in the United States

③
JONG, Erica Mann
    Problems and pleasures of living together; interview, ed by I. Silden. pors Harp Baz 110:116-17 My '77

④
JAPAN Camera Show. See Photography—Exhibitions
JAPAN-United States air agreement. See Aviati...

1—Author entry for illustrated article, "American Furniture in the Milwaukee Art Center," in *Antiques* magazine, volume 111, pages 974–983, May 1977 issue.

2—Subject entry for article by S. Friedman in *Christian Century*, volume 94, pages 348–349, issue of April 13, 1977.

3—Another subject entry, but this subject is a person: the writer Erica Jong. Entry refers to an interview with her, illustrated with several portraits, in *Harper's Bazaar*, volume 110, pages 116–117, May 1977 issue.

4—Cross-reference entry that refers to the Photography section of the *Guide.*

Very useful for topics of current interest as well as for topics that require day-by-day information dating back to 1851 is *The New York Times Index*. The *Index* refers you to articles in the *Times*, giving date of issue and page number. Here is a set of sample entries:

Pk and attached devices to study their behavior; details; Natl Geographic Soc and Natl Science Foundation sponsors, D 19,58:1
BEARSTED, Lord (Marcus Richard Samuel). See Hill, Samuel & Co
BEASLEY, (Asst Sec) D Otis. To retire, D 11,31:5
BEATLES, The (George Harrison, John Lennon, Paul McCartney, Ringo Starr). See Motion Pictures—Revs, Hard Day's Night; Help!.Music—Gen F 13,19, My 19, Ag 11 par. Music—Tours, Foreign. Recordings Je 10, Ag 9, N 9, D 14,17. TV—Programs, Beatles

R Starr weds M Cox, London, F 12,19:1

Queen Elizabeth names Beatles members of Brit Empire Order, Je 12,1:8; Brit reaction, Je 13,3:2; MP H Dupuis (Canada) to return his medal in protest, Je 15,15:1

2 Brit war heroes protest award of Brit Empire Order, Je 16,13:1; Lt Col Wagg returns all 12 of his medals to Queen in protest, Je 17,3:3; comment on dispute; group of Labor MPs signs motion welcoming award, Je 20,IV,5:3

Investiture ceremony, Buckingham Palace; illus, O 27,49:8
BEATON, Cecil. Diaries, 1939-44, revd, N 7,VII, p90

Notes on the "BEATLES" entry:

1—Paragraph 1 compresses much information in a group of cross references to full entries elsewhere: (1) Reviews and other news items about the Beatles' movies *A Hard Day's Night* and *Help!* can be located by looking up the titles under the index heading Motion Pictures—Reviews. (2) News items relating to the Beatles' music printed on February 13 and 19, May 19, and August 11 (paragraph) are described and further indentified under the index heading Music—General, where the entries are arranged in order of dates of news items. (3) News items about the Beatles' tours can be found under Music—Tours, Foreign, alphabetically under "Beatles." (4) Items about the Beatles' recordings printed on June 10, August 9, November 9, December 14 and 17 are described and further identified under the index heading Recordings, where the entries are in order of dates. (5) Items about the Beatles' TV programs can be found under Television—Programs, alphabetically under "Beatles."

Following are a number of actual entries describing and locating general news items:

2—Paragraph 2 refers to a news story about Ringo's marriage to M. Cox in London; the article appears in the February 12 *Times* on page 19, column 1.

3, 4, 5—These paragraphs concern the award of the Order of the British Empire to the Beatles and the uproar this caused among certain British citizens. At the end of paragraph 4, the roman number "IV" refers to section 4 of the paper. At the end of paragraph 5, the abbreviation "illus" means that the article is accompanied by one or more photographs.

The New York Times Index. Copyright © 1965 by The New York Times Company. Reprinted by permission.

Specialized indexes

In addition to the periodical indexes, you can consult a large number of specialized indexes, by subject area. The following is only a partial list:

Agricultural Index
Applied Science and Technology Index
Art Index
Bibliographic Index
Biological and Agricultural Index
Book Review Index
Business Periodicals Index
Education Index
Engineering Index
Essay and General Literature Index
Index of Economic Journals
Index to Legal Periodicals
Music Index
Public Affairs Information Service Bulletin
Social Sciences and Humanities Index
United Nations Documents Index

In addition to these, numerous other, even more specialized, indexes are available, and listed in the card catalog. Look for the cards that follow a subject or author entry that have printed across the top in red the words *BIBLIOGRAPHY* or *INDEX*.

Note: All indexes, including the *Readers' Guide* and *The New York Times Index,* supply the reader with keys to their abbreviations. These "key" pages usually appear at the front of the volume. Looking over these pages before you begin to search the volume can usually save you a great deal of time and confusion.

Government documents

The Federal government publishes an enormous amount of material on numerous subjects. Guides to this literature are the *Monthly Catalog of United States*

Government Publications and the *Monthly Checklist of State Publications*.

TEST YOURSELF ON
Information Sources

Using your research paper topic or a sample topic assigned to the whole class, make a list of subject headings under which you might find information sources. Take the list to the library and look up each subject heading in the following three sources:

1. *Readers' Guide*.
2. *The New York Times Index*.
3. The card catalog.

Add to your list of subject headings as you discover new ones. Which source was best for your particular topic? Why?

Setting up the working bibliography

The mechanics of setting up your working bibliography are simple and may appear to you to be excessively tedious. But if you establish good work habits at this stage, your life (while working on this paper) will be free of stress. Skipping past the meticulousness required here will surely cause you grief later—the experience of millions of researchers attests to that fact.

For this work, you should acquire 3″x5″ lined index cards. Use one card for each book or article or pamphlet—*never* put more than one entry on a single card. Following are sample cards for a book and a magazine article. Note carefully the reasons behind including each bit of information.

Sample bibliographical entries for various kinds of published materials begin on p. 335. You may use these entries as models in setting up your working bibliography. These are later transferred to a typed list and used as your final bibliography (see below for instructions on setting up the final bibliography). Note carefully the order in which information is presented, and the exact punctuation used to separate the items.

PS
3537
T+753
Z6216
  ①

② ⑦

Burney, William.
            ③
<u>Wallace Stevens</u>. Twayne
United States Authors
Series. New York :
Twayne Publishers, 1968

④ Has bibliography of secondary
sources.

AP2.1A
  ①

② ⑧

McPhee, John. ③
"Coming into the Country III."
<u>The New Yorker</u>, July 4, 1977.
Pp. 33-65. ⑤

⑥ 3rd part of four-part
article. Has data on legal
status of Alaskan gold miners.

1—The call number of the book or magazine volume; once you've
noted it here, you need not return to the card catalog every time you
want the book or article.

2—Your own item number. In your rough first draft of the paper, you
can use this number in your rough footnotes. You also use this number on your notecards.

3—Name of author, exact title, facts of publication. Being exact here
can save you trouble: you can use this card for your final bibliography.

4—An important note reminding yourself of an especially useful feature
of the source.

5—Exact page numbers of the article.

6—Note reminding yourself that this article is one of a series and that
it contains data of special interest to you.

A BOOK

Waldhorn, Arthur. <u>A</u> <u>Reader's</u> <u>Guide</u> <u>to</u> <u>Ernest</u>
<u>Hemingway</u>. New York: Farrar, Straus and
Giroux, 1972.

A WORK IN SEVERAL VOLUMES

Jaeger, Werner. <u>Paideia:</u> <u>The</u> <u>Ideals</u> <u>of</u> <u>Greek</u>
<u>Culture</u>. Trans. Gilbert Highet. 3 vols. New
York: Oxford University Press, 1943.

A LATER OR REVISED EDITION

French, Robert Dudley. <u>A</u> <u>Chaucer</u> <u>Handbook</u>. 2nd
ed. New York: Appleton-Century-Crofts, Inc.,
1955.

THE WORK OF SEVERAL AUTHORS

Lynn, Naomi B., Ann B. Matasar, and Marie Barovic
Rosenberg. <u>Research</u> <u>Guide</u> <u>in</u> <u>Women's</u>
<u>Studies</u>. Morristown, N.J.: General Learning
Press, 1974.

NOTE: Where there is more than one author, only the first author's name is inverted.

A GENERAL REFERENCE WORK

"Fleming, Sir Alexander," <u>Chambers's</u> <u>Biographical</u>
<u>Dictionary</u>. New Edition. P. 476a.

AN ARTICLE FROM AN EDITED COLLECTION

Rovit, Earl H. "Ralph Ellison and the American
Comic Tradition." In <u>Ralph</u> <u>Ellison:</u> <u>A</u>
<u>Collection</u> <u>of</u> <u>Critical</u> <u>Essays</u>, ed. John
Hersey. Englewood Cliffs, N.J.: Prentice-
Hall, Inc., 1974.

ARTICLES FROM WEEKLY MAGAZINES

Otten, Jane. "Living in Syntax." <u>Newsweek</u>,
December 30, 1974, p. 9.
"Coming Across." <u>The</u> <u>New</u> <u>Yorker</u>, June 27, 1977,
pp. 26-27.

AN ARTICLE FROM A MONTHLY MAGAZINE

Mattingly, Ignatius C. "Some Cultural Aspects of
      Serial Cartoons, or Get A Load of Those
      Funnies." Harper's, December 1955, pp. 34-39.

AN ARTICLE IN A LEARNED JOURNAL

Erikson, Erik H. "The Problem of Ego Identity."
      Journal of the American Psychoanalytic
      Association, 4 (January 1956), 56-121.

NEWSPAPER ARTICLES

Maitland, Leslie. "Story of an East Side Policeman
      Who Turned in Fellow Officers." The New York
      Times, July 3, 1977, sec. 1, pp. 1, 33.
"Eight Firemen Injured as Tenement Burns." The New
      York Times, July 3, 1977, sec. 1, p. 25.

A PUBLIC DOCUMENT

U.S. Congress. Senate. Committee on the
      Judiciary. Hearings before the Subcommittee
      to Investigate Juvenile Delinquency.
      Washington, D.C.: Government Printing Office,
      1954.

Setting up the final bibliography

To do this job, take your working bibliography cards,
the ones you have actually used in writing your paper,
and alphabetize them according to the authors' last
names. For unsigned articles, alphabetize by the first
letter of the first word, excluding the initial words *the*
or *a*. Then simply type the cards into a list that looks
like the final bibliography shown at the end of the sample research paper (p. 395). Be sure to use a heading and
to follow the spacing and indentation of the sample—in-
denting five spaces for the second and subsequent lines
of the bibliographical citation and double-spacing between entries. Notice that items in a final bibliography
are not numbered.

TEST YOURSELF ON
Bibliography Form

Using the forms just discussed, set up working bibliography cards for each of the following items.

1. A book by Claude Lévi-Strauss called Structural Anthropology, translated by Claire Jacobson and Brooke G. Scoepf and published in New York City in 1963 by Basic Books, Inc.
2. An article by Donald Kaplan called On Preaching Old Virtues while Practicing Old Vices: A Psychoanalytic Perspective on Morality. It was published in the Bulletin of the Menninger Clinic, volume 39, number 2, in March 1975, on pages 113-130.
3. A book in two volumes by Vernon L. Parrington called Main Currents in American Thought, published in New York by Harcourt, Brace & World, Inc., in 1954.
4. A newspaper article by Christopher S. Wren called Soviet Sharpens Criticism of U.S. Plans for Missile, published on page 1 of the New York Times for July 4, 1977 and continued on page 2.
5. A book edited by Mary Jane Moffat and Charlotte Painter called Revelations: Diaries of Women. It was published in 1974 by Random House in New York.

READING AND TAKING NOTES

You are now ready to begin a period of intensive reading of the works you have compiled for your working bibliography.

How do you go about it and how do you take notes on what you've read?

First, avoid crashing; that is, avoid all emergency schedules—such as all-night sessions or forty-eight-hour squeezes. Instead, *plan* a reading period of, say, two work weeks, ten days, in which you read either in the library or in your room for two to three hours a session.

Second, what should you read? Obviously, you

should read the whole of every article you select for your working bibliography, but should you read the whole of every book you have chosen? Not necessarily. How to decide? Look at the table of contents carefully; look at the index of the book carefully. For example, suppose you are writing on John F. Kennedy's handling of the Cuban missile crisis. You might have a book on your list that would take you through Kennedy's entire

---

Totemism

(9)

p. 30

Maoris of New Zealand consider animals, vegetables, and minerals true ancestors. Therefore, "they cannot play the part of totems."

Notes on the "Totemism" card:

1. There is only one note on the card; that is, the note refers to one page of the source and sticks to a single subject; this makes for ease of handling: the card can be shuffled into any number of different positions in your final ordering.

2. The subject heading, "Totemism," is written at the top left and underlined; this also makes for ease of handling when sorting cards later.

3. The note itself *begins* with the page number at the left, above. It is written first so that you will have no trouble in identifying the page reference when you write your footnote.

4. The number in the upper-right-hand corner is the item number in your working bibliography that identifies the source, in this case *Totemism* by Claude Lévi-Strauss.

5. Part of this note is a direct quotation from the source. When you quote directly, be sure to include the quotation marks—*both* sets.

political career. The shrewd move would be to examine the index carefully and read where the subject headings refer you to such topics as "Cuban missile crisis," "attitude toward Russians," "pressure from Republicans regarding Cuba," etc. You might want to read more of such a book—but you should understand that it is not entirely necessary to read from cover to cover every book on your list. The effective researcher learns to pick through the jungle of data to find what is *needed*.

What kind of notes should you take and how should you record this material?

First, the easy part: notes should be recorded on index cards. Researchers who do not use index cards are in for trouble—if not for downright misery; there is simply no way to keep and organize notes on ordinary note paper or in a notebook used for other purposes as well. *No way*. The good size for this job is the 5"x8" *lined* card.* A lined card encourages neat writing (very important when it comes time to decipher what you've written!), and the extra size will enable you to get a good deal of information on the cards while still not sacrificing ease of handling. A rubber band to hold them together is essential.

If you've compiled an efficient set of working bibliography cards, all you need do when you record data on a note card is to use the number of the bibliography card and the page number where you got the data. Two examples are shown on pp. 338 and 340.

What kind of notes should you take? What kinds of information should you record?

The best instrument for determining this is the rough outline of your paper. (See below for more about outlines.) Although you may not have a fully developed outline at this point, you may have either a topic outline or a rough idea of the main divisions of your paper. For example:

---

*If you don't like the idea of carrying around 3x5 cards for your working bibliography and 5x8 cards for your notes, switch to 5x8 for both.

1. Advantages of nuclear power
2. Disadvantages of nuclear power
3. Advantages of solar power
4. Disadvantages of solar power

If you have something like this (and you may want to work in such a way or find yourself working in such a way that you will have), then your notes should of course fill out what you need for these main divisions.

The other instrument you have for determining what kinds of information to record is your instinct; by this

---

Grief and depression   ④
p. 155
Comparing real grief and the state of depression:

real grief = loss by death of real person
= world becomes poor and empty
depression = unconscious loss of image of person
= self becomes poor and empty

Notes on the "Grief and depression" card:

1. Note that this card is written in a kind of shorthand. This system is perfectly acceptable as long as you can interpret the shorthand you decide to use. Actually, this is good note-taking because it summarizes concisely a densely informative page from a difficult source, Freud's essay, "Mourning and Melancholia." It is also possible to summarize *several* pages of a source on a single card.

2. As in the previous card, the subject heading that identifies the card is written at the upper left.

3. Also as in the previous card, the page number is placed above the note itself, and the item number that identifies the source is written at the upper right.

time you *know* something about your topic and you will be working to increase that knowledge. Thus the best advice is that you record whatever you think important, reserving for later the job of sifting through the cards and disregarding what is not useful.

But the biggest question you will face is whether to paraphrase information you gather from a particular page or pages or to quote it exactly onto your cards.

In nearly all cases, your decision should be to paraphrase. There are a number of good reasons for this, beginning with the fact that your paper will (because it *should*) use relatively little direct quotation. Papers that quote extensively appear to be nothing more than strings of undigested pieces of quotation; the reader tires of reading so much quoted material and is not prepared to take in the full significance of a really important quote, because the writer has not been selective in the use of such material.

Direct quotation in your paper should only be used when 1. you need directly to prove something and only the actual words you have read will do that job; when 2. you intend to be critical of the actual words an author has used; or when 3. the words are so appropriate, dramatic, emphatic, or witty that no paraphrase can do them justice. For example, suppose you are reading about an event that took place in the 1950s, a hearing on the use of air power by the United States Air Force. The then commander of our Strategic Air Forces, General Curtis LeMay, Jr., you read, suggested to a Congressional committee that we "bomb them into the Stone Age." You want to record General LeMay's attitude. Do you paraphrase and note that "LeMay favored total destruction of the enemy by air power" or do you quote him directly? No difficulty there.

Naturally, there are harder problems than this example. But as you read and take notes, you will become more expert at making these decisions and you can always go back—after gaining some experience—and check to see what you can do to improve your notes.

After each reading session, you are likely to have a pile of cards—perhaps ten or more. Whatever the number, you must now perform an important task. Read each card carefully and see what its essence is; that is, see if you can summarize each card in one or two words. Take a large felt-tip marker and write this word or words across the top. After your two-week reading period, you will have a large number of cards, ready to organize by the subject headings you've written across the top of each. These words, or subject headings, should correspond—or with slight revision can correspond—to the rough divisions you had already had in mind before you started the period of intensive reading. In any case, they are needed for the next step: preparing an outline.

PREPARING AN OUTLINE

An outline is an instrument for controlling the writing of a paper. It details the order in which you present your material. A *topic outline* is useful for the preliminary stages of a research paper, because it assists you to order your reading and your notes. Here is a typical —and simple—topic outline for a paper on the energy crisis in America:

I. The energy situation in the U.S. before 1973
II. Action by oil-exporting countries in 1973
III. Situation in U.S. between 1974-1977

This is an efficient way to order a chronological set of materials. But notice that while this kind of outline orders the material, it *says* nothing about that which it orders; it expresses no point of view, so that we have no idea of the writer's viewpoint on the material.

Much better for the purposes of the research paper is the *sentence outline:*

I. The energy situation in the U.S. before 1973 was already critical but little noticed.

II. The action by the oil-exporting countries in 1973 made the situation much worse.

III. The situation in the U.S. between 1974 and 1977 has been one of frantically and inefficiently scrambling after "a solution."

What makes this outline more useful than the topic outline is the fact that each of the roman numerals precedes a sentence—a statement that *says* something, that articulates a point of view, and that gives direction to the writer who must use it in writing the paper.

So important is it to develop the sentence outline that many instructors will not permit a student writer to begin composing a paper until this job is done. And at this stage, ready or not, the writer must take the plunge and begin to do the job.

What is most essential for the sentence outline is a thesis—a controlling, central point of view, the conclusion you have come to after all your reading and thinking about your topic. And the thesis can emerge in one of two ways. (1) You have been, as you were engaged in intensive reading and note-taking, an avid reader of your own note cards; each day, after you finished, you thought about the notes you had taken, the subject-headings you had written across them, and the implications of all this. Now you read your notes one last time and suddenly your thesis appears full-blown in your mind. (2) You work on your cards in an organized way until your thesis emerges from your subject headings.

Working with your notecards: toward a thesis and an outline

Let us suppose that you have been researching an aspect of the energy crisis that developed in the United States after 1973. You have have narrowed your topic to "The Relative Merits of Nuclear and Solar Power: Making a Rational Choice." You intend in your paper to answer two questions: (1) Which form of power is the more advantageous to fulfill our needs? (2) What are the prospects for America's adopting the one that seems more advantageous? You have done your reading and now have a batch of note cards under each of the following subject headings:

A. development of nuclear reactors for power needs
B. ancient devices for using the sun
C. nuclear accidents
D. nuclear waste disposal
E. advantages of solar power
F. advantages of nuclear power
G. absence of solar power technology
H. no portable systems for solar power
I. high nuclear costs
J. high solar startup costs
K. solar storage: a problem
L. costs of dismantling nuclear plants
M. industry's attitudes toward solar power
N. industry's attitudes toward nuclear power
O. government's sponsorship of nuclear power
P. government's failure to sponsor solar power

It seems easy enough to impose a preliminary order on these batches of cards. For example, A and B obviously go together in an introduction. M, N, O, and P belong at the end, where you would discuss the prospects for adopting the better choice (either nuclear or solar power). The remaining batches of cards belong in the central part of your paper, but they need to be put together under new subject headings. Logically, batches C through K fall into four separate categories under these headings:

1. advantages of nuclear power
2. disadvantages of nuclear power
3. advantages of solar power
4. disadvantages of solar power

To join these four, we should combine M, N, O, and P into two:

5. government and industry's attitude toward nuclear power
6. government and industry's attitude toward solar power

When you have done this, you are ready for an important task. You must *turn these six subject headings into sentences* that accurately express what *you* think is said by the totality of the cards you've arranged under these new subject headings. To do this, you must read each pack of cards carefully and, from the mass of details they contain, extract a generalization (a sentence) that accurately covers what the cards contain. Your sentence for any one pack need not contain *everything* on the cards—at this stage you may ignore some cards, deciding that some of the information is irrelevant to your sentence. But you do need a sentence for each subject heading.

Let us suppose now that you've done the job and the sentences come out like this:

1. The advantages of nuclear power are few.
2. The disadvantages of nuclear power are considerable.
3. The advantages of solar power are considerable.
4. The disadvantages of solar power are the same as those for any other newly developing technology.
5. The government has sponsored nuclear research, and industry is inclined to follow the path of nuclear development.
6. The government has given little aid to solar power research, and industry is reluctant to pay the costs of solar power development.

The reader who examines these sentences carefully will see that it is possible to find embedded in them a plausible thesis. What is required now are the *words* to express that thesis. As an exercise, before you read any further, try writing a rather longish sentence, using the materials in 1 through 6 above, that you think would do for a thesis.

Compare what you have written with the following:

The advantages that solar power has over nuclear power make it seem more suitable for America's energy needs, but government and industry are not inclined to press for its wide-scale adoption.

Now that you have a thesis, you are ready to "divide" it into an outline.

I. Introduction: Solar energy has been used successfully for thousands of years; nuclear energy is a recent development dating from 1945, when it was first used in the atomic bomb.

II. The advantages of nuclear energy are far outweighed by its disadvantages.
   A. The advantages of nuclear energy are few.
      1. There is a relatively stable supply of fuel.
      2. There is an available and developing technology.
      3. There is a body of engineers and workers trained in nuclear technology.
   B. The disadvantages of nuclear energy are considerable.
      1. It is thermodynamically inefficient.
      2. It needs extraordinary handling because of its deadly character, and its waste products remain deadly for centuries.
      3. It can give rise to catastrophic accidents.
      4. Its recycled products can be made into dangerous weapons.

III. The advantages of solar power far outweigh its disadvantages.
   A. The advantages of solar power are considerable.
      1. Its fuel, the sun, is in endless supply at no cost.
      2. It is thermodynamically efficient.
      3. It results in no deadly waste products.
      4. It cannot give rise to catastrophic accidents.
   B. The disadvantages of solar power are virtually the same as those of any other newly developing technology.
      1. It will be fairly expensive to integrate solar power with current systems.
      2. It is not yet efficient to store solar power.
      3. It is not yet efficient to use solar power for transportation.

IV. Since government and industry are not enthusiastic about making the effort solar power will require and since both have heavy investments in nuclear technology, it seems unlikely that solar power will be adopted on a large scale in America in the near future.

Notes on the outline

1. Note that the introduction rephrases into a sentence the materials on the original notecards, batches A and B (see p. 344).

2. Note that Roman numerals II, III, and IV literally divide up the thesis statement on p. 345. Note too that as we go from the A's and B's to Arabic numerals, the dividing and specifying process continues.

3. Note that sentences II and III are parallel in form. Note too that the parallelism extends to the A's and B's, and that the numerical entries under these are also parallel.

4. The materials, the specific points made, in the statements marked by Arabic numerals come, of course, from the notecards.

Of course, a different set of notecards for a different paper will present different problems, but the process is essentially the same: consider your material until it yields more and more inclusive generalizations, from subject headings to sentences and from these sentences to a thesis. From the thesis to the outline is a matter of proper division and adding details from the cards.

The following few rules may be useful if you want to check your outline against some standard before submitting it to the instructor.

1. No outline should be written unless you are sure the thesis is a satisfactory one. (For more on Thesis Statements, see that entry in Part 2.) For example, here is an example of an unsatisfactory thesis for the nuclear-solar power outline we have just discussed:

There are many advantages and disadvantages to using nuclear power and solar power.

This is unsatisfactory because it is too vague—and would remain so even if it named some of the advantages and disadvantages it speaks of. It is also a failure in not saying specifically what the writer thinks *after* doing the research; a statement like this one could have been made *before* reading about the subject. Compare it to the thesis statement on pp. 000-000.

2. The outline should always divide its material logically. For example, consider this piece of outline:

II. By hard work, Woodward and Bernstein tracked down their important sources.
   A. They tracked down a secretary at CREEP.
   B. They found an important source in the F.B.I.
III. They located a "leak" in the White House itself.

Notice that Roman numeral III should be capital C. It clearly refers back to Roman numeral II and is in parallel form with A and B.

3. The outline should present its material in logical order. Consider this preliminary outline:

I. Modern methods of early diagnosis cut down on heart disease fatalities.
II. Treatment of heart disease was hampered before 1950 by inadequate diagnostic understanding.
III. Treatment of heart disease cases used to consist of rest and only rest.
IV. Modern treatment of heart attack is based on the theory of prevention by physical and psychological conditioning.

Can you rearrange these into a more logical order? If you changed I to III, kept IV, and changed II and III to I and II, respectively, you have a good eye for logical order.

WRITING THE PAPER

If you have done your work efficiently to this point, you now have an outline in hand and batches of notecards in the same order as the divisions in that outline—and you are ready to write.

The mechanics

You should be prepared to write at least two drafts. It is not inappropriate to suggest, in fact, that you write as many drafts as you need to write; it is hard to imagine extra attention spoiling your work. Depending on your preference in work habits, you may either write your drafts in longhand or type them; either way, be sure to keep careful track of your footnotes from draft to draft. (See below, Footnotes, for detailed information about them.)

When you are ready for a final draft, it should be typed on good white bond, 8½"x11", on one side of the page only, with foonotes at the foot of the page or all together at the end, as your instructor requests. You should supply a title page (see Sample Paper) and a final bibliography. All of these should be proofread carefully.

Finally, you should know that there are a variety of words and phrases available to use in introducing quoted material. It is useful rhetorical strategy, for example, to introduce a quote with an expression like "as the noted astronomer and cosmologist Carl Sagan has observed. . . ." In this way, you let the reader know that an authority's words are about to be spoken, and the reader might be properly impressed. In any case, there are many ways to introduce quotes and you should think about the values inherent in each. For your convenience, here is a small list (there are many others):

As Prof. X *declared*
Dr. Falk *notes*
Winston Churchill *observed*
As Pablo Picasso *put it*
Nietzsche *has written that*

In Kennedy's *analysis*
By Freud's *definition*
Edward Heath *asserted that*
Nixon *summarized it as*

The rhetoric

Everything you know about writing should, of course, be applied to the writing of the research paper. But this paper presents a special problem that you have not encountered before: the necessity to weave into your paper materials taken from a number of sources.

The way to deal with this problem is to take the approach that these materials are *not* in and of themselves the heart of your paper; the heart of your paper is *your* purpose in writing, the thesis that you have set out to present. Once you have made the decision to take this approach, the materials you have been collecting will fall into their proper place. That is, you will see that they are to be used for your purposes, *woven* into the texture of your paper to support and illustrate your thesis and *not* strung together like strange beads because these pieces are all you have to present.

DOCUMENTATION

The mechanics

Documentation is substantiation, providing proof or evidence. In a research paper, documentation is in the form of footnotes that specify the source of something you have used in your paper. The things in your paper that require a footnote for documentation are the following:

1. A direct quote from a source.
2. Statistics, including graphs, tables, charts, or diagrams taken from a source.
3. A discussion in your own words based on someone else's words.
4. Your paraphrase of someone else's opinion.

You need *not* footnote specific details that you did not know before you began work on the paper *provided they are such that in the field of your topic they are common knowledge*. For example, you need not document the fact that Robert Kennedy was Attorney General of the United States during his brother's presidency; this fact is considered common knowledge in the history of the United States from 1960 to 1963.

You should consult your instructor if you have questions about documentation, because one of the goals of writing a research paper is to learn the accurate documentation of research materials, and the instructor's guidance in the matter can help you improve your skills.

Ethics

In working with other people's material—an invariable part of writing a research paper—you may be faced with two ethical considerations. The first is the necessity to acknowledge the debt you owe to a source for words, ideas, or facts. The failure to make such acknowledgments is a serious breach of ethics known as plagiarism. For plagiarism, published writers are subject to court action and student writers to disciplinary action by the schools they attend. The second is the duty you have to present with absolute fairness the essential meaning of what you are quoting. Failure to make such a presentation has no name but deception.

To ensure that you are not guilty of plagiarism, you should be scrupulous in acknowledging the source of whatever you quote—whether you paraphrase it or quote it directly. Moreover, you should transcribe quoted material exactly as you find it in your source, being sure to include every punctuation mark, because even a misplaced comma can alter the meaning of a passage.

To avoid deceiving a reader, you should quote a passage without distorting its essential meaning. For example, suppose you had on one of your notecards a quoted passage such as this one:

The American parent seems solidly behind his teen-age child, though numerous research studies and cultural articles like novels and television shows indicate that he is greatly troubled by his child's participation in the drug culture or his early involvement with sex. He is proud of his teen-ager's accomplishments and is likely to support teen-age pursuits in sports, hobbies, or socializing, but he admits to little awareness of how to provide discipline or vocational guidance.

Since you have at your disposal ellipsis points, three spaced periods (. . .), to indicate an omission, you might quote in your paper a version of the above that goes like this:

The American parent seems solidly behind his teen-age child
. . . He is proud of his accomplishments and is likely to support teen-age pursuits . . .

But this would be a deceptive distortion, since the original passage clearly shows the parent to be much more
uncertain than the abbreviated quotation would suggest.

To be sure that your work follows the highest ethical
standard, the best guidelines are these: quote with accuracy, convey the essential meaning of what you are
quoting, and acknowledge the source of the quotation.

Footnotes

The physical form of footnotes follows one or another
convention. No single convention is universally adhered to above another, so the form suggested here is
based upon one widely adhered to: the *MLA Handbook
for Writers of Research Papers, Theses, and Disserta-
tions* (New York: Modern Language Association,
1977).

A footnote consists of two parts: 1. the superscript
number you use in the body of your text to mark the
passage to be documented and 2. the note itself, which
normally goes at the *foot* of the page (hence *footnote*),
but which may also go on a separate sheet of paper at
the end of your text before the final bibliography. Of
course, the note proper is numbered to correspond with
the superscript number in the text.

If you place your notes at the foot of the page, separate the note or notes from the text with a triple space
(set off by a line typed across the page). Wherever you
place the notes, separate them from each other with a
double space. Footnotes should also be indented, as in
the examples below, and the numbers should run con-
secutively throughout the paper; do not start a fresh set
of numbers on each page.

It is important to note that a footnote reference is similar in form to that used on your bibliography cards —*but it is not identical*. Compare the sample footnotes given below with the bibliography samples given above on pp. 335–336 and with the final bibliography of the sample research paper on pp. 395–396.

The following sample footnotes give you the form of the first citation of a reference, and the short form of each subsequent reference to the same source. You may use these as models for your own footnotes. In doing so, notice the order in which the information is presented and the exact punctuation that separates the bits of information.

REFERENCE TO A BOOK
   [1]Arthur Waldhorn, A Reader's Guide to Ernest Hemingway (New York: Farrar, Straus and Giroux, 1972), p. 98.

SUBSEQUENT REFERENCE Waldhorn, p. 123.

REFERENCE TO A WORK IN SEVERAL VOLUMES
   [2]Werner Jaeger, Paideia: The Ideals of Greek Culture, trans. Gilbert Highet (New York: Oxford University Press, 1943), II, 13.

SUBSEQUENT REFERENCE Jaeger, III, 215.

Note: Note that in the Waldhorn references, the abbreviation "p." is used for the page number while in the Jaeger it is not. This is because the Roman numeral for the volume number is used in the Jaeger. Wherever a volume number is used, the page number is cited *without* the "p." See below, under note 10.

REFERENCE TO A BOOK IN WHICH THE EDITION IS CITED
   [3]Robert Dudley French, A Chaucer Handbook, 2nd ed. (New York: Appleton-Century-Crofts, Inc., 1955), p. 327.

SUBSEQUENT REFERENCE French, p. 299.

REFERENCE TO A BOOK WITH TWO OR MORE AUTHORS

[4]Naomi B. Lynn, Ann B. Matasar, and Marie Barovic Rosenberg, <u>Research Guide in Women's Studies</u> (Morristown, N.J.: General Learning Press, 1974), p. 32.

SUBSEQUENT REFERENCE Lynn, et al., p. 90.

Note: For more than three authors, use this form: "Naomi B. Lynn, et al. . . ." omitting the names of the other authors; the abbreviation *et al.* means "and others." Note, too, that this is done in subsequent references to the work of three authors —as a convenient short form.

REFERENCE TO A GENERAL REFERENCE WORK

[5]"Fleming, Sir Alexander," <u>Chambers's Biographical Dictionary</u>, New Edition, p. 476a.

SUBSEQUENT REFERENCE <u>Chambers's</u>, p. 476a.

Note: You need not supply publication facts in the case of a well-established general reference work, but only specify the edition and the page number.

REFERENCE TO A CLASSIC PLAY, GIVING ACT, SCENE, AND LINE NUMBERS

[6]<u>Hamlet</u>, II.i.36

SUBSEQUENT REFERENCE: FOLLOW SAME FORM

REFERENCE TO AN ESSAY INCLUDED IN AN EDITED COLLECTION

[7]Earl H. Rovit, "Ralph Ellison and the American Comic Tradition," in <u>Ralph Ellison: A Collection of Critical Essays</u>, ed. John Hersey (Englewood Cliffs, N.J.: Prentice-Hall, Inc., 1974), p. 152.

SUBSEQUENT REFERENCE Rovit, p. 153.

REFERENCE TO SIGNED ARTICLE IN A WEEKLY MAGAZINE

[8]Jane Otten, "Living in Syntax," <u>Newsweek</u>, December 30, 1974, p. 103.

SUBSEQUENT REFERENCE Otten, p. 103.

REFERENCE TO UNSIGNED ARTICLE IN A WEEKLY MAGAZINE

[9]"Coming Across," The New Yorker, June 27, 1977, p. 26.

SUBSEQUENT REFERENCE "Coming Across," p. 27.

REFERENCE TO AN ARTICLE IN A MONTHLY MAGAZINE

[10]Ignatius C. Mattingly, "Some Cultural Aspects of Serial Cartoons, or Get a Load of Those Funnies," Harper's, December 1955, p. 35.

SUBSEQUENT REFERENCE Mattingly, p. 38.

REFERENCE TO AN ARTICLE IN A LEARNED JOURNAL

[11]Erik H. Erikson, "The Problem of Ego Identity," Journal of the American Psychoanalytic Association, 4 (January 1956), 57.

SUBSEQUENT REFERENCE Erikson, p. 60.

REFERENCE TO SIGNED NEWSPAPER ARTICLE

[12]Leslie Maitland, "Story of an East Side Policeman Who Turned in Fellow Officers," The New York Times, July 3, 1977, sec. 1, p. 1.

SUBSEQUENT REFERENCE Maitland, p. 33.

REFERENCE TO UNSIGNED NEWSPAPER ARTICLE

[13]"Eight Fireman Injured as a Tenement Burns," The New York Times, 3 July 1977, sec. 1, p. 25.

SUBSEQUENT REFERENCE "Eight Firemen," p. 25.

REFERENCE TO A PUBLIC DOCUMENT

[14]U.S. Congress, Senate, Committee on the Judiciary, Hearings before the Subcommittee to Investigate Juvenile Delinquency (Washington, D.C.: Government Printing Office, 1954), p. 112.

SUBSEQUENT REFERENCE Senate Hearings, p. 200.

Subsequent references and Latin abbreviations

For many years it was customary to use a number of Latin abbreviations in footnote citations. For example, in those years a set of footnotes might have looked like this:

⁶Jones, op. cit., p. 26.

Op. cit. is an abbreviation of *opere citato,* "in the work cited," and so the footnote would mean "in the work of Jones that was previously cited, on p. 26."

⁷Ibid., p. 76.

Ibid. is short for *ibidem,* "in the same place," and so this footnote would mean "in the same book (Jones) note 6 cites, only this time on p. 76."

⁸Smith, op. cit., p. 23.

⁹Loc. cit.

Loc. cit. is an abbreviation of *loco citato,* "in the place cited," and so this footnote would mean "in the same book (Smith) cited in the previous footnote and on the same page (23)."

However, the more recent trend is to eliminate Latin abbreviations like *ibid., op. cit.,* and *loc. cit.* and treat the same set of footnotes as follows:

⁶Jones, p. 26.

⁷Jones, p. 76.

⁸Smith, p. 23.

⁹Smith, p. 23.

The less complicated system of footnote citation has many advantages, not the least of which are an uncluttered set of footnotes and a style of reference that produces clarity.

If you refer in your footnotes to works by two authors with the same name, say Thomas Jones and Richard Jones, then in order to avoid confusion you would use the full name of each when you give their names in short, subsequent references (after the first, full citation).

⁶Thomas Jones, p. 75.

⁷Richard Jones, p. 112.

If your sources include two different works by the same author, then the form of your subsequent references to each cannot consist merely of this author's name. Let us suppose that your two books are Peter Clapps, *How Workers Triumph Over Unions,* and Peter Clapps, *Finding the Way Through Union Pension Funds.* Subsequent references to these would require the author's last name and an abbreviated title:

⁷Clapps, <u>Workers</u> <u>Triumph</u>, p. 179.

⁸Clapps, <u>Pension</u> <u>Funds</u>, p. 105.

Abbreviations used in footnotes

The following list of abbreviations for terms used in footnotes may be useful. Note that abbreviations are followed by a period and that the abbreviations for Latin words are not italicized.

anon.	anonymous
c., ca. (*circa*)	about (c. 1485)
cf. (*confer*)	compare
ch., chs., chap., chaps.	chapter(s)
diss.	dissertation
ed., eds.	edited by, edition, editor(s)
e.g. (*exempli gratia*)	for example
et al. (*et alii*)	and others
f., ff.	and the following page(s)
ibid. (*ibidem*)	in the same place
i.e. (*id est*)	that is
intro.	introduction
l., ll.	line(s)
loc. cit. (*loco citato*)	in the place cited
MS., ms., MSS., mss.	manuscript(s)

n.	note
n.d.	no date (of publication)
n.p.	no place (of publication)
numb.	numbered
op. cit. (*opere citato*)	in the work cited
p., pp.	page(s)
passim	here and there; throughout
rev.	revised
tr., trans.	translated by, translator
v. (*vide*)	see, consult
vol., vols.	volume(s)

SAMPLE RESEARCH PAPER

The sample research paper that follows is shown in final typed form. Commentary on the text, keyed to the numbered paragraphs, appears facing the appropriate paragraphs.

VIOLENCE ON TELEVISION:

WHAT DO WE KNOW ABOUT

HOW IT AFFECTS US?

Tamara Pakes

English 40 B

November 15, 1977

Statement of Purpose

The purpose of this paper is to examine
research that has been done on the connections
between the depiction of violence on television
and its effect on an audience, to determine what
is scientifically known about the subject, and to
comment on this state of knowledge.

I. Introduction: As of this writing a 15-year-
old in Miami offers TV violence as defense
in his murder trial, and violence on
television has been an issue for decades.
  A. There is disagreement on exactly what the
effects are.
  B. Public opinion has sometimes held that
there are definite effects.

II. Early research and social critics have said
there was an effect.
  A. Studies in 1933 thought movies produced
criminals.
  B. A Senate committee thought TV was linked
to juvenile delinquency.
    1. Most evidence came from professional
opinion, not research.
    2. Some evidence came from research, but
it suggested some aggression on TV was
healthful.
    3. The evidence also suggested that the
greatest effect was on children and
adolescents.

III. The first extensive research, by Himmelweit
and later by Schramm and his associates,
indicated that violence on TV did not cause
violence in children but rather frightened
them; no effort was made to reduce the
amount of watching after this information
was available.
  A. To the children, verbal aggression on TV
was more disagreeable than physical
violence.

B. Although sometimes able to distinguish the real from the fictional on TV, those exposed to many TV shootings were frequently unable to distinguish the two.
C. Schramm's conclusions were similar to Himmelweit's, but he thought that it was impossible to predict exactly which scenes would upset a child and that a child predisposed to violence, rather than TV itself, was the chief element in delinquency--television would aid such a child to become aggressive.

IV. Bandura's studies of the preschool child and studies by the Media Task Force of the National Commission on the Causes and Prevention of Violence suggested that children can learn aggression; that violence, portrayed as successful on television, is partly responsible for violence in society; and that children of low-income families were more likely to believe what they saw because they watched more than other subgroups.

V. The Surgeon General's report suggested that violence can be mimicked by children, but it could not conclude that television violence uniformly affects a majority.

VI. Liebert's group, reporting at the same time as the Surgeon General, made similar qualifications.

VII. Conclusion: Although there is no scientific proof that television violence affects us all adversely, there are potentially more dangerous effects: fear, the mixing of reality and fiction, and the depiction of violence as successful; intuitively, we know we have a problem--the only question is the question of degree.

Par. 1. Tammy refers to a recent case—a dramatic opening that links her paper to current news.

After consultation with her instructor, Tammy has chosen to place all her footnote citations together at the end of the paper. (See p. 352 under Footnotes.) Of course, she might have placed them at the foot of each page. The advantage of her choice is that readers may proceed from the beginning to the end of the paper without interruption. The disadvantage is that if readers want to see a note, they must turn to the back of the paper. The method you choose will depend on how you evaluate these conflicting claims, and on one other thing: if your notes are rather full of supplementary information (for example, see footnote 3), you might want to put them at the foot of the page. (You should not in any case overuse this type of supplementary note.)

VIOLENCE ON TELEVISION:
WHAT DO WE KNOW ABOUT
HOW IT AFFECTS US?

1   At the end of September 1977, 15-year-old
Ronny Zamora went on trial in Miami, Florida,
charged with robbing and then shooting to death
his next-door neighbor, an 82-year-old woman.
The defense was an unusual one: not guilty,
because the defendant had seen so much violence
on television he had lost the ability to tell
right from wrong. "If you judge Ronny Zamora
guilty," his lawyer told the jury, "television
will be an accessory."[1] For, as he pointed out
repeatedly during the trial, Ronny was just an
average young American; and the average young
American can see more than 18,000 hours of
television before reaching the age of 18. Ronny,
in fact, had been watching television since he
was a baby, and his mother estimated that by the
time he reached high school he watched six hours
a day. An ironic aspect of the trial was that <u>it</u>

Par 2. Despite its being a "giveaway," the second paragraph spells out her thesis in detail. Offering readers the thesis at the outset is good strategy, however, for it permits them to follow the paper's development with clarity and ease.

was televised. Someone could then ask a
complicated question: if witnessing television
murders motivates real-life murders, would
watching television punishment act as a deterrent?

2   Nevertheless, the case is sure to stimulate
still another investigation into the troublesome
relations between television and its depiction of
violence. Yet violence on television has been a
controversial issue for more than two decades.
The debate has focused on whether violent
material affects its audience, especially
children and adolescents. Research to date
indicates that television violence may have an
effect on some viewers, but there is disagreement
on the exact nature of the influence and who is
most affected. Research has failed to find
evidence to support or refute those critics who
blame "mayhem in the media"[2] for the upward turn
of the crime curve. No direct causal connection
between television violence and juvenile
delinquency has been established. It may be more
important, however, that this same research
raises the possibility that television's effects
may be less obvious but potentially more
dangerous.

Par. 3. Notice how Tammy has woven into her text the quotation beginning "70 percent." Notice the placement of footnote number 4.

Par. 4. The long quotation in this paragraph is handled the same way as other long quotations throughout the paper. That is, it is indented, single-spaced, and given without quotation marks. Tammy has used a number of such long quotations—perhaps more than you will see in most student papers. The reason for her choice is that the subject matter of her paper and the nature of the investigation demand that she report what is known; thus she is being scrupulous when she reports conclusions in the words of the researchers she is reporting on.

3   Television was introduced as popular
entertainment in 1949, and within five years, the
majority of Americans became its audience.[3]
Although they had enthusiastically accepted the
medium, they were unwilling to approve
uncritically everything which it presented.
Programing was criticized for depicting violence,
which, some felt, aroused aggressive impulses in
young viewers. A Gallup survey that was
published in 1954 reported that "70 percent of
the adults questioned place at least part of the
blame for the 'upsurge in juvenile delinquency'
on crime-type comic books and on mystery and
crime programs on television and radio."[4] It was
not without precedent that the American public
chose to attribute moral decay to the mass media.

4   In 1933, for example, convicted criminals
were interviewed and studied; their examiners
concluded that motion pictures had often been
instrumental in leading these individuals astray:

> Through the display of crime techniques and
> criminal patterns of behavior; by arousing
> desires for easy money and luxury; by
> suggesting questionable methods for their
> achievement; by inducing a spirit of
> bravado, toughness, and adventurousness; by
> arousing intense sexual desires; and by
> invoking daydreams of criminal roles, motion

pictures may create attitudes and furnish techniques conducive, quite unwittingly, to delinquent behavior.[5]

Various social commentators of the 1940s and 1950s thought similarly; children's nightmares, nervousness, and naughtiness were the less harmful effects of media exposure.[6] A prominent professor wrote that "daily broadcasting . . . cannot but be destructive of ideals that have proven wholesome and worth of preservation."[7]

5 Criticism of the media was not restricted to the fare available on radio or on big and little screens. Fredric Wertham declared: ". . . the bad effects of crime comic books exist potentially for all children."[8] However, the easy accessibility of television led to the conclusion that its effects might be the worst. A United States Senate subcommittee that investigated juvenile delinquency concluded that "Television crime programs are potentially much more injurious to children and young people than motion pictures, radio, or comic books. . . . Television, available at the flick of a knob and combining visual and audible aspects into a 'life' story, has a greater impact on its child audience."[9] This claim was based primarily on

Par. 6. Notice the neat handling of a difficult problem. The "catharsis hypothesis" has come up in Tammy's discussion. She judges, correctly, that she must explain the term, but rather than interrupt the flow of her paper she defines it expertly within parentheses.

<u>Low-income TV watching</u>   <u>TEJ</u>, 169-171

Low-income children watch TV 5-1 hrs. a day, according to study of 4<u>th</u> and 5<u>th</u> graders; estimated twice as much as middle-income children.

<u>Advertisers believe TV</u>   <u>TEJ</u>, 166
    <u>has influence</u>

Advertisers spend more than $2.5 billion annually in the belief that TV viewing influences buying habits. Some advertisers believe that if they stopped advertising on TV, they would be at great competitive disadvantage! Cigarette companies.

the testimony of psychiatrists and law enforcement officials. These witnesses were relying on their judgment, however, because there was little research data on the effects of television violence.

6   Only one subcommittee witness related actual experimental data.[10] In her testimony, Eleanor Maccoby disagreed with the catharsis hypothesis (i.e., the viewing of "vicarious violence on film or television will 'discharge' the aggressive energy of the individual"[11]). She felt that television violence might increase the frustrated child's aggressive impulses. However, televised violence, if presented in the proper context, had the potential to dissuade the child from violently releasing his or her own aggression. Maccoby maintained: "The child may learn that aggressive action is permissible under certain conditions (for example, in battle, when the action is directed against an enemy), but can also learn that unprovoked aggression against one's own society will bring retribution."[12]

7   It was believed that television violence had the greatest effect on children and adolescents, but there was no research dealing with the manner

It is worthwhile to examine four of Tammy's notecards shown on p. 372 and this page. See if you can understand how and why she worked this material into her text. In one case, you should try to understand why she did *not* use the material.

<u>Kids and aggression</u>   Liebert, 117–118

Bandura says that kids did not learn from TV violence things like how to shoot, how to attack physically, how to destroy property, steal, etc. Rather than the exact details of behavior, they learn how to be rough on environment.

<u>On setting of violence</u>   Schramm, et. al., 140

Violent content not frightening to kids. "rather it was the dark and mysterious scenes — for example a picture that was mostly in the dark, and a scene in which persons dug for a body in a cellar — or the scenes into which they could easily put themselves, such as a person uncovering tarantulas by over-turning a rock."

in which they were affected, or if certain children were more likely to be influenced than others. Despite a lack of statistical evidence to support them, psychiatrists and psychologists asserted that media violence would only affect children who were already emotionally disturbed. Dr. Otto Billig presented the case this way:

> My clinical experience has led me to believe that television programs, movies, etc., have a very limited influence on the child or juvenile. We have performed rather exhaustive psychiatric and psychological studies on juvenile delinquents. Most youngsters do not seem at all influenced by such outside factors. The well-adjusted personality can resist them without difficulties. A very occasional case was triggered into some delinquent act, and possibly received specific ideas on how to carry out a crime. But only the emotionally disturbed and insecure individual appears susceptible to outside forces. Other outside pressures have probably greater significance, such as recognition by neighborhood gangs, inadequate or lack of group activities.[13]

Furthermore, Billig was convinced that the effort to find a solution to the juvenile delinquency problem would be hampered by the extreme claims of some media critics. Too much attention had been focused on "surface appearances"; rather, a more intensive study had to be made of "principal causative factors."

8 In 1958, a British research team published

the first extensive report on the effects of
television on a young audience. Himmelweit,
Oppenheim, and Vince had studied 1,854 children
(946 13- and 14-year-olds and 908 10- and 11-year-
olds), who were divided into a viewer and a
nonviewer group. In their investigation, the
researchers found no evidence to suggest that
television violence encourages children to be
aggressive. They did discover, however, that
many (though not a majority) of the children
seemed to be frightened by such material. The
researchers, in determining what had scared these
children, noted that the amount of violence which
they had seen was of less significance than "the
setting in which the violence occurred, . . . the
manner of its presentation . . . and the
complexity of the characterization of the two
sides in the struggle."[14] They also observed
that only a few of the children were frightened
if they were familiar with the formats in which
violence was presented.

9   In the children's estimation, verbal
aggression was far more disagreeable than
physical violence; questioned about "which acts

376

of violence they 'dislike' on television, 6
percent or less of the children mentioned
shooting, and from 19 percent to 23 percent
mentioned 'fighting with other weapons,' but 23
percent to 30 percent mentioned such things as
'when the sheriff tells the good cowboy off
because he is not catching the bad man quickly
enough,' and 'when someone is told off when it is
not really his fault' and 'when grown ups are
angry with one another and shout.'"[15]

10   Violence (e.g., shooting, rioting, and
fires) in documentaries and newsreels had as
little effect as did similar events portrayed in
Westerns (or any format with which the child was
familiar). It was demonstrated that the children
could differentiate between the fictional and the
real, and that they were much more afraid of the
real if the situation was one in which they could
conceivably find themselves. However, the
researchers found that children who were
frequently exposed to fictional shootings had
difficulty in recognizing the significance of the
real event (shades of Ronny Zamora!): "by the age
of 11-12 they should be able to separate more

clearly in their minds the tragedy of real
~violence from its inconsequential character in
fictional programmes. We suggest that this
distinction may be retarded through the steady
stream of fictional violence, especially
shooting, that they witness."[16]

11   This study had been designed so that
immediate reactions might be observed. It could
not be determined if the most outstanding
response, fright, could and would affect future
attitudes and behavior. Himmelweit indicated
that an inquiry into this area was needed. Their
data led these researchers to conclude:

> . . . Seeing violence on television is not
> likely to turn well-adjusted children into
> aggressive delinquents; there must be a pre-
> disposition for them to be affected in this
> way. Nor do children as a whole translate
> television experience into action. It may
> happen in extreme cases where children have
> a strong desire to be aggressive or to
> perform a delinquent act, and for whom
> constant watching of programmes with an
> explosive content may be the last straw.
>   Even in extreme cases the influence of
> television is small. The child's emotional
> make-up and the total of his environmental
> influences determine his behaviour.
>   Our findings and those of Maccoby
> suggest, then, that these programmes do not
> initiate aggressive, maladjusted or
> delinquent behaviour, but may aid its
> expression. They may not affect a stable
> child, but they may evoke a response in 5-10
> percent of all children who are disturbed or
> at least emotionally labile . . .[17]

12   After three years of research in ten
communities in the United States and Canada,
American investigators announced their findings
in <u>Television</u> <u>in</u> <u>the</u> <u>Lives</u> <u>of</u> <u>Our</u> <u>Children</u>.[18]
Schramm and his associates (although their study
was of a different design), reached conclusions
that were similar to those of Himmelweit. Again,
it was found that when children were frightened,
the degree of their fear was dependent upon the
context in which the incident occurred; however,
"dark and mysterious scenes,"[19] rather than
violent ones, had upset these children. It was
also suggested that certain children will be
affected by unlikely material. The observations
of Dr. Fritz Redl were cited. While working with
delinquents, he noticed that television shows
which portrayed "warm family relationships"[20]
could trigger sleeping disturbances in these
children. Schramm maintained that, in most
instances, it is impossible to specify which
television themes will affect children: "For some
children, under some conditions, some television
is harmful. For other children under the same
conditions, or for the same children under other
conditions, it may be beneficial. For most

children under most conditions, most television
is probably neither particularly harmful nor
particularly beneficial."[21]

13   Schramm believed, however, that certain
predictions could be made about television's
effects on a child who is considered to be more
aggressive than his peers. Most significant is
the likelihood that when he feels aggressive in a
real-life situation, he will be able to recall
and employ violent methods which a fictional
character had used successfully; the
nonaggressive child is less likely to react in
this way.

14   Schramm emphasized that children are active
rather than passive entities, and are not
helplessly bombarded by television. If their
behavior has been adversely affected, they were,
prior to exposure, different from children whose
conduct remained socially acceptable:

          . . . the kind of child we send to [watch]
          television, rather than television itself,
          is the chief element in delinquency. . . .
          [T]he delinquent child (unless he is
          psychopathic) is typically not different
          from other children in standards or
          knowledge or intelligence, but rather in the
          speed with which he can rouse his aggressive
          feelings, and the intensity and violence of
          his hostility. He has typically come from a
          home that has not given him the security and

> warmth children need. He often has peer
> group trouble, too, and sometimes has felt
> that he had to do extraordinary things to be
> recognized by his peers. . . . [C]onflict of
> this kind leads a middle-class child to seek
> more television; a lower-class child is
> already seeing a great deal of it.
> Television then interacts with the needs and
> emotions a child brings to it.[22]

15   According to the results of these major

studies, average, well-adjusted children and

adolescents are not likely to be permanently

affected by television violence. Investigators,

however, were not willing to endorse daily

presentations of murder and assault, or to

declare that this type of entertainment could not

influence a particularly impressionable viewer,

such as a young child. Psychologists have long

been aware that observational learning plays a

principal role in a youngster's development. It

was known, too, that before most children acquire

new behaviors, they follow a predictable pattern:

observation, imitation, and repetition. Children

are attracted to novelty, and become quite

attentive when they are confronted with it. They

are not yet able to distinguish between fantasy

and reality. Television, it is argued, offers

numerous unfamiliar situations which will arouse

the curiosity of inexperienced children.

Par. 16. "The now famous Bobo doll experiments." Within the context of her subject, these *are* famous experiments and by saying so, Tammy indicates once again her familiarity with the field.

The square brackets in the third sentence indicate that the material within is supplied by the writer of the paper and not by the person being quoted.

Researchers speculated that children may imitate what they see on television. Although they continued to study television viewers of various ages, by the early 1960s, their attention was being focused on the pre-school child.

16   Initial data in this new area of inquiry was gathered in 1961 by Albert Bandura. His series of studies demonstrated that young children can learn aggression from live performances and films in which either a cartoon character or an adult behaves aggressively. In one of the now famous Bobo doll experiments, he found that "88 percent of the children [3- to 5-year-old boys and girls] who saw an aggressive television program displayed imitative aggression in a play situation though they had not been asked to do so and were free to play with attractive non-aggressive toys. . . ."[23] Other researchers employed Bandura's techniques and obtained similar findings.

17   As Bandura himself has remarked, these studies only showed that children can learn aggression.[24] There was no indication that they had learned modes of behavior, or that they would transfer aggression from their play activity into real life.

18   Although there were many expressions of concern about the possible effects of television violence, little was being done to reduce it. Parents claimed that it was impossible to constantly monitor the programs their children watched and to specify ones to be avoided. Network officials claimed that children do not isolate violent incidents from the stories in which they occur. They were quick to point out that aggressors were punished for their actions; it would have been more accurate to say that this happened only when they were caught.[25]

19   In a survey conducted by the Media Task Force of the National Commission on the Causes and Prevention of Violence during the weeks of October 1 through 7 in 1967 and 1968, it was discovered that

> Nearly half of all the leading characters who kill (25 of 54) and more than half of all the leading characters who are violent (126 of 241) achieve a clearly happy ending in the programs. To this extent, violence is portrayed as a successful means of attaining a desired end. . . . It is not usually shown as legally or socially unacceptable.[26]

20   The Commission, which had been established in 1968, believed that television might be partly responsible for violence in society. It

Par. 21. Note the effect of the quotation in this paragraph. Could it have been paraphrased? How?

criticized studies which had only recorded the
frequency of aggressive acts, and acknowledged
that many complex problems had been encountered
in the attempt to find a connection between human
behavior and media content. The Commission
evaluated the existing data, and while admitting
that much was not clear, concluded that "the
preponderance of available research evidence
strongly suggests that violence in TV programs
can and does have adverse effects upon audiences--
particularly child audiences."[27]

21   Low-income families were known to watch more
television than their middle-class counterparts.
In one of its investigations, the Commission
found that low-income adolescents were more
likely to believe what they saw:

> Of teenagagers asked whether they agreed or
> disagreed with such statements as: "The
> programs I see on television tell me about
> life the way it really is" and "The people I
> see on TV programs are just like the people
> I meet in real life," 40 percent of the poor
> black adolescents and 30 percent of the poor
> whites strongly believed in the true-to-life
> nature of television content, as compared
> with only 15 percent of the middle-class
> white youngsters.[28]

22   The significance of the Bandura studies and
the Hicks[29] after experiment was properly
apprehended. The more violence children observe,

the more they potentially can learn. On the

basis of a good amount of supporting evidence,

the Commission reported:

> We believe that it is reasonable to conclude
> that a constant diet of violent behavior on
> television has an adverse effect on human
> character and attitudes. Violence on
> television encourages violent forms of
> behavior, and fosters moral and social
> values about violence in daily life which
> are unacceptable in a civilized
> society. . . . Television is a particularly
> strong force . . . in low-income areas or
> where violent life styles are common. . . .
> The strong preference of low-income
> teenagers for crime, action, and adventure
> stories . . . is a fact of considerable
> social importance, especially in light of
> the time low-income youngsters spend with
> television and the credence they place in
> what they watch. The television experience
> of these children and adolescents reinforces
> a distorted, pathological view of society.[30]

23   Finally, as had been the case with cigarette

smoking, the Surgeon General of the United States

was called in to have his say. The result was a

six-volume study by the National Institute of

Mental Health. Any attempt to summarize the

findings adequately would be impossible in this

limited space. But certain themes familiar to

the reader of this paper were repeated:

> . . . violence depicted on television can
> immediately or thereafter induce mimicking
> or copying by children. . . . [U]nder
> certain circumstances television violence
> can instigate an increase in aggressive
> acts. The accumulated evidence, however,

does not warrant the conclusion that television violence has a uniformly adverse effect on the majority of children. It cannot even be said that the majority of children in the various studies we have reviewed showed an increase in aggressive behavior.[31]

24   But as a final demonstration of how the evidence reported in this paper accumulates uncertainties, here are conclusions of another study published at about the same time as the Surgeon General's:

The evidence does indicate that televised violence may lead to increased aggressive behavior in certain sub-groups of children, who might constitute a small portion or a substantial portion of the total population of young television viewers. We cannot estimate the size of the fraction, however, since the available evidence does not come from cross-section samples of the entire American population of children.[32]

25   Thus we can see that, strictly speaking, there is no scientific proof that violence on television does harm to those who watch it. But we are speaking of human behavior, not a mechanical device, and human behavior has never submitted itself to scientific proof. In that light, it is reasonable to assume that no amount of research can or will provide the kind of proof that science is used to. What then do we know of this subject?

26   We know that hundreds of studies have
suggested <u>some</u> link between television violence
and the behavior of the television audience.
Moreover, as was suggested at the beginning of
this paper, the same research that is divided on
the main question has indicated potential harmful
effects apart from that question. The reader is
reminded that Himmelweit and his associates
discovered that television violence arouses fear
in children and that this material may retard a
child's ability to distinguish the real from the
fictional (see above, pp. 7-9). The reader is
further reminded that the National Commission on
the Causes and Prevention of Violence saw a grave
danger in television violence being depicted as
successful.

27   The implications of these dangers accord
well with what we know in our bones. For
millions of us feel intuitively that we have a
television-violence problem, and it seems
unlikely that we are all hallucinating together.
What we know is that Ronny Zamora claims violence
on television altered his behavior and made him a
murderer. What we do not know is what, precisely,
television violence does to the rest of us.

FOOTNOTES

[1]B. Drummond Ayres, Jr., "TV Is on Trial, and at Trial, in Miami," The New York Times, October 7, 1977, p. A18. All the information in the paragraph comes from this source.

[2]Fredric Wertham, A Sign for Cain (New York: The Macmillan Company, 1966), p. 193.

[3]By January 1948, there were 102,000 sets in the United States. As of 1954, more than half of all American families had acquired a television set. It is estimated that today some 97 percent have at least one set. David M. Rein, "The Impact of Television Violence," Journal of Popular Culture, 7 (Spring 1974), 934-935.

[4]Leo Bogart, The Age of Television, 3rd ed. (New York: Frederick Ungar Publishing Co., Inc., 1972), p. 273.

[5]Joseph T. Klapper, The Effects of Mass Communications (Glencoe, Ill.: The Free Press, 1960), p. 142. This is the conclusion of Herbert Blumer and Phillip Hauser, as quoted by Klapper.

[6]Klapper, pp. 140-143, and Bogart, pp. 273-282. Both works present many of the charges that were leveled against the media.

[7]Nicholas Murray Butler, former president of Columbia University, quoted by Bogart, p. 274.

[8]Fredric Wertham, Seduction of the Innocent (New York: Rinehart & Company, Inc., 1954), p. 118. Klapper observes (p. 142) that the Report of the New York State Joint Legislative Committee to Study the Publication of Comics contains similar denunciations.

[9]Television and Juvenile Delinquency: An Interim Report of the Subcommittee to Investigate Juvenile Delinquency, quoted by Bogart, p. 278. This is vol. 2 of John P. Murray, Eli A. Rubinstein, and George A. Comstock, eds., Television and Social Behavior: Reports and Papers: A Technical Report to the Surgeon General's Scientific and Advisory Committee on Television and Social Behavior, 5 vols. (Washington, D.C.: U.S. Government Printing Office, 1972).

[10]Bogart, p. 284.

[11]Dennis Howitt and Guy Cumberbatch, Mass Media Violence and Society (New York: John Wiley & Sons, Inc., 1975), p. 34.

[12]Maccoby, quoted by Bogart, p. 285.

[13]Dr. Otto Billig, quoted by Wilbur Schramm, Jack Lyle, and Edwin B. Parker, Television in the Lives of Our Children (Stanford, Calif.: Stanford University Press, 1961), p. 165.

[14]Klapper, p. 146.

[15]Hilde T. Himmelweit, A. N. Oppenheim, and Pamela Vince, Television and the Child (London: Oxford University Press, 1958), p. 147.

[16]Himmelweit et al., p. 216.

[17]Himmelweit et al., p. 215.

[18]Schramm, et al.; see note 13.

[19]Schramm, et al., p. 140.

[20]Schramm et al., p. 143.

[21]Schramm et al., p. 1.

[22]Schramm et al., pp. 165-166.

[23]Robert M. Liebert, Emily S. Davidson, and John M. Neale, "Aggression in Childhood: The Impact of Television," in Victor B. Cline, ed.,

Where Do You Draw the Line? (Provo, Utah: Brigham Young University Press, 1974), p. 118.

[24]Liebert et al., p. 119.

[25]Bradley S. Greenberg and C. Edward Wotring, "Television Violence and Its Potential for Aggressive Driving Behavior," Journal of Broadcasting, 18 (Fall 1974), 473-475.

[26]To Establish Justice, To Insure Domestic Tranquility: The Final Report of the National Commission on the Causes and Prevention of Violence (New York: Praeger Publishers, 1970), pp. 165-166.

[27]To Establish Justice, p. 166.

[28]To Establish Justice, p. 168.

[29]Liebert et al., p. 118: "Hicks (1965) found that children shown a simulated television program similar to those used by Bandura and his associates learned many new aggressive behaviors after a single viewing and could still produce them when tested again, without further exposure, six months later."

[30]To Establish Justice, pp. 169-170.

[31]Television and Growing Up: The Impact of Television Violence, Report to the Surgeon General (Washington, D.C.: U.S. Government Printing Office, 1972), p. 123.

[32]Liebert et al., p. 122.

BIBLIOGRAPHY OF WORKS CITED

Ayres, B. Drummond, Jr. "TV Is on Trial, and at Trial, in Miami." The New York Times, October 7, 1977, p. A18.

Bogart, Leo. The Age of Television. 3rd ed. New York: Frederick Ungar Publishing Co. Inc., 1972.

Greenberg, Bradley S., and C. Edward Wotring. "Television Violence and Its Potential for Aggressive Driving Behavior." Journal of Broadcasting, 18 (Fall 1974), 473-480.

Himmelweit, Hilde T., A. N. Oppenheim, and Pamela Vince. Television and the Child. London: Oxford University Press, 1958.

Howitt, Dennis, and Guy Cumberbatch. Mass Media Violence and Society. New York: John Wiley & Sons, Inc., 1975.

Klapper, Joseph T. The Effects of Mass Communication. Glencoe, Ill.: The Free Press, 1960.

Liebert, Robert M., Emily S. Davidson, and John M. Neale. "Aggression in Childhood: The Impact of Television." Where Do You Draw the Line? Ed. Victor B. Cline. Provo, Utah: Brigham Young University Press, 1974.

Rein, David M. "The Impact of Television Violence." Journal of Popular Culture, 7 (Spring 1974), 934-945.

Schramm, Wilbur, Jack Lyle, and Edwin B. Parker. Television in the Lives of Our Children. Stanford, Calif.: Stanford University Press, 1961.

Television and Growing Up: The Impact of Television Violence. Report to the Surgeon

General. Washington, D.C.: U.S. Government
Printing Office, 1972.

Television and Social Behavior: Reports and
Papers: A Technical Report to the Surgeon
General's Scientific and Advisory Committee
on Television and Social Behavior. Ed. John
P. Murray, Eli A. Rubinstein, and George A.
Comstock. 5 vols. Washington, D.C.: U.S.
Government Printing Office, 1972.

To Establish Justice, To Insure Domestic
Tranquility: The Final Report of the
National Commission on the Causes and
Prevention of Violence. New York: Praeger
Publishers, 1970.

Wertham, Fredric. A Sign for Cain. New York: The
Macmillan Company, 1966.

-----. Seduction of the Innocent. New York:
Rinehart & Company, Inc., 1954.

Where Do You Draw the Line? Ed. Victor B. Cline.
Provo, Utah: Brigham Young University Press,
1974.

Glossary of Usage

Each of the entries in this section discusses words or phrases that are frequently usage problems for student writers—as well as for more experienced ones. Suggestions for correct usage given in the entries describe current usage among educated writers and are based on the best dictionaries and recent studies in usage. Naturally, not every problem is treated here. If you are unable to find the word, expression, or rule you are interested in, you should consult either a good dictionary or your instructor. The following labels are used in the glossary:

Formal: Words or expressions of standard educated usage; appropriate to a high level of serious writing. Students are expected to produce this kind of writing in most colleges and in most courses.

Informal: The language of the everyday world. Informal words and expressions occur widely, but are also widely avoided in formal writing.

Colloquial: The language used in conversation, mainly informal; used by writers and speakers both educated and uneducated; but should, in most cases, be avoided in all but the most informal writing.

Standard: The language used in most printed matter; includes formal and informal, but is understood to stand closer to formal.

Nonstandard: Applies to words or expressions that good dictionaries label as *Illiterate, Nonstandard, Obsolete, Slang, Dialect,* or *Substandard.* These are to be avoided in all kinds of writing.

Illiterate: A species of the nonstandard occurring only in the most uneducated writing and speaking; of course, items so labeled are to be avoided.

Slang: Also a species of nonstandard writing. Slang aims to be fresh, funny, and forceful. Often, slang develops into a kind of shorthand language and quickly becomes overused. Exercise care in using slang; it belongs only in informal writing and should be used there sparingly.

a, an   Use *a* before a word beginning with a consonant *sound* —even when the word begins with a letter classified as a vowel, as in *a university*. Use *an* before a word beginning with a vowel sound (*an egg, an orange*) or a word with a silent *h* (*an hour, an honor*).

absolutely   Overworked when used as an intensifier: "It was *absolutely* the greatest experience of my life."

accept, except   *Accept* is a verb, meaning "to receive" or "to agree to," and *except* is a preposition, meaning "other than" or "but."

I *accept* your invitation
I have invited everyone *except* Charlie.

actually   Overworked as an intensifier—like *absolutely* and *really*. Instead of "They were *actually* happy" use "They were very happy" or "They were happy."

ad   An abbreviated form of *advertisement*, not appropriate to formal writing. Similarly shortened forms are *auto*, *exam, photo, math*, and *phone*.

adapt, adopt   To *adapt* is to be able to adjust to a situation or set of circumstances; to *adopt* is to take in or to agree to a course of action.

Fred was not able to *adapt* to college life.
We would like to *adopt* a child.

advice, advise   *Advice* is the noun, *advise* the verb.

I can give you good *advice*.
Let me *advise* you.

affect, effect   Usually, *affect* is a verb, meaning "to influence." The verb *effect* means "to bring about or achieve"; the noun *effect* means "the result."

The music *affected* me deeply.
We can, through political action, *effect* a change in government.
The *effect* of a shave is to open little cuts on the face.

aggravate   Means "to make worse" or "to intensify." Used colloquially to mean "annoy" or "provoke."

Formal   The argument *aggravated* my headache.
Colloquial   I was *aggravated* by his attitude.

ain't   Contraction of *am not*. Extended frequently to *is not, are not, has not*, and *have not*. Not only nonstandard, but also strongly disapproved by most educated speakers and writers.

all, all of Use *all of* before proper nouns or pronouns, as in *all of Africa, all of these*. The *of* may be omitted to make expression more concise in constructions like *all of his energy* (better: *all his energy*) or *all of her strength* (better: *all her strength*).

allusion See **illusion, allusion.**

almost See **most, almost.**

all ready, already *Already:* "before" or "by a certain time"; *all ready:* completely prepared."

When I arrived, she was *already* in the shower.
The Cosmos are *all ready* for the big game.

all right, alright Most dictionaries say *alright* is nonstandard for *all right.*

all that Colloquial when used in constructions like "I didn't like the course *all that* much." How much is *all that*?

alot Should be two words: *a lot.*

all together, altogether *All together* means "in a group." *Altogether* means "entirely," or "thoroughly."

We were *all together* in our decision.
Smoking is an *altogether* unhealthy vice.

among, between *Among* is usually reserved for more than two persons or things. *Between* is commonly used only for two. However, it is possible to use *between* for three or more items when they are regarded as having a reciprocal relationship or to express the relationship of one to the others.

Among those at the meeting, there wasn't a single Democrat.
The choice *between* ice cream and pie is easy to make.
There's much competition *between* the three major car companies.
We sailed directly *between* the three big rocks.

amount, number *Amount* refers to quantities, like water and air, that cannot be counted individually; *number* refers to things, like trees, that can be counted individually.

The *amount of traffic* on the road is staggering.
The *number of cars* going through the tunnel is staggering.

an, a See **a, an.**

analyzation Illiterate for *analysis.*

and etc. A redundancy, since *etc.* means "and so forth"; together the words would mean "and and so forth."

ante, anti *Ante* means "before" (as in *antedate*); *anti* means "against" (as in *anti-American*). Use the hyphen after *anti* when it precedes capital letters and when it precedes a word beginning with *i*—as in *anti-intellectual.*

anyone, any one Not interchangeable. *Anyone* means "any person at all"; *any one* refers to a specific individual or thing in a group.

Anyone can learn to drive a car.
Any one of those drivers can teach you to drive a car.

Note: This distinction also applies to *everyone* and *someone.*

anyways Nonstandard for *anyway.*

apt, likely, liable *Apt* refers to a habitual tendency or a natural talent; *likely* means "probable" or "to be expected"; and *liable* means "legally responsible" or "susceptible to."

Correct She is apt at solving equations
Correct She is not *likely* to go to college this fall.
Correct He is *liable* to prosecution for grand larceny.

Informal usage sometimes confuses these meanings.

Informal She is *apt* to go to college this fall.
Informal She is *liable* to go to college this fall.

around Colloquial for "about" or "near."

Formal It was *about* four o'clock.

as, as if, like See **like, as, as if.**

at Nonstandard after *where*, as in the following:

Where is he *at*?
I know where he's *at*.

auto See *ad.*

awful See **real.**

awfully Commonly used in speech to mean "exceedingly," but not preferred in writing.

Formal She was *very* late.
Colloquial She was *awfully* late.
  The play was *awfully* good.

be sure and, try and Colloquial for *be sure to, try to*.

beauty See **real**.

being that, being as how Illiterate. Use the correct subordinating conjunctions *as, since, because*.

beside, besides Writers should be careful to distinguish between *beside* meaning "at the side of" and *besides* meaning "in addition to" or "also."

He was *beside* me as we entered the room.
Besides, I'm tired.

between See **among, between**.

breakdown Standard when used to mean "collapse," but colloquial when used instead of "itemization" or "analysis."

Standard She suffered a nervous *breakdown*.
Colloquial He made a *breakdown* of our receipts from the dance.

bunch Colloquial when used to mean a *group* or a *gathering* of people, as in *a bunch of people*, but standard when appropriately applied to, for example, *grapes*, as in *a bunch of grapes*.

burst, bursted, bust, busted *Burst* is the standard past tense and past participle form of *burst*. *Bursted* is no longer standard. *Bust* and *busted* are slang.

Standard The water main *burst* last night.
Nonstandard The water main *bursted* last night.
Slang The water main *busted* last night.

commence Pretentious. Use *begin* or *start*.

compare with, compare to Similar items are compared *with* one another; dissimilar ones are compared *to* each other.

Compared with Florence, New York is ugly.
Compared to an airplane, a bird is a model of flight efficiency.

compliment, complement A *compliment* is an expression of praise; a *complement* is something that makes up or completes something else.

The remark was a *compliment*.
The remarks were a *complement* to the previous speaker's.

contact There is some feeling against the use of *contact* as a verb meaning "to meet with" or "to talk to," but it is in wide use just the same. The trouble with the word is that it is too general, and it is better replaced in writing by more specific terms such as *meet, consult, talk to.*

continual, continuous That which is *continuous* proceeds without interruption in time or space; the *continual* proceeds with some interruption.

The Alaska pipeline provides a *continuous* flow of oil.
We had a *continual* debate over the energy crisis.

could of Nonstandard. Use *could have.*

couple Should be followed by *of*, whether used to mean *a few* (in colloquial use) or *two* (in formal use).

cute Very much overworked to indicate general approval.

data, phenomena Plural forms of *datum*, "a fact used to draw a conclusion" and *phenomenon*, "a fact or event perceptible to the senses." Informally, *data* is used as a collective noun and agrees with a singular verb.

Formal These *data are* invaluable.
Informal This *data is* invaluable.

deal Colloquial, but bordering on slang when used to mean *transaction (a good deal on a car), secret contract (a deal with the D.A.),* or *treatment (a bad deal from the teacher).*

different from, different than *Different from* is idiomatic. *Different than* is becoming widely used, but should be restricted to introducing a clause.

Rugby is *different from* football.
Rome was *different than* I had expected.

See also Idioms under **Diction** in Part 2.

differ from, differ with To differ *from* someone or something is to be unlike that person or thing; to differ *with* someone is to have a dispute with that person or hold an opposite opinion.

disinterested, uninterested *Disinterested* means "without bias"; *uniterested* means "without interest." These words are often used interchangeably to mean "without interest," but the distinction is worth preserving.

don't The contraction of *do not*—not of *does not.*

He *doesn't* (not he *don't*) have much money.

dose, does A *dose* is a specified quantity of medication; *does* is the third person singular present tense form of the verb *to do*.

due to Opinion is divided on this. Some authorities criticize the construction used in the sense of *owing to* or *because of*. The criticism objects to its use as a preposition at the head of an adverbial phrase, but this use is becoming widespread and can be used in all but the most formal circumstances.

Formal Our picnic was cancelled *because of* rain.
Informal Our picnic was cancelled *due to* rain.

each other, one another *Each other* refers to two people; *one another* to more than two people.

Tom and Jerry congratulated *each other*.
The Yankees congratulated *one another* after the victory.

each and every Redundant for either *each* or *every*.
effect See **affect, effect.**
eminent, imminent, immanent *Eminent* means "distinguished"; *imminent* means "about to happen"; *immanent* means "within a realm of reality or discourse."

Colin is an *eminent* sociologist.
Marvin's arrival is *imminent*.
David's book is on history as *immanent*.

enthuse, enthused An informal construction. Recast the sentence and use *enthusiastic* instead.
etc. Latin abbreviation for *and so forth*. Use it in formal writing only when its meaning is perfectly clear. Since etc. already includes *and*, never write *and etc*. See **Abbreviations** in Part 2.
everyone See **anyone, any one**
every so often Colloquial for *frequently*.
exam See **ad.**
expect Sometimes used colloquially to mean "suppose" or "think."

Formal I *suppose* I should go to bed.
Colloquial I *expect* I should go to bed.

except See *accept, except*.
fact, the fact that A wordy way to say *that*.

Wordy   Are you aware of *the fact that* she's leaving?
Better   Are you aware *that* she's leaving?

fantastic, fabulous   Avoid these terms of exaggerated astonishment.

farther, further   *Farther* is the correct word to use to express physical distance; *further* the correct term for all other distance.

His house is *farther* down the road than mine.
In politics, he is *further* to the left than I am.

In informal usage, *further* is widely used in both senses.

fewer, less   *Fewer* is used when countable units are discussed; *less* is proper when an uncountable amount is discussed.

There are *fewer* calories in diet soda than in regular.
If the pollution stories are true, we'll soon have *less* water to drink.

field   Much overworked, frequently unnecessary.

Wordy   He was an expert in *the field of* computers.
Better   He was an expert in computers.

figure   Colloquial for words such as *believe, think, suppose, calculate,* and *expect.*

fix   Colloquial for *predicament.*

flunk   Colloquial for *fail.*

folks   Colloquial when used to refer to members of one's family or relatives as in the sentence "The *folks* all thought I looked well." Standard when it refers to people in general or a specific group: *young folks.*

foot, feet   As units of measurement, standard usage requires *a man six feet tall* or *a four-foot plank. A man six foot tall* is nonstandard.

funny   Colloquial for *odd, queer,* or *strange.*

gentleman   See **lady, gentleman.**

get   There are many colloquial and slang expressions of which the verb *get* is part. These are not appropriate in formal writing. Among them are the following: *get with it, get smart, get wise, get lost, get going.*

good   A good adjective that should not be used as an adverb.

Good   The weather is *good* today.
Not Good   She dances *good.* (should be *well*)

good and Colloquial when used in phrases like "*good and* hungry."

great See **real.**

guess In a construction like "I *guess* you'll be happy with your motorbike," formal usage would prefer *think* or *suppose* to *guess*.

guy Colloquial for *man, boy,* or *fellow*.

had ought to Illiterate for *ought to*.

Illiterate   He *had ought to* change his oil.
Standard   He *ought to* change his oil.

half a *Half a* and *a half* are good usage; *a half a* should be avoided.

Half a loaf is better than none.
I have *a half* hour to spare.

hanged, hung In formal writing, use *hanged* to refer to executed people, *hung* to refer to pictures or other objects.

he or she This is a construction used to compensate for the alleged sexist use of *he* to refer to both males and females. The construction is clumsy and logically leads to equally clumsy compromises such as *his or hers* and *him or her*.

Clumsy   When a student is well-motivated, *he or she* earns good grades.
Better   When a student is well-motivated, *he* earns good grades.

It is possible, of course, and often desirable to avoid the use of *he* to mean both sexes. This is done by rephrasing in some appropriate way:

Rephrased   When students are well-motivated, *they* earn good grades.
Rephrased   A student who is well-motivated earns good grades.

hopefully Used to mean "It is to be hoped" or "Let us hope," as in the sentence, "Hopefully, it won't rain while we're on vacation," *hopefully* is strongly disapproved by most educated speakers and writers. Nevertheless, it is widely used in those senses. Used as an adverb meaning "in a hopeful manner," it is correct.

The teacher entered the classroom hopefully.

if, whether Either *if* or *whether* may be used after such words as *say, ask, doubt, know, wonder,* or *understand*.

She asked if [whether] she could join us.
I wonder if [whether] you have a pencil to lend me.

In standard usage, choose *whether* when your sentence expresses alternatives.

I don't understand whether you're going or not.

illusion, allusion   *Illusion* means a "false image or impression"; *allusion* means an "indirect reference to" something or someone.

It is an *illusion* to think you'll get a job this summer.
She made an *allusion* to the fact that she needed the money.

immanent, imminent   See **eminent, imminent, immanent.**
imply   See **infer, imply.**
in terms of   A vague and wordy expression; to be avoided.

Wordy   In terms of power, Aaron can hit home runs.
Better   Aaron has the power to hit home runs.

in the case of   A vague and wordy expression; to be avoided.

Wordy   In the case of my Shakespeare class, it's boring.
Better   My Shakespeare class is boring.

infer, imply   *Infer* means "to draw conclusions from evidence"; *imply* means "to suggest obliquely without actually saying" something.

He *implied* he wouldn't go on the trip with us.
Therefore, we *inferred* that he didn't like the people who were going.

inside of, outside of   Mainly, the word *of* in these constructions is unnecessary. *Outside of* is also informal for *except* or *besides*.

Informal   She'll be here inside of an hour.
Formal   She'll be here *inside* [or *within*] an hour.

Informal   Outside of me, nobody can operate the tractor.
Formal   Except me, nobody can operate the tractor.

irregardless   Nonstandard. Use plain old *regardless*.
is when, is where   Clumsy and illogical expressions when *where* and *when* are used to introduce noun clauses as the complement of *is*.

Clumsy   Capitalism *is where* there is private ownership of capital.
Better   Capitalism is a form of economic development with private ownership of capital.

Clumsy A neurosis *is when* there is a disturbance of ego function.
Better A neurosis is a disturbance of ego function.

it is me, it is I The latter is very (almost too) formal; the former is widely used informally. See **Case** in Part 2.

it's, its *It's* is the contraction of *it is*. *Its* is a possessive pronoun.

kind of a Leave out the *a*.

know, no, now Know is "understand"; no is the negative particle; now means "at present."

lack, need, want As nouns, a *lack* is a shortage; a *need* is a condition brought on by a *lack;* and a *want* is a lack of things that are necessary combined with an awareness of that lack.

New York City has a *lack* of funds.
He had a *need* for friendship and affection.
The people feel a *want* of responsiveness to their problems.

lady, gentleman *Man* and *woman* are plainer and therefore preferred to the pompous *lady* and *gentleman*—unless you are using the terms to make real distinctions in refinement. *Ladies and Gentleman* is a conventional phrase used in addressing various gatherings.

lay, lie This pair of verbs continues to give trouble. *To lie* is to "rest in or place oneself into a horizontal position." *To lay* something is "to set it or place it somewhere." The only way to correct the trouble is to memorize the forms of this pair.

Infinitive	Past Tense	Past Participle	Present Participle
to lie	lay	lain	lying
to lay	laid	laid	laying

Here are correct examples of the use of each form:

Lie
I want to lie down.
After I lay there a while, I had an idea.
After I had lain there for an hour, I made my decision.
After lying down past lunch hour, I got up and made myself a snack.

Lay
Please lay the package on the table.
He laid the package on the table.

She had laid the package on the table.
I was laying the package on the table.

Note: Lay, unlike *lie*, has a passive voice:

The package had been laid neatly inside the drawer.
The body has been laid to rest.

leave, let *Leave* means "to depart from"; let means "to permit." Nevertheless, "leave (or *let*) me alone" is a standard idiom. The trouble comes when you use *leave* for *let*.

Nonstandard I won't *leave* you go with me.
Standard I won't *let* you go with me.

less See **fewer, less.**
let's us Redundant, since *let's* already means *let us*.
liable, likely See **apt, likely, liable.**
lie See **lay, lie.**
like, as, as if In formal use, *like* is a preposition; *as* and *as if* are conjunctions. *Like* is much used in conversation as a conjunction, but in writing this usage should be avoided.

Correct My daughter looks *like* me. (preposition)
Avoid My daughter speaks *like* I do. (conjunction)
Correct My daughter speaks *as* I do. (conjunction)

Avoid He spends money *like* he's rich. (conjunction)
Correct He spends money *as if* he were rich. (conjunction)

likely, liable See **apt, likely, liable.**
lose, loose *Lose* means "misplace; no longer having," or, in betting terminology, the opposite of *win. Loose* is an adjective meaning "free or unattached."

If I don't make an "A" average, I'll *lose* my scholarship.
My notes are on some *loose* sheets of paper.

mad Colloquial for "angry."
marvelous Avoid this overworked term of insincere approval.
math See **ad.**
maybe, may be *Maybe* means "perhaps"; *may be* is a two-part verb form.

It *may be* necessary to take Vitamin C in large amounts.
Maybe he hasn't got the money.

mighty   Informal for "very" or "exceedingly." *Mighty* means "powerful."

Informal   This is *mighty* good coffee.
Formal   Hank Aaron was a *mighty* home run hitter.

moral, morale   *Moral* as a noun is "a lesson" or "a conclusion to be drawn from a story"; the adjective *moral* means "pertaining to right or ethical conduct." *Morale*, a noun, refers to "the enthusiastic state of mind of an individual or a group."

Does this story have a *moral*?
His action was considered to be *moral* behavior.
The *morale* among the workers was high.

most, almost   *Most* is an informal substitute for *almost*.

Informal   *Most* every time I see you, you're well dressed.
Formal   *Almost* every time I see you, you're well dressed.

Mr.   Never spell out *mister* except for special emphasis. In America, a period follows the abbreviation (unlike the custom in Britain, where it is omitted).

Ms.   A recently adopted abbreviation to identify women, married or unmarried. It answers the needs of those who believe it unfair that women—but not men—should have their marital status made public in the usual way (that is, *Mrs.* or *Miss*). Ms. is in widespread use. It can be used when you are uncertain of a woman's marital status. In other cases, the individual's preference should be respected.

must of   Illiterate for *must have*.

myself (himself, etc.)   Do not use *myself* where you would normally use *I* or *me*. *Myself* is used 1. reflexively, 2. for emphasis, 3. in absolute constructions, or 4. to indicate the normal, healthy state of the self. All other uses should be regarded as informal.

1. I'm going to buy *myself* a new car.
2. I *myself* will go to the station.
3. *Myself* a professor, I nevertheless avoided other professors.
4. I'm not *myself* today.

Informal   Joanna and *myself* went to visit her parents. (formal: *I*)
Informal   The property was left to my sister and *myself*. (formal: *me*)

need See **lack, need, want.**

no, now See **know, no, now.**

nohow Nonstandard for *not at all.*

nowheres Nonstandard for *nowhere.*

number See **amount, number.**

off of No need for the *of.*

okay This or abbreviations like O.K. or OK are all okay—standard—but use a more specific word in formal writing.

one and the same Stale and wordy for *the same.*

one another See **each other, one another.**

ought to of Illiterate for *ought to have.*

outside of See **inside of, outside of.**

over with Colloquial for *over* and *ended.*

Colloquial I'm glad the game is *over with.*
Formal I'm glad the game is *over.*

percent, percentage Both mean "rate per hundred"; *percent* may be written as two words or as one, but *percentage* is always written as one. In formal writing, use *percent* to follow a numeral *(75 percent).* Do not use either word when you simply mean *part.*

Formal A small *part* of my home is used as an office.
Formal A small *percentage* of the team lacks spirit.
Informal A small *percent* of government officials are corrupt.

phenomena See **data, phenomena.**

phone See **ad.**

photo See **ad.**

plenty Informal when used to mean "very."

plus As a preposition, means "increased by." It is informal when used in place of *and.*

Informal Irv had a high fever *plus* he was breaking out in red spots.

pretty Overworked when used as an intensifier to mean *somewhat,* e.g., *pretty good, pretty happy.*

principal, principle *Principal,* a noun meaning "person in controlling authority" or an adjective meaning "main" or "chief," should be distinguished from *principle,* a noun, meaning "fundamental law" or "concept."

The *principal* idea was to begin our vacation in January instead of June.
The *Principal* of the high school came to dinner.
With him, it was a matter of *principle.*

prior to   Overblown usage for *before;* avoid it.

provided, provided that, providing   All three are now considered correct conjunctions.

I will go on the trip *provided that* you take your camera.
He will invite you to lunch *providing* you apologize.

quite a few, quite a bit, quite a little   Colloquial and wordy when used to substitute for *many, a substantial amount,* or *more than a little.*

raise, rise   Two different verbs. *Raise (raised, raised, raising)* is a transitive verb meaning "to cause or help to rise to a standing position." *Rise (rose, risen, rising)* is an intransitive verb meaning "to assume an upright position" or "to wake up from sleep."

He had *risen* at five and gone straight to work.
She *raises* chickens and sells eggs.

rap   Informal for "talk" or "chat," but slang when used to mean "punishment" or "blame."

real, swell, great, terrific, beauty, awful   However you may use these, they are becoming—or have become—vague and tired. Try for more specific words.

reason is because   *Because* in this construction should be replaced by *that.*

Informal   The *reason* he can't see you tonight *is because* he has to make up a chem lab.
Formal   The *reason* he can't see you tonight *is that* he has to make up a chem lab.
He can't see you tonight *because* he has to make up a chem lab.

seeing as how, seeing that   Colloquial for *since* or *because.*

shape up   Colloquial for "proceeding or developing in a satisfactory manner."

My vacation plans are *shaping up.*

set, sit   Frequently confused pair. *Sit (sat, sat, sitting)* means "be seated." *Set (set, set, setting)* means "place" something somewhere.

The dog was *sitting* at my feet.
She *set* the dog down at my feet.
The package *was set* down beside me.

Note: Set has a passive voice; *sit* does not.

show up Colloquial when used to mean "appear" or "prove."

Formal   John did not *appear* at the dance.
Colloquial   John did not *show up* at the dance.

Formal   Charles *proved* superior to Frank.
Colloquial   Charles *showed up* better than Frank.

so   In clauses describing purposes, *so* used in place of *so that* is colloquial.

Formal   We met in a hotel room *so that* we could discuss our plans in private.
Colloquial   We met in a hotel room *so* we could discuss our plans in private.

So used instead of "very" is colloquial and overworked.

Formal   She seems *very* sad.
Colloquial   She seems *so* sad.

someone   See *anyone, any one*.
sort   See **these kind**.
stationary, stationery   *Stationary* means "at rest" or "in a fixed posture or position." *Stationery* is "paper, envelopes" and other such materials.
such   Colloquial when used as an intensifier.

Formal   He owned a *very* handsome dog.
Colloquial   He owned *such* a handsome dog.

supposed to, used to   Don't forget the final *-d* in the words *supposed* and *used*.
sure   Colloquial for *surely* or *certainly*.
swell   Slang when used to mean "excellent" or "very good." See **real**.
terrific   See **real**.
than, then   Two different words. *Than* is a conjunction; *then* is an adverb or adverbial conjunction.

His grades are better *than* mine.
He had a long, cool drink; *then* he plunged into a cold shower.

their, there, they're   Frequently confused. *Their* is the possessive pronoun; *there* is an adverb or expletive; *they're* is a contraction of *they are*.

Their eyes stared straight at the flag.
There is no reason to be afraid.
They're going off on a holiday in July.

theirself, theirselves Nonstandard. Use *themselves*.

these kind Should be *this kind* (or *that kind*) or *these kinds* (or *those kinds*). Same holds true for *sort*.

thing Too often used for everything. Where possible, a more specific word should be used.

this here, that there, these here, them there Nonstandard all. Just use the first word of each pair.

through Informal when used instead of *finished*.

Formal He is *finished* studying.
Informal He is *through* studying.

to, too, two Distinguish between the preposition *to*, the adverb *too*, and the number *two*.

If it isn't *too* much trouble, I'd like *two* pounds of candy to give *to* my mother.

transpire Although the word means "to become known," it is widely used to mean "come to pass," "happen," or "occur," as in "It transpired that my scholarship check was late this month." Some authorities disapprove of this usage.

try and See **be sure and, try and.**

type Colloquial for *type of*.

Formal This *type of* air conditioner eats energy.
Colloquial This *type* air conditioner eats energy.

uninterested See **disinterested, uninterested.**

used to See **supposed to, used to.**

want See **lack, need, want.**

ways When referring to distance, *ways* is informal, *way* formal.

Informal Davenport is a long *ways* from here.
Formal Davenport is a long *way* from here.

where, were Pronounced differently, these are two different words. *Were* is the plural verb; *where* is an adverb, a conjunction, and a noun. Do not substitute *where* for *that*.

Informal He could see *where* she was getting ready to leave.
Formal He could see *that* she was getting ready to leave.

whether, if See **if, whether.**

which, who, that Use *who* or *that* to refer to persons, *which* or *that* to refer to all other things.

who, whom See **case** in Glossary of Grammatical Terms or **Case** in Part 2.

-wise Characteristic of governmental, business, or advertising jargon is the practice of converting a noun to an adverb by tacking on *-wise*. In formal writing, this is a vulgar practice.

Jargon   Moneywise, it's not a good deal.
Better   Financially, it's not a good deal.

Jargon   Defensewise, we need an early warning system.
Better   For defense purposes, we need an early warning system.

worst way Use *very much*, the formal way of saying *in the worst way*.

Informal   He wanted to go to the movies *in the worst way*.
Formal   He wanted *very much* to go to the movies.

would of Illiterate for *would have*.

Glossary of
Grammatical Terms

This glossary is intended to provide brief explanations of grammatical terms used in this book as well as others that might be of interest to students of language. Many of the entries refer to other parts of the book for expanded treatment of their subjects. Also see the index for this purpose.

absolute construction A group of words not related grammatically to the rest of the sentence. When the construction is a phrase, commonly a noun followed by a participle, it is frequently referred to as a *nominative absolute*.

The air being nippy, we decided to take our heavy sweaters.
To tell the truth, I'm very tired.

See also Part 2, **Dangling Modifiers.**

active voice See **voice.**

See also Part 2, **Voice.**

adjective A part of speech regularly used to modify, describe, or limit a noun or a pronoun.

blue shirt	*pretty* dress	*bigger* trees
that garage	*less* time	*this* place
African art	*Moroccan* leather	

A *predicate adjective* modifies its subject through the use of a linking verb.

The swan is *graceful.*
Airplanes are *noisy.*

See also pp. 16–19.

adjective clause A subordinate clause used as an adjective.

His position, *which he explained carefully,* favored ecology. (modifies *position,* the subject)

See also pp. 48–53.

adverb A part of speech regularly used to modify, describe, qualify, or limit a verb or verbal, an adjective, another adverb, or a whole sentence.

Lucia is *greatly* interested in the art of weaving. (modifies adjective *interested*)
John works *purposefully*. (modifies verb *works*)
Fortunately, he is efficient. (modifies whole sentence)

See also pp. 19–23.

adverb clause A subordinate clause used as an adverb

Because he likes fruit, he often eats fruit salad.
He sees his mother *whenever he is in Boston.*
Although he is only a student, his research has impressed his professors.

See also pp. 53–54.

agreement The correspondence in form between a verb and its subject or a pronoun with its antecedent.

He plays the clarinet. (singular pronoun agrees with third person singular verb)
The *workmen* carried *their* tools. (plural pronoun agrees with plural antecedent)

See also Part 2, **Subject-Verb Agreement, Pronoun References, Shifts.**

antecedent The name given to a word or group of words to which a pronoun refers.

David, who promised to do the carpentry, had to change *his* plans because *he* got a better job out of the city.
(*who, his* and *he* all refer back to the antecedent *David*)

See also Part 2, **Pronoun References.**

appositive A noun or something that can take the place of a noun which is set beside—in apposition to—a noun to further explain or define it.

My English *professor, Edward Quinn,* studied at NYU.
Ted's *room, the one with the balcony,* looks out over the sea.

See also Part 2, **Appositives.**

articles There are three: *a* and *an* (indefinite articles) and *the* (definite article).

auxiliary verb Also called helping verbs, auxiliaries are used to make various forms of main verbs. The most common auxiliaries are forms of *be* and *have;* others are *do, can, shall, will, would, could, should, may, might, must, ought to.*

We *are* playing. She *may* play. He *must* play.

case The inflectional forms of nouns and pronouns that indicate their function in a sentence. The three cases are the nominative (*girl, I, we*), the possessive (*girl's, my, our*), and the objective (*girl, me, us*). Case is most important when using pronouns. Six pronouns have case forms in all three cases.

Personal Pronouns

	Nominative	Singular Possessive	Objective
First Person	I	my, mine	me
Second Person	you	your, yours	you
Third Person	he, she, it	his, her, hers, its	him, her, it
		Plural	
First Person	we	our, ours	us
Second Person	you	your, yours	you
Third Person	they	their, theirs	them

Relative or Interrogative Pronouns

singular	who	whose	whom
plural	who	whose	whom

See also Part 2, **Case.**

clause A group of related words that contains both a subject and a verb and that functions as a part of a sentence or stands by itself as a sentence. The clause that can stand alone is called a *main* or *independent clause;* the clause that cannot stand by itself is called a *subordinate* or *dependent clause* and may function either as a noun, an adjective, or an adverb.

You were meant for me. (complete sentence)
You were meant for me, and *I was meant for you.* (two main clauses connected by a conjunction)
Because you were meant for me, I asked you to marry me. (subordinate clause, used as an adverb modifying *asked*)

See also Part 1, **Clauses.**

cluster There are two types: a *noun cluster,* consisting of the subject of the sentence and the string of words that surrounds and modifies it; and the *verb cluster,* the string of words surrounding and including the verb. The slash in these examples separates the two.

The best players on the team/often practice late in the afternoon.
Some of the biggest dogs in my neighborhood/play very gently with children.

collective noun   A word such as *team, committee, audience, herd*. A collective noun takes the singular verb when the group is considered as a single entity; it takes a plural verb to indicate that members of the group are acting individually.

The committee *flies* to San Francisco today.
The committee *are fighting* among themselves.

See also Part 2, **Subject-Verb Agreement.**

colloquial   A level of usage that describes the informal conversation of most people.

See also Part 2, **Diction.**

comparison   A word describing changes in the form of adjectives and adverbs to indicate changes in degrees of quality or quantity. There are three degrees: positive, comparative, and superlative.

Positive	Comparative	Superlative
happy	happier	happiest
good	better	best
rarely	more rarely	most rarely

See also Part 1, Adjectives and Adverbs.

complement   A word describing the word or words that complete the sense of a verb. A complement can be an object (direct or indirect), a subject complement (predicate adjective or predicate noun), or an object complement.

Objects   Fred gave *Myra* his *schedule.* (*schedule* is direct, *Myra* indirect object)

Subject Complements   Fred is *charming.* (predicate adjective) Fred is an *artist.* (predicate noun)

Object Complements   We elected Fred *chairman.* (noun as complement of *Fred*) We painted the fence *white.* (adjective as complement of *fence*)

See also Part 1, Sentences.

complete predicate See **predicate**.
complete subject See **subject**.
complete sentence See **sentence**.
compound A word or a group of words with two or more
  parts that act as a single entity.

Compound Nouns   shakedown, second base, master-of-ceremonies

Compound Subject of a Sentence   *Mary* and *Arthur* were in love.

Compound Predicate of a Sentence   Mary and Arthur *were in love* but
  had never married.

Compound Sentence   *You are very young,* but *you are very wise.*

compound-complex sentence See **sentence**.
compound sentence See **sentence**.
conjugation A list of all the forms of a verb, indicating tense,
  person, number, mood, and voice. Here is an example.

INDICATIVE MOOD

Present Tense

ACTIVE VOICE
I *hear*   we *hear*
you *hear*   you *hear*
he, she, it, *hears*   they *hear*
PASSIVE VOICE
I *am heard*   we *are heard*
you *are heard*   you *are heard*
he, she, it *is heard* they *are heard*

Past Tense

ACTIVE VOICE
I *heard*   we *heard*
you *heard*   you *heard*
he, she, it *heard*   they *heard*
PASSIVE VOICE
I *was heard*   we *were heard*
you *were heard*   you *were heard*
he, she, it *was heard* they *were heard*

Future Tense

ACTIVE VOICE
I *will hear*   we will *hear*
you will *hear*   you will *hear*
he, she, it will *hear* they will *hear*
PASSIVE VOICE
I will *be heard*   we will *be heard*
you will *be heard*   you will *be heard*
he, she, it will *be heard* they will *be heard*

Perfect Tense

ACTIVE VOICE
I have *heard*
you have *heard*
he, she, it has *heard*

we have *heard*
you have *heard*
they have *heard*

PASSIVE VOICE
I have *been heard*
you have *been heard*
he, she, it has *been heard*

we have *been heard*
you have *been heard*
they have *been heard*

Past Perfect Tense

ACTIVE VOICE
I had *heard*
you had *heard*
he, she, it had *heard*

we had *heard*
you had *heard*
they had *heard*

PASSIVE VOICE
I had *been heard*
you had *been heard*
he, she, it had *been heard*

we had *been heard*
you had *been heard*
they had *been heard*

Future Perfect Tense

ACTIVE VOICE
I will have *heard*
you will have *heard*
he, she, it will have *heard*

we will have *heard*
you will have *heard*
they will have *heard*

PASSIVE VOICE
I/you/he, she, it/we/you, they will have *been heard*

SUBJUNCTIVE MOOD

Present Tense

ACTIVE VOICE
that I/you/he, she, it/we/they *hear*
PASSIVE VOICE
that I/you/he, she, it/we/they *be heard*

Past Tense

ACTIVE VOICE
that I/you/he, she, it/we/they *heard*
PASSIVE VOICE
that I/you/he, she, it/we/they *were heard*

Perfect Tense

ACTIVE VOICE
that I/you/he, she, it/we/they *have heard*
PASSIVE VOICE
that I/you/he, she, it/we/they *have been heard.*

Note: The past perfect tense is the same as the indicative forms.

IMPERATIVE MOOD

Present Tense
ACTIVE VOICE
hear
PASSIVE VOICE
be heard

See also Part 2, **Verbs**, and Part 1, Verbs.

conjunction   A part of speech used to connect and relate words, phrases, clauses, and sentences. There are two kinds of conjunctions:

coordinating conjunctions: and, but, for, or, nor, so. These are used to connect structures of equal grammatical rank.

subordinating conjunctions: after, although, as, as if, because, before, if, since, unless, until, when, whenever, while, and so forth. These are also called *clause markers* and serve to introduce a dependent or subordinate clause and connect and relate it to the main clause.

For a longer list of these, see pp. 25–29.

conjunctive adverb   An adverb used to connect and indicate the relationship between two main clauses. Common conjunctive adverbs are *also, besides, consequently, furthermore, however, similarly, moreover, nevertheless, and therefore.*

See also Part 1, Conjunctions.

coordinating conjunction   See **conjunction.**

correlatives   The name given to coordinating conjunctions used in pairs, e.g., *both . . . and, either . . . or, neither . . . nor, not only . . . but also.*

demonstrative pronouns   There are four—*this, that, these, and those;* they often function as adjectives in a sentence.

dependent clause   Another name for *subordinate clause.* See **clause.**

determiner   A word that signals the reader a noun is coming, such as *a, an, the, my, this.*

See also Part 1, Determiners.

direct object   See **object.** See also Part 1, Sentences.

direct quotation   The words of others, either spoken or written.

double negative   Two negative signifiers within the same unit of meaning. *She was not unknown to me* uses two negatives (*not* and *unknown*) to say in a particular way *I knew her* (a positive statement) and is an acceptable usage. Most cases of double negatives are uneducated usage. The writer of *He didn't do nothing* wants to indicate that *He didn't do anything*.

See also Part 2, **Double Negative.**

expletive The words *there* and *it* are called expletives when they are used to change the structure but not the meaning of a sentence.

After midnight *there* were four people left at the party. [you could say, "After midnight four people were left at the party" and omit the word *there*]

It is clear that the rain will soon be pouring down. [you could say, "That the rain will soon be pouring down is clear" and omit the word *it*]

finite verb The verb that can stand alone as the main verb of the sentence. Gerunds, infinitives, and participles are not finite verbs.

Finite Verb They have no idea I plan to visit them. (correct)
Nonfinite Verb They *having* no idea I plan to visit them. (incorrect)

gerund A verb ending in *-ing* that functions as a noun.

Flying can be exhilarating. (subject of the sentence)
He took pleasure in *walking* through his old neighborhood. (object of the preposition *in*)

headword The principal word in a group of words—such as the main verb in a cluster that includes auxiliaries and modifiers, or the noun subject in a cluster that includes its modifiers.

noun cluster
The TV *documentary* on crime/disappointed us. (noun head)

verb cluster
Our team/could have *challenged* Brandeis High to a championship game. (verb head)

idiom An expression peculiar to a particular language, in which the meanings of the words that make up the expression are not necessarily a clue to the meaning of the idiom.

We *took off for* Rome in the afternoon.
He was caught *holding up* a gas station.

See also Part 2, **Diction.**

imperative See **mood.**

independent clause See **clause.**

indicative See **mood.**

indirect object See **object.**

infinitive The form of the verb with the word *to* in front of it, as in *to draw, to work,* and so forth. Most often the infinitive is a noun, occasionally an adjective or an adverb. See also pp. 56–59; 294.

intensifier A word that acts like the word *very* (*very good, very happy, very sad*). Intensifiers include words such as *somewhat, pretty, rather, quite, more, most,* and *really*

somewhat sad, rather old

See also Part 1, Intensifiers.

interjection A part of speech used to express emotion directly. *Oh, Wow,* and *ouch* are examples.

intransitive See **verb.**

inversion Changing the usual word order of a sentence for special effect.

Normal Word Order Just at that moment, the principal walked in.
Inversion Just at that moment, in walked the principal.

irregular verb A verb that does not form its past tense and past participle by the addition of *-d* or *-ed*. A few examples: *swim, swam, swum; take, took, taken; sit, sat, sat.* See also Part 2, **Verbs.**

linking verb A verb that relates the subject to either a predicate noun or a predicate adjective. These include all the forms of the verb *be,* along with such other verbs as *become, appear, seem, feel, look, taste, smell, and sound.* See also pp. 11–12.

main clause See **clause.**

modifier An adjective or adverb that modifies, qualifies, describes, or limits either another word or a word group. See also Part 2, **Modifiers.**

mood One of three ways in which a verb states its action or conception. They are the indicative, the imperative, and the subjunctive moods. Use the indicative to make statements and ask questions; the imperative to issue commands, make requests or give directions; the subjunctive for contrary-to-fact or wishful expressions.

Indicative   I'm going to the party.
Will you come with me?

Imperative   Don't be gone too long.
Please let me have a glass of water.
Turn right at the stop sign.

Subjunctive   If I *were* rich, I'd be happy.
I suggested that the barn *be* painted red.

See also pp. 295–296.

nonfinite verb   A verb form that cannot stand alone as the main verb of a sentence. Another word for this form is a *verbal*.

nonrestrictive   The name given to a part of a sentence that is not essential to the meaning but that adds information. This type of parenthetical construction should be enclosed in commas.

The tiger in the cage, *pacing powerfully,* looked menacing. (nonrestrictive phrase)
The tent, *which was made of nylon and canvas,* was a welcome addition to our camping gear. (nonrestrictive clause)

See also **restrictive** and Part 2, **Comma Rules.**

noun   A part of speech that names something: a person, place, thing, idea, quality, and so forth. Nouns change form to make plurals and possessives.

See also pp. 4–7.

noun clause   A subordinate or dependent clause that functions as a noun in a sentence.

That he cares about her is obvious. (subject of the sentence)
She fears *that John is getting too serious about her.* (object)
The College will award a B.A. to *whoever completes the requirements.* (indirect object)

See also pp. 54–56.

noun phrase   See **phrase.**

number   The indication that a noun, pronoun, or verb is singular or plural. All verbs in the third person singular present tense change form to indicate the singular.

See also Part 2, **Verbs, Shifts.**

object Four types are important:

A *direct object* is any noun or noun substitute that receives the action of a finite verb that is also transitive and active in voice. Asking of the verb the question *what* or *whom* will usually locate the direct object, as in this sentence:

Havlicek pulled down the rebound. (Havlicek pulled down *what*? Answer: the *rebound*: the direct object)

A direct object can be converted into the subject when you change the verb to the passive voice. See **voice.**

The *indirect object* is a noun or a noun substitute that indicates to or for *whom* or *what* the action of the verb is done. Usually, the indirect object comes *before* the direct object.

She gave *me* a camera.
I told *her* a story.

The indirect object can usually be converted into a prepositional phrase with either *to* or *for*.

She gave a camera *to me*.

The *object of a nonfinite verb*—a participle, a gerund, or an infinitive—is also a noun or a noun substitute. It follows and completes the meaning of these constructions.

Jogging a *mile* is easy when you're in shape.
To love *somebody* is not always easy.
Walking *home,* I had an idea.

The *object of a preposition* is a noun or a noun substitute that the preposition relates to another group of words in the sentence.

We ate our lunch at the *beach*. (object of *at*)
Whom are we waiting for? (object of *for*)

See also pp. 23–25.

object complement See **complement.**

objective See **case.**

See also Part 2, **Case.**

participle A verb form that may appear in a compound verb (was *running,* should have *gone*), as an adjective (the *completed* book, the *driven* man), or as a verbal (*running* along the street, he became breathless).

See also Part 2, **Verbs, Modifiers.**

parts of speech Classes into which grammarians place words according to their form and function in sentences: nouns, verbs, adjectives, adverbs, pronouns, prepositions, conjunctions, and interjections.
See also pp. 4–36.

passive voice See **voice**.

person The form of a pronoun and verb that identifies the speaker as the one speaking (*I am:* first person), the one spoken to (*you are:* second person), or the one spoken about (*he, she, it, is*).

personal pronoun See **pronoun**.

phrase A group of words that does not have both subject and verb—except that a two- or three-part verb (for example, *could have walked*) is called a verb phrase.
See also Part 1, Phrase.

possessive See **case**.

predicate One of the two basic parts of a sentence—everything in the sentence that is not the subject. The *complete predicate* is the main verb, any auxiliaries it might have, and whatever other words modify or complement these.

Birds *sing.* (sing is the predicate)
Birds *sing when they are well-fed and have an appropriate environment in which to fly.* (the italicized words constitute the complete predicate; sings is the headword)

predicate adjective See **adjective** and **complement**.

predicate noun A noun that acts as a subject complement.
See **complement**.

preposition A part of speech consisting of words that relate a noun or a noun substitute to other words in the sentence. Prepositions are such words as *across, after, as, at, because of, before, beside, between, by, for, from, in, like, near, next to, of, on, over, through, to, under, until, up and with*.
See also pp. 23–25.

prepositional phrase See **phrase**.

principal parts The three forms of a verb from which any of its tenses can be formed: the present infinitive (*look, see*), the past tense (*looked, saw*), and the past participle (*looked, seen*).
See also Part 2, **Verbs**.

progressive verb form   A group of verbs consisting of the present participle and an auxiliary verb that is a form of *to be*.

I *am working.*
You *were drawing.*

See also Part 2, **Verbs.**

pronoun   A part of speech; a pronoun functions as a noun does in a sentence. The principal types are as follows:

Personal   you, me, us, we, and so forth.

Demonstrative   this, that, those, these.

Relative   who, whom, that, which

Indefinite   anybody, everybody, one, somebody, another, and so forth.

See also Part 1, Pronouns.

proper adjective   An adjective, spelled with a capital letter, formed from a proper noun, as *Chinese* is formed from *China*.

See also Part 1, Adjectives.

quotation   See **direct quotation.**

See also Part 2, **Quotation Marks.**

regular verb   A verb that makes its past tense and past participle by adding *-d* or *-ed* to the stem of the infinitive, as *play, played, played; wait, waited, waited.*

See also Part 2, **Verbs.**

relative pronoun   One of a group of words, noun substitutes, used to introduce subordinate clauses: *who, whom, whose, that, which, what, whoever, whomever, whichever, whatever.*

He has a car *that is ready for the junk heap.* (adjective clause)

restrictive   A construction so essential to the meaning of the sentence that it cannot be omitted. Also, it must *not* be set off by commas.

The man *leaning against the wall* is my father. (restrictive phrase)
The team *that plays hard today* will be tired tomorrow. (restrictive clause)

See also Part 2, **Comma Rules.**

sentence   The unit of complete expression that includes both a subject and a predicate. Sentences are classified in two ways: 1. according to an expected response, as *statements, questions,* or *requests.*

Statement   I'm going to the movies. (responder acknowledges)

Question   Are you going to the movies? (responder answers)

Request   Please go to the movies. (responder acts)

2. According to the type and number of clauses they contain, as *simple, compound, complex,* or *compound-complex.*

Simple   Eagles fly. (a subject and a simple predicate, consisting here of a single verb)

Compound   We left the party early, but we had a good time. (two main clauses)

Complex   Although we left the party early, we had a good time. (a subordinate clause and a main clause)

Compound-Complex   Although we left the party early, we had a good time, and we'll remember all the fun we had. (one subordinate and two main clauses)

See also Part 1, Sentences.

sentence modifier   A word or a word group that modifies the whole of the sentence rather than some part of it.

Ordinarily, I go to bed at a late hour.

See also Part 2, **Modifiers.**

subject   A basic grammatical part of a sentence; what the sentence is *about.* Subjects are nouns or noun substitutes. Predicates make an assertion about nouns to form sentences. A *complete subject* is the *simple subject* together with all the words that modify it. In the imperative mood, the subject is implied.

See also Part 1, Sentences.

subject complement   See **complement.**

subjective   See **case.**

subjunctive   See **mood.**

subordinate clause   See **clause.**

subordinating conjunction   See **conjunction.**

tense   A specific form of a verb that indicates its relation to time. Changing the ending and adding auxiliaries alter the verb to show the different tenses.

See also Part 2, **Verbs,** and Part 1, Verbs.

transitive   See **verb.**

verb   A part of speech. Verbs describe either action or a state of being. A *transitive* verb is one that needs an object to complete its meaning.

His chimney *rains* soot on the whole neighborhood. (direct object: soot)

An *intransitive* verb is one that does not need an object to complete its meaning.

Mary Ellen *sat.*

Many verbs can be used transitively in one sentence and intransitively in another.

Karl *works* crossword puzzles.
Barbara *works* hard.

A *linking verb* indicates the relationship between a subject and either a noun, a pronoun, or an adjective in the nominative case. The principal linking verbs are *be, become, appear, seem,* and verbs denoting the senses: *taste, smell, feel, look, sound.*

She *looks* sad. They *are* policemen. It *is* he.

See also Part 2, **Verbs,** and Part 1, Verbs.

verb phrase   See **phrase.**

verbal   The name given to any one of three verb forms (*gerund, participle, infinitive*) when it is used as a noun, an adjective or an adverb.

voice   Transitive verbs have either an *active* or a *passive* voice. A passive verb consists of some form of the verb *be* together with the past participle.

Active

Professor Johnson *taught* the class.
Grizzly Adams *trained* the bear.

Passive

The class *was taught* by Professor Johnson.
The bear *was trained* by Grizzly Adams.

Note that in each case, the direct object of the active verb becomes the subject of the passive verb.
See also Part 2, **Voice.**

Index

NOTES

NOTES

NOTES

NOTES

NOTES

NOTES

NOTES

NOTES